Applied Historical Studies
An Introductory Reader

Applied Historical Studies
An Introductory Reader

Edited by Michael Drake
at The Open University

Methuen & Co Ltd
in association with
The Open University Press

First published 1973
by Methuen & Co Ltd
11 New Fetter Lane London EC4 P4EE
in association with
The Open University Press
Walton Hall Milton Keynes Bucks
Printed and bound in Great Britain by
Richard Clay (The Chaucer Press) Ltd
Bungay Suffolk

SBN hardback 416 79100 X
SBN paperback 416 79110 7

Contents

Acknowledgements

The editor and publishers thank the following authors and publishers for permission to reprint the material listed below:

Russell Sage Foundation for 'Sociology and the historical perspective', by Kai T. Erikson in Wendell Bell and James A. Mau (eds.), *The Sociology of the Future: Theory, Cases and Annotated Bibliography* (1971), pp. 61–77; David C. McClelland for pp. 132–49 of Chapter 4 in *The Achieving Society* (1961); E. G. West for 'Resource allocation and growth in early nineteenth-century British education', *The Economic History Review*, 2nd ser., XXIII, No. 1, April 1970, pp. 68–95; J. S. Hurt for 'Professor West on early nineteenth-century education', *The Economic History Review*, 2nd ser., XXIV, No. 4, November 1971, pp. 624–32; E. G. West for 'The interpretation of early nineteenth-century education statistics', *The Economic History Review*, 2nd ser., XXIV, No. 4, November 1971, pp. 633–42; Robert William Fogel and the Royal Economic Society for 'Railroads as an analogy to the space effort: some economic aspects', *The Economic Journal*, LXXVI, March 1966, pp. 16–43; John T. Krause for 'Some implications of recent work in historical demography', *Comparative Studies in Society and History*, I, 1958–9, pp. 164–88; Richard A. Easterlin for 'Implications of the demographic history of developed countries for present-day under-developed nations', *Comparative Studies in Society and History*, II, 1959–60, pp. 374–8; John T. Krause for 'On the possibility of increasing fertility in the under-developed nations', *Comparative Studies in Society and History*, II, 1959–60, pp. 485–7; C. F. Küchemann, A. J. Boyce and G. A. Harrison for 'A demographic and genetic study of a group of Oxfordshire villages', reprinted from *Human Biology*, XXXIX, No. 3, 1967, pp. 251–76 (copyright 1967 by Wayne State University Press);

Stephan Thernstrom for 'Notes on the historical study of social mobility', *Comparative Studies in Society and History*, X, 1967–8, pp. 162–72; Stuart Blumin for 'The historical study of vertical mobility', *Historical Methods Newsletter*, I, No. IV, September 1968, pp. 1–13; T. J. Nossiter for 'Voting behaviour 1832–1872', Political Studies, XVIII, September 1970, pp. 380–9.

Introduction

Applied Historical Studies are explorations of the past undertaken with the explicit purpose of advancing social scientific enquiries. To 'participate in the overall scholarly enterprize of discovering and developing general laws of human behaviour';[1] to test the models of the social scientist 'by running them through the dimension of time';[2] to help 'clothe' the propositions of social science so as to make them both 'verifiable and applicable';[3] are all facets of the applied historian's task. It is a task which involves a search for appropriate historical data; the devising of ways to exploit it and, not least important, the presentation of findings in a form that is acceptable to social scientists. It is the purpose of this introduction to examine these three tasks in turn: the rest of the book is designed to illustrate them.

I would like to thank a number of my colleagues for assisting in the preparation of this book, (needless to say they bear no responsibility for its shortcomings): they are – John Annett, Hedy Brown, Paul Lewis, David Potter, Dennis Mills, Rees Pryce, Geoffrey Edge, Dick Stevens, David Boswell, Ken Thompson, Jeremy Tunstall, and Ken Jones. I would also like to thank Noelle Whiteside of the Public Record Office for patiently ferreting out a mass of relevant material.

[1] Lee Benson, 'Quantification, scientific history and scholarly innovation', in Robert P. Swierenga (ed.), *Quantification in American History. Theory and Research* (New York, Atheneum, 1970), p. 26.
[2] H. R. Trevor-Roper, 'The past and the present: history and sociology', *Past and Present*, 42 (1969), p. 12.
[3] Michael M. Postan, (speaking of economic propositions), in 'Time and change', in William Robson (ed.), *Man and the Social Sciences* (London, Allen and Unwin, 1972), p. 37.

I

As Erikson notes below, p. 15, the historian is usually regarded as operating in an area of scarce resources. Historical data are seen as unique items which have survived the passage of time, the fact of their survival bearing no obvious relationship to their value. This myth of scarcity derives from a failure to distinguish between history conceived of as data generated in the past and history as the selection and interpretation of that data by the historian. If historians have chosen to focus their attention on what they regard as 'important' events or people for which documentation is slight, it does not follow that there are not large caches of data of interest to the social scientist. One suspects too that some of these have been ignored, partly because historians are not normally trained to handle large quantities of data and partly because, for many historians, half the fun of their discipline is in making do with scattered fragments of evidence. This myth of scarcity dies hard. McClelland, in his introduction to *The Achieving Society*, from which an extract appears below (pp. 31–51), tells a story against himself which epitomizes this idea of history as limited and finite. He remarks that he asked a colleague 'an eminent Harvard historian, to recommend "a" book that would bring me up to date on English history. . . . He simply looked at me aghast, murmured "my God!" and turned away.'[4]

McClelland himself, in writing *The Achieving Society*, drew on one data cache, the size of which is relatively large. Wishing to measure the 'need for achievement' (abbreviated to *n* Achievement) in different societies, he devised a method of applying content analysis to various types of literature in order to see whether achievement imagery was, among other things, more frequent just prior to periods of rapid economic growth. The passages from his book reprinted here illustrate the technique in the context of England from the late sixteenth to the nineteenth century. Whatever one may think of McClelland's work as a whole (and he has not been without his critics) or of the particular example cited below, there can be no doubt that the use of content analysis for measuring attitudes of various kinds will not fail through any shortage of appropriate materials.[5] A second potentially rich source

[4] David C. McClelland, *The Achieving Society* (New York, The Free Press paperback edition, 1967), p. vii.
[5] See T. F. Carney, 'Content analysis: a review essay', *Historical Methods Newsletter*, vol. iv, no. 2, (March, 1971), pp. 52–61. For a study of the timing of the development of a distinctively American self-consciousness see Richard L. Merritt, 'The emergence of American nationalism: a quantitative approach',

of historical data for the social scientist is to be found in the enumerators' returns of the various censuses that were taken in most western countries from the early nineteenth century onwards. The published census volumes offer a great deal of information,[6] but the enumerators' returns can be made to yield even richer results. Included in this volume are two articles, by Thernstrom (pp. 22–32) and Blumin (pp. 233–49) which exploit the manuscript schedules of the United States Federal Census. For Britain, the enumerators' returns of the censuses of 1841, 1851, 1861 and 1871 are now available. Later returns are embargoed under the hundred year rule. From 1851 onwards the enumerators' returns give the age, sex, name, address, occupation, marital condition and relationship to the head of the household for virtually the entire population of the country. Historians have been mining this material for some years.[7] A sociologist, Michael Anderson, has also used it to throw light on the impact of urban-industrial life on the role of the family.[8] He, together with Peter Laslett and associates, have as a result of the analysis of census and census-type documents in England and other countries, radically altered our views of the development of the family. Two findings will suffice to show the value of their work. First it appears that the small, nuclear conjugal household was the norm in England long before the industrial revolution, and second that, contrary to the normally held view, there has been 'a massive *increase* over the past two centuries in co-residence of married couples and their parents'.[9]

American Quarterly, xvii (Summer, 1965), pp. 319–35. This is reprinted, with an introduction reviewing briefly the use of content analysis on American historical data, in Robert P. Swierenga (ed.), *Quantification in American History: Theory and Research* (New York, Atheneum, 1970), pp. 77–95.
[6] For an inventory of the nineteenth century volumes of the British census together with a critique of their reliability see Michael Drake, 'The census, 1801–1891', in E. A. Wrigley (ed.), *Nineteenth-century Society: Essays in the Use of Quantitative Methods for the Study of Social Data* (Cambridge, Cambridge University Press, 1972) pp. 7–46.
[7] See the chapters by Tillott and Armstrong in E. A. Wrigley, *op. cit.*, pp. 82–145 and pp. 191–310.
[8] Michael Anderson, *Family Structure in Nineteenth Century Lancashire* (Cambridge, Cambridge University Press, 1971) and 'The Study of Family Structure' in E. A. Wrigley, *op. cit.*, pp. 47–81. Dr Anderson is currently taking a national sample from the 1851 census of Great Britain. It is intended that from mid-1975 onwards scholars contacting Dr Anderson will be able to receive 'specially prepared tabulations and/or data sets for their own research'. For further details write to Dr Anderson at the Department of Sociology, Edinburgh University.
[9] Michael Anderson, 'Household structure and the industrial revolution: mid-nineteenth-century Preston in comparative perspective', in Peter Laslett

In the United States Stephan Thernstrom has examined the so-called 'blocked mobility' hypothesis within a historical context.[10] The hypothesis, which suggested that upward social mobility in the United States had slowed down over the last century, was found wanting.[11] Not only that, his study, and that of Blumin (see below pp. 233–49) added much to the actual analytical techniques used to understand this problem of social mobility.

In addition to the census enumerators' returns the Public Record Office has a vast amount of nominative data of relevance to the interests of social scientists. This has been comparatively little used.[12] Two kinds of material will be noted here by way of illustration. First there are papers emanating from the War Office and the Admiralty. Among the former are Militia Attestation Papers, 1,522 boxes of them, covering the years 1806–1915. These comprise questionnaires presented to each man on enlistment. Arranged alphabetically by surname and by regiment and year of enlistment, they give for each individual militiaman, his age, birth place, occupation, size of chest, height and (sometimes) weight, the name and address of his employer, his present residence and his residence during the previous twelve months. A further 4,231 boxes contain similar information about regular soldiers from 1760–1900. Among the Admiralty papers are 267 large volumes containing a detailed account of each and every ordinary seaman enlisted between 1873 and 1895. These give the kind of information mentioned in the army attestation papers above but also provide detailed information about each man's career. Attestation forms for the marines going back to 1790 are contained in 659 boxes. Some 67 volumes give even more detailed information about naval officers. Covering the period 1777–1915 these include details of parentage, marriage, examination results, the length of service, career, a report from the commanding

(ed.), *Household and Family in Past Time. Comparative Studies in the Size and Structure of the Domestic Group over Time* (Cambridge, Cambridge University Press, 1972), p. 216.
[10] Stephan Thernstrom, *Poverty and Progress: Social Mobility in a Nineteenth Century City* (Cambridge Massachusetts, Harvard University Press, 1964).
[11] Thernstrom has subsequently modified his views, in the light of his research on social mobility in Boston from the years 1880 to the present, in a paper, 'Working class social mobility in industrial America' delivered to the Anglo-American Colloquium of the Society for Labour History in London, 23 June 1968.
[12] See *Guide to the Contents of the Public Record Office*, 3 vols. (London, H.M.S.O., 1963–68): and Brenda Swann and Maureen Turnbull, *Records of Interest to Social Scientists, 1919–1939* (London, H.M.S.O., 1971).

officer of each ship in which the officer served and details as to health and cause of death.

More relevant for readers of this volume, perhaps, are the various educational returns held at the Public Record Office. Professor West, (see below pp. 53–91) has re-interpreted British education in the nineteenth century in the light of his study of primary sources, particularly the published statistics. His findings are no doubt controversial. One way of testing them would be to look at reports on individual schools and teachers. (Many can be found in the *published* minutes (1839–58) and the Reports (1859–99) of the Committee of Council on Education.) The Public Record Office holdings include 172 boxes contain questionnaires completed by all elementary schools seeking government support from 1846 onwards. Each questionnaire contains such information as to whether the school was of a public, private or 'adventure' type; the amount of fees charged (showing the range of fees where there was one) and the number of pupils paying them; the size of the school building and when built; the expenditure on salaries, books, fuel, repairs, etc. The completed questionnaire also contained short biographies of each of the principal teachers including such information as age, length of service, where trained and class of certificate. In 1871 a return was made by all London elementary schools whose fees were under 9*d* a week. The questionnaires, which fill 28 boxes, give extensive information on the fee structure, the age of the school children, the numbers doing each subject, the size of the school, number of class rooms, its religious affiliation and short biographies of each head teacher. For detailed reports on schools, their physical condition, curricula, competence of their staff (in the eyes of the inspectors at least!), from 1857–1946 one can turn to some 68,000 files. (It is pointless giving a precise figure as files are continually being added.) The files are complete, none having been weeded or thrown away.

For political scientists, especially those of the behavioural school, one of the richest sources of information lies in the poll books produced in the years before the Secret Ballot Act of 1872. Until that year voting in parliamentary elections was public. On polling day the vote of each registered elector was entered in the poll book. Until 1844 these books were preserved in the various county Quarter Session Records. From that year custody was transferred to the clerk of the crown in Chancery.[13] They were destroyed in 1896. The loss of the manuscript poll books is not, however, as grievous as it might have been because it was not

[13] House of Commons, Accounts and Papers (1852), XLII, p. 301.

unusual for local printers to publish a copy of them immediately after the poll had closed. A recent review indicates the whereabouts of 841 printed poll books in the period 1832–72:[14] thus just under a third of the 2,640 contests are covered. Personal acquaintance with the contents of local libraries and record offices suggests there are many more.

Poll books show considerable variation in the amount of material they contain. At the very least they give the name of the voter and the way he cast his vote or votes (many constituencies had two members). Some, however, contain much more than this. *The Bath Reform Poll Book for 1841* not only gave the names and addresses of all those entitled to vote in the general election of 28 June 1841 and the way they cast their votes but also, entered against each elector's name, how he had voted in the elections of 1832, 1835 and 1837. *The Bath Poll Book* for 1855, as well as giving the name and address of each elector and the way his vote was cast, (it was a by-election), also gave his occupation and the amount he was assessed for the poor rate. What appeared in printed poll books depended largely on what the manuscript poll book contained. In addition to printed and manuscript poll books, it is not unusual to come across annotated registers of voters, used, it appears, for canvassing purposes. For instance, the Banbury Public Reference Library has a *Register of Electors entitled to vote in 1865*. This contains in printed form the name and address of each voter, arranged by street. Manuscript addenda show how each voter cast his vote in the *two* elections held in 1859 and a prediction of how he would vote in 1865. Since the library also contains a printed poll book for 1859 giving the occupation of each voter and his poor rate assessment, the possibility of some interesting exercises in historical psephology are apparent.[15]

---

[14] *Dod's Electoral Facts*, edited by H. J. Hanham (Brighton, Harvester Press, 1971), pp. lxxix–cxiv. The main central repositories are the Institute of Historical Research; the British Museum; the Guildhall Library and the Society of Genealogists – all in London – and the Bodleian Library, Oxford.

[15] For work by historians on poll books see J. Vincent, *Poll books. How Victorians Voted* (Cambridge, Cambridge University Press, 1967); and 'The electoral sociology of Rochdale', *The Economic History Review*, Second Series, vol. xvi (1963–64) pp. 76–90; R. S. Neale, *Class and Ideology in the Nineteenth Century* (London, Routledge and Kegan Paul, 1972) especially Chapter 2, 'Class and ideology in a provincial city: Bath 1800–50' and Chapter 3, 'Class conflict and the poll books in 'Victorian England'; W. A. Speck and W. A. Gray, 'Computer analysis of poll books: an initial report', *Bulletin of the Institute of Historical Research*, xliii, No. 107 (May, 1970), pp. 105–12; D. C. Moore, 'Concession or cure: the sociological premises of the First Reform Act', *The Historical Journal*, ix, No. 1 (1966), pp. 39–59, 'Social structure, political structure and public opinion in Mid-Victorian Britain', in Robert Robson (ed.), *Ideas and Institutions*

One other major data source will be considered here. This is the one that has been extensively used by historical demographers over the last twenty years, namely the parish registers of baptisms, marriages and burials kept by the Church of England from 1538 onwards though not always preserved since then. Responsibility for the upkeep of these registers has been that of the individual incumbent, but in recent years many have been removed to county record offices for safe keeping. It is, therefore, not uncommon to find offices having either the original registers or transcripts of them for a half or more of all the parishes in their respective counties.

It will be apparent from the foregoing that not only are there large deposits of data suitable for analysis by social scientists, but also that much of it is accessible with relative ease. More important, however, than the physical accessibility of the material is the fact that in many cases it provides the social scientist with the only opportunity he has of getting hold of certain kinds of data. Take for instance the study of voting behaviour. Not only is the ballot now secret, but, in Britain, for parliamentary elections, all the voting slips are shuffled together on a constituency wide basis before being counted. This latter requirement effectively puts paid to the kind of ecological analysis of voting behaviour that is common in the United States. Confidentiality rules also prevent the social scientist analysing contemporary census forms, the reports on individual schools made by the government's inspectors, and the personal files of public or private employees.

There is another aspect to this question of accessibility. It is demonstrated both by the work of E. G. West and C. F. Küchemann *et al.* printed below. In both cases the only way of finding empirical data for the pursuit of their particular enquiries was by going to the historical record. West was interested in exploring 'the social and economic principles of intervention', in this instance intervention by the state in primary education.[16] The historical record gave him the opportunity of

---

of Victorian Britain: Essays in Honour of George Kitson Clark (London, G. Bell, 1967): George Rudé, 'The Middlesex electors of 1768–1769' *English Historical Review*, lxxv (1960), pp. 601–17; Peter Jupp, 'County Down elections, 1783–1831', *Irish Historical Studies*, xviii, No. 70 (September, 1972), pp. 177–206. For work by one of the few political scientists operating in this area see T. J. Nossiter below pp. 251–64 and his 'Aspects of electoral behavior in English constituencies, 1832–1868', in Erik Allardt and Stein Rokkan, *Mass Politics: Studies in Political Sociology* (Free Press, London-New York, 1970), pp. 160–89.
[16] E. G. West, *Education and the State: a Study in Political Economy*, 2nd ed. (London, Institute of Economic Affairs, 1970), p. xx.

contrasting the pre-1870 situation when, he alleges, there was a system of universal access to private schools, with the post-1870 situation when the state took over the provision as well as the financing of education. As for Küchemann *et al.*, they were able to reconstruct the genetic structure of a community over several hundred years, thus providing a check on the studies of purely contemporary communities.[17]

To sum up then, it has been suggested that not only does the past, in Britain at least, provide us with large quantities of relevant, and readily accessible[18] data, but also that some of it is superior to what the contemporary world can supply.

II

We have noted that social scientists have possibly misunderstood the nature of much historical data, believing it to be in short supply, irrelevant and difficult to obtain. Some undoubtedly is, and as it appears that many historians have focused their attention on just such data, the misunderstanding is not a surprising one. The same confusion seems also to have arisen over the nature of historical analysis. Because historians have tended to be non-quantitative, relying on literary evidence of an impressionistic nature and arguing from supposedly salient instances (these being intuitively determined), there is no reason why social scientists should approach historical data in the same way. Indeed many historians are no longer content with the traditional approaches of their craft. In the United States the *Historical Methods Newsletter*, published by the Department of History at the University of Pittsburgh, is now in its sixth year. Its readership of 2,300 in 30 countries is indicative of the interest in the application of social science techniques to historical data.[19] Social scientists too have worked on

[17] For analagous demographic studies see A. Constant, 'The geographical background of inter-village population movements in Northamptonshire and Huntingdonshire, 1754–1943', *Geography*, 33 (1948), pp. 78–88 and P. J. Perry, 'Working-class isolation and mobility in rural Dorset, 1837–1936: a study of marriage distances', *Transactions of the Institute of British Geographers*, 46 (1969) pp. 121–74.
[18] On the question of accessibility and the problems involved in getting hold of some types of data at the present time see Robert Sommer, 'Some costs and pitfalls of field research', *Social Problems*, 19, No. 2 (1971), pp. 162–6. Sommer mentions such problems as maintaining anonymity, avoiding being thought to be prying and spying as well as suffering danger, discomfort, disillusionment and potential legal problems.
[19] Recently it has dropped from its masthead the subtitle 'Quantitative Analysis of Social Economic and Political Development'. This, readers were assured,

historical material. There is much work, for instance, by geographers on migration.[20] There are now sufficient examples of these new interpretations to fill several Readers.[21]

All this activity has paved the way for Applied Historical Studies, but it must not be confused with them. It has paved the way by unearthing data suitable for analysis and it has conducted such analysis at the micro level, according to the canons of social science. But it has been a one-way traffic. It has been a case of the social scientist adding to our understanding of the past *for its own sake*. To that extent the objectives have been those of the traditional historian, despite the novelty of the methods. Allan G. Bogue has remarked that:

> Few behavioural historians are consciously looking for findings with predictive value, or purposefully giving their research a theoretical frame which the results may in part verify, modify or contradict. Instead, most are still problem or topic-oriented, using social science techniques or theory to refute or build on the work of past historians or to probe new areas which catch their fancy.[22]

The 'new economic historians' have been criticized along similar lines by Professor M. M. Postan:

> To employ economic theory and econometric tests in the interpretation of famous historical events such as the emancipation of the Negro slaves, or the decision to open up the American interior by

---

was not because of any reduction in zeal for quantitative methods, but rather to emphasize a broadening of emphasis to embrace articles 'on social science concepts, approaches and techniques which in themselves are not necessarily quantitative'. *Historical Methods Newsletter*, 5, No. 4 (September 1972), p. 144.

[20] See H. C. Darby, 'The movement of population to and from Cambridgeshire between 1851 and 1861' *Geographical Journal*, Vol. ci (1943), pp. 118–25; C. T. Smith, 'The movement of population in England and Wales in 1851 and 1861', *Geographical Journal*, Vol. cxvii (1951), pp. 200–10; R. Lawton, 'Population movements in the West Midlands, 1841–1861', *Geography*, 43 (1958), pp. 164–77. For a wider range of subject matter see also the essays in Alan R. H. Baker, John D. Hamshere and John Langton (eds.), *Geographical Interpretations of Historical Sources: Readings in Historical Geography* (Newton Abbot, David and Charles, 1970).

[21] See Robert P. Swierenga (ed.), *Quantification in American History: Theory and Research* (New York, Atheneum, 1970); Seymour Martin Lipset and Richard Hofstadter (eds.), *Sociology and History: Methods* (New York, Basic Books, 1968); Peter Temin (ed.), *New Economic History* (Harmondsworth, Penguin, 1973).

[22] Allan G. Bogue, 'United States: the "new" political history', *Journal of Contemporary History*, III (January, 1968), pp. 5–27. Reprinted in Robert P. Swierenga *op. cit.* pp. 36–52.

railway construction, is a useful but perhaps an over-modest enterprize. It is over-modest not only because it tries to do what economists could always do without the assistance of historians, but also
because it concerns itself more with historical episodes than with
economic problems. For this and other reasons it does not offer to
economists the kind of collaboration which, whether they know it or
not, they most need. What economists require or ought to require
from the social scientists nearest to them, and especially from economic historians, is not that they should verify the established propositions of economics or use them to illuminate episodes of general
history, but that they should help to make economic propositions
verifiable and applicable.[23]

There is increasing evidence to suggest that the 'needs' Postan talks
about are coming to be felt by social scientists generally. Erikson's
article below pp. 13–30 is one indication of this. In another recent
piece Gabriel A. Almond remarked that 'it goes without saying that
historical evidence will constitute a principal body of data which
development theory will have to rely on. It is in history (which includes
contemporary history) that one encounters man's "natural experiments" with development.'[24] Within this present volume two expressions appear which sum up much of the disquiet now felt about
ahistorical social science. Thernstrom (p. 221) talks of 'the parochialism
of presentism', whilst Krause, (p. 193) speaks of 'disembodied demography'.

The benefits which the use of historical data can bring to voting
studies, 'the chief intellectual god child of behaviouralism in political
science',[25] may serve as an illustration of the general point made above.
First by drawing on the poll book material one can avoid reliance on
voters' memories as to how they voted in particular elections. That such
memories are both short and fallible is well documented.[26] Since the

[23] Michael M. Postan, 'Time and Change' in William Robson (ed.), *Man and
the Social Sciences* (London, Allen and Unwin, 1972) pp. 36–7.
[24] Gabriel A. Almond, 'Determinacy-choice, stability-change: some thoughts
on a contemporary polemic in political theory', *Government and Opposition*, 5
(1969–70), p. 27. For a further discussion, and for a comment on the above see
Trowbridge H. Ford, 'Towards a better relationship between history and
political science', *Government and Opposition*, 7 (1972), pp. 207–29.
[25] Evron M. Kirkpatrick, 'The impact of the behavioural approach on traditional political science', in Austin Ranney (ed.), *Essays on the Behavioral Study
of Politics* (Urbana, University of Illinois Press, 1962) p. 18.
[26] An Office of Public Opinion Research Survey asked voters in April 1944 how
they had cast their votes in the 1940 United States Presidential election. Some

poll books, allied to other nominative data derived from census enumerators' returns, tax assessments, directories and the like, in effect
permit one to conduct a survey of voting behaviour in the past, one can
avoid the problems of aggregative analysis.[27] The difficulty of deriving
knowledge about individual voting behaviour from aggregative data
is now well known.[28] The use of the poll books also facilitates the longitudinal analysis of individual voting behaviour (a much neglected
area of analysis according to Talbot[29]), as many constituencies have the
records of a consecutive sequence of polls. Finally, since there is a great
deal of material available, and since in many cases it is laid out in a way
that facilitates sampling, there is little trouble or expense in replicating
psephological studies done on it.

III

The social scientist requires particular kinds of material and particular
kinds of skills to exploit it. It has been suggested that the past can
provide such data and that, with care, traditional social scientific
methods are appropriate for analysing it. The essays in this volume have
been chosen, in part, with a view to the various ways practitioners of
Applied Historical Studies might communicate their findings. The three
main elements are first, the need to spell out one's assumptions, to be
explicit wherever possible, to forswear what Fogel (p. 131) calls 'casual

---

36·3% said they had voted for Dewey: 62·8% for Roosevelt. The actual votes
cast in 1940 were respectively 44·8% and 54·7%. Frederick F. Stephan and
Philip J. McCarthy, *Sampling Opinions: an Analysis of Survey Procedure* (New
York, John Wiley, 1958), p. 140.

[27] It is likely to save one from say exaggerating the overall stability of voting
patterns as Norwegian political observers had done until Valen and Katz did a
survey and found that one-third of their sample had changed their party
allegiance since the time they cast their first vote. Henry Valen and Daniel Katz,
Political Parties in Norway (Oslo and London, Universitets-forlaget and Tavis-
tock Publications, 1964), p. 185.

[28] The classic article by W. S. Robinson, 'Ecological correlations and the
behavior of individuals', *American Sociological Review*, Vol. xv (June 1950),
pp. 351–7, first drew attention to the so-called 'ecological fallacy'. For a brief
review and illustration of this see Charles M. Dollar and Richard J. Jensen,
Historian's Guide to Statistics: Quantitative Analysis and Historical Research
(New York, Holt Rinehart and Winston, 1971) pp. 97–103. For a recent statement upbraiding scholars for exaggerating the problem of the 'ecological fallacy'
see Paul Kleppner, 'Beyond the "new political history": A review essay',
Historical Methods Newsletter, 6, No. 1 (December, 1972), p. 25; footnote 13.

[29] Robert H. Talbot, 'Consistency in patterns of individual voting behavior',
Social Science Quarterly, 52, No. 2 (1971), p. 417.

procedures', to watch carefully for the impressionistic or qualitative statement. The everyday use of implicit quantification (with words like 'slight', 'typical', 'significant', 'widespread', 'common', 'representative') has been carried over into traditional history. It has no place in Applied Historical Studies. A second requirement is the use of appropriate statistical techniques. Examples appear throughout this volume – Spearman's Rho; Kendall's Tau; one-tailed significance tests; multiple regression analysis; chi square. Thirdly, findings must be cradled in theory. Again, examples can be drawn from this volume. E. G. West regards his work as a 'trying out of new theory in the context of old data' (p. 53); Krause sets his findings in the context of an element of contemporary demographic theory (p. 155); Thernstrom sees his task as that of refining 'social theory to make it more sensitive to social reality, past and present' (p. 232).

Applied Historical Studies can be seen, then, as providing 'historical answers to basically unhistorical questions.'[30] This volume seeks to illustrate what it is all about – 'warts and all'. Wringing findings from historical data that are of interest to the social scientist is not easy. Interpretations are quickly challenged – one reason why we have included some polemic arising from the articles by Krause and West. The data too are never perfect, as Küchemann battling with the reconstitution of families technique (p. 196) or Blumin ('the Philadelphia data remain inscrutable to the last', p. 248) admit. However, when all is said and done, the analysis is not impossible, some progress can be made and the occasion is not so rare when the findings of Applied Historical Studies are of a greater value than those provided by an analysis of purely contemporary data.

[30] The phrase, though not the context, is that of Edward Shorter, *The Historian and the Computer: a Practical Guide* (Englewood Cliffs, N.J., Prentice-Hall, 1971), p. 4.

1 Sociology and the historical perspective

KAI T. ERIKSON

The relationship between sociology and history has interested scholars from both disciplines for a long time. By now a considerable library of materials is available on the subject, ranging from involved philosophical essays on the nature of the borderline separating the two fields to ceremonial addresses of various kinds urging a greater volume of traffic across that line. Literature from the sociological side of the border, at least, has been almost unanimous in its insistence that sociologists should devote more attention to history – so much so that the argument would appear to have lost much of its urgency for simple lack of opposition. Nevertheless, sociology in the United States continues to lack historical focus. One can cite the works of men like Bellah, Bendix, Lipset, Merton, Moore, Nesbit, Smelser, Swanson, and Tilly to demonstrate that sociology sometimes reflects a strong sense of history; but these distinguished names only serve to suggest by contrast that most of what passes for sociological research in this country is not informed by much in the way of a historical perspective.

I should perhaps begin by explaining that I once spent a period of several years working with historical records, even though I was involved in a project that seemed eminently 'sociological' to me at the time. Like others before and since I went into that experience fully convinced that the study of history and the study of social life are logically different forms of scholarship. I emerged from the experience,

Kai T. Erikson, in Wendell Bell and James A. Mau (eds.), *The Sociology of the Future: Theory, Cases and Annotated Bibliography* (New York, Russell Sage Foundation, 1971).

This article was originally a MacIver Lecture presented at the annual meeting of the Southern Sociological Society, Atlanta, Georgia, 1968.

however, in a more confused frame of mind. On the one hand, it seemed obvious that the traditional distinctions we usually draw between history and sociology do not pose any real barriers to the actual conduct of social research, whatever merit they may have in abstract principle. On the other hand, I thought there must be a number of other obstacles and inhibitions lying elsewhere in the structure of the field that make it difficult for a sociologist to deal comfortably with historical data, and this is the line of thought I hope to pursue in this chapter.

FORMAL DISTINCTIONS

The sociologist who elects to use historical records in his work is likely to approach the assignment with some misgiving. For one thing, if he has been recruited into the profession in the usual manner and has been exposed to the usual kind of professional training, he does not know very much about history. Beyond that he carries with him as part of his intellectual equipment a set of distinctions that confirm the separate identity of sociology by differentiating it from other fields like history; and yet it is not at all clear to him how these distinctions are supposed to orient his research.

The most familiar of these distinctions, of course, is that historians are interested in something called 'the past' and sociologists in something called 'the present'. As a practical matter, this simply means that students in each of the two fields customarily address themselves to different locales in time – a point of no importance here. As a methodological matter, however, the distinction is somewhat more complicated. Generally speaking, historians depend upon the passage of years to inform them what moments in the past have influenced the course of future events and are, for that reason, 'historic'; and to that extent, at least, historians can be said to rely on fate to determine not only what data shall filter down to them but what portion of the past shall engage their attention. Sociologists, on the other hand, are apt to be more suspicious of fate. They are generally encouraged by the logic of their method to generate their own information, extracting it from the contemporary social setting themselves because they hope to reach *behind* the historical appearance of things and have no reason to suppose that the information they require will be deposited in the ordinary run of historical records. In theory, then, historians should find it easier to make sense of data that have been seasoned by the effects of time, and sociologists should find it easier to make sense of data over which they can exercise some immediate measure of control.

This distinction, if it ever meant anything, is almost surely losing force, partly because it is no longer so clear that historians and sociologists rely upon different sources of information. Historians are beginning to generate their own data by procedures developed in the social sciences; and sociologists, in turn, are frequently deriving their material from documents of precisely the sort employed by historians. The whole character of historical data has changed anyway because sociologists are currently in the business of data gathering; sociological reports are now sent to the archives for storage along with state papers and official records, and there they have simply become a new species of historical document. In general, it is difficult to see how a reasonable line can be drawn between the two fields on that score alone.

Yet the feeling persists within both disciplines that the kinds of intellectual orientation necessary for studying the past are somehow different from those necessary for studying the present, and one must look for the sources of that feeling in the professional climates of the two fields themselves. The past has generally been studied in an atmosphere of scarcity: the traditional task of the historian has been to sift through a finite supply of data as thoroughly and as carefully as he can, and the working arrangements he has devised for that purpose – the quiet reserve of his workshops, the vigor of his arguments over seemingly small matters of texture and detail – can be both unfamiliar and a little intimidating to the sociologist. The present, however, is generally studied in an atmosphere of abundance: the traditional job of the sociologist is to take rough and approximate samplings of the data as they splash around him in an endless flow, and the working arrangements he has fashioned for that purpose – the abstractness of his vocabulary, the impersonality of his procedures, the spare geometry of his charts and tables – can be strange and sometimes offensive to the historian. Carl Bridenbaugh, the distinguished American historian, was once horrified when a sociologist asked him: 'What is *your* method of sampling?' The question may have been shrewder than Bridenbaugh recognized, but the notion that one can examine a problem responsibly by selecting a tiny fraction of the available evidence lies far outside what more traditional historians would define as proper scholarship. Sampling is the strategy of persons who work with vast universes of data; it is a strategy of plenty.

As a result of these differences in atmosphere, students often over-estimate the degree to which the working arrangements of the other field are governed by some hidden method of approach, some implicit logic not readily apparent to outsiders. For what it is worth, I can report that I drifted through the beginning stages of the study mentioned earlier thinking that there must be ways to 'do' history that I could learn if I only consulted the right scholar or read the right book; and now, several years later, I frequently encounter students of history looking for inside hints on how to 'do' sociology, as if some manageable recipe were involved. Students often hesitate to move across the border between the two fields, then, because they mistake the professional postures they confront on the other side for a formidable and exclusive set of methods.

A second and more telling distinction between the two fields is an old and honored tradition that sociologists should concern themselves with the more *general* properties of social experience, the everyday patterns of activity that appear again and again in the life of the social order, while historians should concern themselves with those *specific* moments in the flow of time that have influenced the character of an age or tempered the course of the future. According to this academic division of labor, the sociologist's assignment is to look for regularities and correspondences in the conduct of men in the hope of discovering general 'laws'. The historian's assignment, in turn, is to look for the unique and distinctive in the conduct of men in the hope of capturing as accurately as possible what actually happened in the past. Sociology is nomothetic, history idiographic.

This distinction makes a good deal of sense in the abstract, but it is sometimes difficult to know what to do with it in any given case. On the one hand, it seems perfectly reasonable that some events in the past (decisive elections, for example) should attract the attention of historians because they literally 'made' history, while other events (say the voting activities of housewives in Omaha) should attract the attention of sociologists precisely because they are undistinguished acts, representative acts, passing instances of some more inclusive social pattern. On the other hand, it is also important to recognize that human actions them-selves are neither generic nor specific. Every event has properties that can be subsumed under a more general heading: if this were not so, we would be unable to identify the event in the first place. Yet every event is also peculiar to *some* historical sequence, whether it be the life history of one of those housewives in Omaha, the emergence of Western civilization, or a sweep of time as broad in scale as the evolution of the human species. This division of labor, then, fails because it obscures the extent to which each of the two fields employs the perspective attributed to the other. Historians generalize all the time, as numbers of them have pointed out; and sociologists are always dealing with particularities, no matter how energetically they cut and trim the data to fit the abstract logic of their procedures.

Whenever a sociologist looks carefully at a human scene, he is actually observing a unique moment in historical time as well as an instance of some broader regularity; and thus the social landscape he surveys does not differ in any appreciable way from the landscape viewed by the historian. Why is it, then, that sociologists and historians usually produce works that are so distinct from one another in style and content? One reason, presumably, is that each attends to different features of the common landscape and reports on different activities taking place within it. A sociologist is more likely to note the structure of the scene than the character of its leading actors, he is more likely to be interested in the activities of civil society than in the actions of governments, and, in general, he is more likely to be concerned with some underlying pattern in the events he is studying than with the moments of crisis: the sudden shifts of fortune, the contests among commanding adversaries, the ironies of fate, and all the other human dramas around which the conventional historical narrative is organized.

Still, this is not the only reason accounts written by historians are so easy to distinguish from those written by sociologists. Even the barest analysis of sociological prose would probably confirm the suspicion held by many critics both inside and outside the profession that the abstract quality of sociological work is conveyed as much by the prevailing conventions of sociological reporting as by the contents of the reports themselves. Take titles, for example: sociology must be one of the few scholarly fields where a study of hospital rates in Massachusetts could be called *Psychosis and Civilization* or where a study of young men and women in industrial England could be called *Youth and the Social Order*. Or take prefaces: it is a standard practice in sociological reporting to introduce a set of findings by simply naming the academic species to which it hopefully belongs, whether or not any further connections are drawn between the two ('the following is intended as a contribution to the sociology of . . .'). Or the presentation of data: even where an author is careful to note that his evidence on delinquency comes from a working-class section of Scranton during the third and fourth months of a steel strike, the next person to mention that evidence may very well treat it as a 'finding' about delinquency everywhere, a standard item in 'the literature'.

Other usages, too, have the sometimes inadvertent effect of wrapping sociological merchandise into nomothetic packages. In the interests of protecting the anonymity of their informants, for example, sociologists frequently omit from their published reports exactly the kind of identifying information that would place the study in its proper historical context. When one invents names like 'Western Hospital' or 'Southern City' for his research sites and then is purposefully vague about persons and dates and locations, he is introducing a note of generality and abstractness into the finished product that does not accurately reflect the substance of the findings themselves. The presumption, of course – sometimes stated, more often not – is that the site in question is somehow representative of other locales and other times; yet the researcher does not ordinarily know whether this is so. If he simply states or implies that the scene he has studied is 'typical' and then deals only with those features that make it appear so, he is making it almost impossible for the reader to arrive at his own reasoned conclusion. The problem for the responsible investigator, then, is twofold. He cannot distinguish the regular pattern from the unique happening unless he is careful to study both, in which case his research procedures are necessarily similar to those of the historian. And if he hopes to show the reader how he made that discrimination, he must include a good deal of local color and 'historical' detail in his report.

These, then, are two of the formal boundaries dividing sociology from history – the notion that sociologists are anchored to the present by the special logic of their methods and the notion that sociologists have a particular investment in the more general contours of social life. I would say, to repeat, that these distinctions do not in themselves represent a very compelling difference between the two fields at the operational level; but I would also say that they sometimes serve to mask a network of other barriers that lie below the visible surface and help keep the sociologist confined within his own academic preserve. These barriers have not been declared in philosophical essays on the nature of knowledge: they are built into what we might call the 'professional reflexes' of the sociologist – those habits of mind and temper that become the hidden products of a sociological apprenticeship and constitute the normative climate of the discipline. We have noted two or three of these implicit barriers. It is time now to consider several

others by backing away from the subject for a moment and returning
to it along a different line of approach.

PROFESSIONAL REFLEXES

Sociology, in common with several of the social sciences, claims the
entire range of human experience as its proper subject matter and thus
does not observe very many jurisdictional limits in its search for relevant
data. Therefore, the niche occupied by sociology in the structure of
academic life is sometimes difficult to portray. When a sociologist is
asked to describe his profession, he is likely to say in terms that sound
a little vague to students in neighboring fields that sociology is a
'perspective' rather than a subject matter, an 'approach' rather than an
inventory of known facts. What he means by this, normally, is that
sociologists do not have a natural territory in the world of human
phenomena and can only be distinguished from students in other fields
by the *way* they pursue data – by the way their senses are conditioned,
the way their imaginations are tuned, the way their minds are disciplined.

To think sociologically, then, is not simply a matter of rehearsing
certain theories or developing certain skills: it is a matter of learning new
devices for sorting out the various details that crowd one's consciousness
and of learning new ways to determine what impressions in the world of
human experience are worth one's attention. When a sociologist studies
a conversation between two people, for instance, he is presumably
trained to note the patterning of the relationship rather than the contributions of the individual participants – the words and gestures that
are drawn from a common cultural vocabulary rather than those that
suggest personal idiosyncrasies. He is trained to look at the *space
between* the interacting pair rather than at the spaces they occupy as
separate persons, to visualize the two as a single social unit rather than as
discrete objects in space that happen to intersect for a passing moment.
He sees the actors as reflections of one or another abstract position in
the social order – as occupants of statuses, players of roles, representatives of class interests, or ethnic traditions.

This (or something like it) is what sociologists normally have in mind
when they talk about their perspective or approach. When we say that
groups of scholars share a common discipline, we are suggesting, among
other things, that they turn their attention to the same universe of
detail and try to screen out from their line of vision all other details that

might interfere with that concentration. It is the essence of all special-
ization, presumably, that students will deliberately limit the number of
variables they take into account for the explicit purpose of sharpening
their focus on those they accept as their proper concern; in that respect,
at least, the disciplined eye is one that sees both more and less than the
untutored eye.

The difficulty here is that members of a discipline do not always
recognize the price they have paid to achieve this clarity of focus, and
they sometimes act as if the variables they have screened out in an
attempt to improve their concentration have conveniently disappeared in
the meantime. In the case of sociology, it might be argued that our
ability to appreciate the effects of general social forces on human conduct has often been purchased at the cost of reducing our awareness of
personality processes: the social man who appears in many of our
reports, at any rate, is a creature who does not seem to be governed in
any important way by unconscious impulses and who yields his auto-
nomy rather easily to the demands of the social environment. Or, again,
it might be argued that our ability to appreciate the influence of culture
on human conduct has been purchased at the cost of dulling our sensi-
tivity to *biological processes*: indeed, it is taken for granted in many
sociological circles that serious discussions about the effect of genetic
factors on behavior are not only scientifically unsound but politically
suspicious.

These professional screens have played an important part in the
emergence of sociology and will continue to do so as long as we remember what they are. But there is another screen in common use which
probably serves to impair rather than improve the quality of sociological
vision: the ability sociologists have developed to perceive relationships
between persons and events and institutions that coexist in time by
muting their sense of time altogether. I do not mean to suggest that
sociologists are less aware of the passage of years than other men, or
that dour theorists from Columbia and Harvard have somehow managed
to force time out of our imagery in the interests of promoting a
structural-functional view of the universe, as some commentators have
implied. I mean, rather, that it has been one of the professional reflexes
of the sociologist (in the United States, at least) more or less to freeze
time in order to get a more leisurely look at the patterns of relationship
obtaining at a given moment. In this sense, sociologists are often poorly
equipped to handle historical data, not simply because they are unres-
ponsive to the persisting pleas that they learn to think more historically,

but because the conceptual language of the field and the standards of relevance that are built into its models do not always lend themselves conveniently to that purpose.

It follows, then, that one of the more important hidden barriers dividing the two fields is a matter of conceptualization and terminology. As a general rule, sociologists and historians tend to invest their energics differently when they look at *connections between* the variables they study, sociologists spending more time on relationships that are essentially *lateral* in time and historians on relationships that are essentially *sequential*. This insight may seem something less than profound, but sociologists who work with historical data in a sustained way often discover that a large part of the vocabulary they have been trained to use when portraying the connection between social objects makes sense principally when those objects coexist. Sociologists who incline toward a structural-functional vision of social life have a vocabulary at their disposal – interaction, exchange, balance, equilibrium, function, consensus, and the like – that does not translate easily into narrative figures. Sociologists who lean toward a somewhat less symmetrical view of social life approach historical data with much the same disadvantage; terms such as coercion, conflict, tension, ambivalance, antagonism, and dissensus, like terms featured in the language of structural-functionalism, deal almost entirely with objects present at the same moment in time. I do not mean to imply that the schools of thought in which these vocabularies have developed are themselves frozen in timelessness, for some of our richest work on 'institutionalization' say, or 'socialization' – two areas of study that depend very much on a sense of time – have come out of the same conceptual frameworks. But it is probably fair to point out that the everyday vocabularies of sociology are very largely geared to lateral connections in social life.

The various formulations one finds in American sociology under the heading of 'social change' may be a case in point, for the very *idea* of change can sometimes sound awkward when expressed in conventional sociological prose. Many of our standard descriptions of change – check any current text – draw attention to successive stages in the development of a given institution or structure, almost as if the only way we can introduce the element of time into our calculations is to visualize several different stages of equilibrium or several different states of conflict stacked one on top of the other like so many building blocks. A historian, on the other hand, is more inclined simply to take for granted the fact that change takes place in the life of the social order – that people mature, that institutions age, that generations replace one another, that one event gives way to another in a relentless sweep of time. His language deals with continuities, ours with discrete shifts in the arrangements of society. His language is tuned to growth and decline as genetic processes built into the very nature of social order; ours is tuned to the linkages among social objects that happen to fit together in the same temporal frame.

Another of the hidden barriers between sociology and history, closely related to the first, is that each field entertains a somewhat different set of notions as to what constitutes a plausible 'explanation'. To *explain* a fact, of course, means to *account for it* – to align it with other facts in such a way that the appearance of this one seems logical, reasonable, perhaps even inevitable. In general, historians are likely to feel that a given outcome is explained if they can relate a credible story about the sequence of events that led up to it or the motives that impelled it, while sociologists are likely to feel that an outcome is explained if they can trace its connection to other institutions and forces in the surrounding environment. I do not want to get into this enormously complex problem at any length, but I do want to note one of its less visible consequences for styles of academic work – namely, that historians and sociologists tend to fall back to different methodological shelters whenever their data prove thin and inconclusive. When a historian is unsure of his data, he is invited by the conventions of his trade to fill in the missing information with a fairly deliberate exercise of sympathy and intuition, on the theory that the facts of the case are forever lost and that, in any case, the imagination of a disciplined professional mind is itself a research tool of no mean power. It is surely no accident that history is the one social science recognizing a muse. When a sociologist is unsure of *his* data, however, he is under a certain constraint from the conventions of his trade to withdraw to a more secure and sometimes more trivial ground where his position can be defended and his conclusions substantiated. The records of history cannot always be counted on to furnish information of the sort a sociologist thinks he requires to explain his findings, and this realization often quickens his retreat from the awkward past to the more accommodating present.

The most subtle and yet most compelling of the hidden barriers dividing the two fields, however, is that scholars who deal with the historical past usually visualize their own relationship to the data they study in a different way from scholars who deal with the social present. I shall devote a moment to this subject because I suspect it relates importantly to the kinds of collaboration we can reasonably expect in the future between sociology and history.

Sociologists often proceed as if they have experienced the data they use in their studies at first hand: after all, they can reach out and touch the walls of the institutions they are interested in, speak to people they are trying to understand, observe the social scenes they are writing about, and consult the records of their own era. Because we have prominent examples of field work to cite, we may forget that working sociologists are often just as remote from their sources of information as are historians, since their data are so often gathered for them by intermediaries of one sort or another: student assistants, institutional surveys, official agencies, and so on. Nevertheless, sociologists are often inclined to take a certain methodological comfort from the illusion that they remain close to their data, and as a result they are sometimes rather vague and unreflective about the kinds of concern that belong in the realm of epistemology when they are actually engaged in research. Whatever we teach in courses on the 'sociology of knowledge', we generally approach data with the idea that the world is pretty much as it seems and that the evidence we happen to obtain about the world is a fair enough representation of reality.

When an investigator turns to historical data, however, and loses his anchor in the present, he is in a more precarious position – if only because he cannot sustain any further illusion of sensory contact with the human experience he is studying. Because his evidence is second-hand and his subject matter remote, he is more or less forced to be more thoughtful about the evidence at his disposal and more skeptical about his relationship to it. To begin with, he is fated to work with documents of uncertain ancestry and must ask several questions about the material even before he examines it. Why were these particular scraps of information recorded? Who wrote them down and why? How accurate an observer was the writer? How well did he represent the mood and spirit of his age? This is only the beginning of the problem, for the one quality all these documents have in common is their survival; and even though a researcher has complete faith in the authenticity and reliability of the documents, he must wonder by what law or accident they came to be preserved. They are not the random remains of a dead age, like the debris found at an archeological site. Every generation of men that has lived meantime has served for a period as custodian of those records, and thus the surviving library of materials is in many ways a record of all the intervening years as well.

To use the example with which I am most familiar, a large number of documents are available to the student of seventeenth-century New England, rich in texture and broad in coverage; but one cannot spend more than a few hours in their company without wondering whose history they record. Not only were they originally composed by men with a vested interest in the events they were reporting, but they have been passed along to us by a succession of other men, each of whom has taken a turn sifting, rearranging, and even rewriting those materials. The surviving records, then, register not only what impressed John Winthrop in the early years of settlement, but what Cotton Mather regarded as worth remembering in the second half of the seventeenth century, what Thomas Hutchinson considered 'historic' in the eighteenth century, and what whole generations of chroniclers and antiquarians decided to place on the shelves in the nineteenth century. The attitudes as well as the fingerprints of many men are attached to this (or any) set of documents. The problem does not end here, for any investigator who learns in this demanding school how one generation of persons can influence the work of another will sooner or later begin to wonder how he, in his own turn, is liable to influence the work of students yet to come.

In short, working with historical materials requires an approach to data tempered by a kind of skepticism and uncertainty – an awareness of self, perhaps – that comes naturally to many experienced historians but fits uneasily among the professional reflexes of many sociologists. Historians are aware that their own minds are the spheres in which the past comes alive again and that the data of their researches are converted into 'histories' by a process involving personal qualities of insight, sympathy, and imagination. I do not mean by this that every journeyman historian stays awake at night worrying about the degree to which his personal susceptibilities intrude upon the larger character of his work, but rather that it is generally understood throughout the discipline that written history is bound to reflect the talent and temper of the mind that produced it. When a historian reviews the available data and draws new conclusions from them, for instance, the work he publishes is likely to be called an 'interpretation' – suggesting both that the intellectual posture of the author is an important feature of his work and that the work itself is apt to be replaced in time by another interpretation. Should someone conclude that historians are subject to all the private subjectivities and social biases that flesh is heir to, the historian can reasonably respond that this is not always a handicap. If he is an interpreter of history *for* his generation, he may find it helpful to share the perspectives *of* his generation; if as a scholar he relies upon some measure of insight and intuition to breathe life back into pasts that are forever dead and gone, he may find it fully appropriate to employ the arts of the dramatist as well as the skills of the scientist. This argument, at least as it appears in some of the more idealistic discussions of historical method, sometimes trails off into a form of mysticism that most sociologists and many historians find uncongenial, but the main point is widely accepted throughout the profession.

It is probably unnecessary to add here that considerations of this sort have not figured prominently in sociological discussions of method. The energies of those sociologists concerned with method have been largely spent in an attempt to neutralize whatever qualities of insight and sympathy an investigator brings to his work – and this on the basis of two very questionable assumptions: the first, that proper scientific procedure requires one to systematically reduce one's own influence on the data; the second, that it is humanly and technically possible to do so. We shall return to these two assumptions in a moment.

HISTORY AND METHOD

It has become more important to take a careful look at the boundary dividing sociology and history because the traffic across that line has been increasing over the past several years. Historians have moved across the border in search of new techniques to help them handle the large masses of data that are increasingly being recognized as their main concern and in search of new conceptualizations to help them order the past in more 'social' terms. Sociologists have moved across the border primarily because they are interested in the rich caches of data located in the historians' archives. The rapid pace of change in the modern world, among other things, has encouraged sociologists to view the present as history, and they are beginning to search in the records of the past for older parallels to the processes of industrialization and urbanization and revolution they see in the world around them. In a sense, then, what sociologists have tried to gain from their commerce with history has been additional information that can be analyzed by standard sociological methods and used in the service of standard sociological hypotheses.

The final paragraphs of this chapter will suggest, however, that sociologists might profit from a different form of commerce with history

– one in which they consider the degree to which *historical methods* can help in the analysis of *sociological data*. Perhaps 'methods' is not the proper term: some historians bristle at the suggestion that their work is governed by anything so strict and binding as a method, and many sociologists are only too ready to endorse that judgment. Still, scholars who study the past in a systematic way can be said to share a certain cast of mind, a certain set of professional reflexes, and I would like to propose that these qualities can broaden and inform the scope of sociological inquiry.

One way in which sociologists might profit from paying closer attention to the historical method is to acquire a sharper sense of the relationship between social events over time. In order to appreciate how the institutions we study are molded by the passage of years, we probably need to learn how to think in narrative terms, to develop a feeling for the temporal nature of social forces; and the only way we are likely to attain these skills is to become more 'historical' ourselves.

C. Wright Mills, among others, has insisted that the sociologist is really a contemporary historian. Whether he is studying a school district or analyzing election returns or observing the activities of a religious sect or conducting experiments with laboratory groups, the sociologist is observing the history of his own age as well as looking for broader indicators of regularity and law. Unless he becomes aware of this, he runs the risk of losing not only his historical but his *sociological* command of the social scenes he is studying. For one thing, a setting that appears to reflect general social properties may later prove to have been but an instance of some wider arc of change. As one looks back on some of the truly remarkable studies coming out of American sociology a generation or more ago, for example, they sometimes seem a little antiquated and (to use a curious but meaningful expression) *dated*. This is not because the methods or the vocabulary employed in those works have become obsolete, but because it is clearer to us than it was to the original writers that their works reflect the age in which they were produced – an age of immigration, an age of prohibition, an age of depression and collapse. These studies offer particular insights into the history of places like urban Chicago and rural North Carolina as well as general insights into the anatomy of society; and yet it is not at all evident that the sociologists who did those projects were aware of the difference – or, indeed, that investigators on the scene are themselves *ever* aware of the difference. It is easy to imagine that a number of contemporary classics now honored as monuments to the craft will seem equally dated, equally anchored in time and place once another generation has passed. If so, it will demonstrate again that the greatest difficulty we face in determining whether a given set of findings should be counted as 'generic' or 'specific' is that, like most of the other data of history, their actual contours become apparent only at a distance.

This problem becomes even more complicated when we consider that sociologists continually change the history of the settings they study by the very act of paying attention to them. However representative and typical an institution may appear at first, it takes on a special character simply because an investigator has introduced himself into it; and the investigator is liable to misunderstand the information he obtains unless he sees *himself* as a unique historical event in the life of the institution and remains aware that the report he writes may change the structure he is viewing. In both of these senses, then, the sociologist is something of a participant historian whether the title appeals to him or not, and it seems reasonable to suggest that he can best understand his data if he accepts both roles.

A second way in which sociologists might profit from paying attention to the historical 'method' is to take a somewhat closer look at the relationship between an observer and his data. As suggested earlier, sociologists often seem to derive a certain comfort from the illusion that their evidence is close at hand and that their procedures are largely automatic. There are living populations of subjects to draw upon, tables of significance values to consult, and elaborate hardware to employ in the processing of data; and on the whole we are not especially troubled by the degree to which our own posture as social beings intrudes upon our results. Yet sooner or later the data we use have to be sifted through the soft tissues of a human mind; and when this occurs, the matter of how these tissues operate and how they relate to the rest of the social order becomes an important technical concern rather than an artistic whim. This is an issue to which historians (or philosophers of history, at any rate) have devoted a good deal of attention, but it has provoked little systematic thought in sociology.

It is probably fair to observe that sociologists who worry about this matter are regarded by their fellows as 'soft' and humanistic, while those who do not – who think that their use of standard measures and mechanical procedures protects them from subjective bias – are regarded as 'hard' and scientific. Yet this contrast is very likely a misreading of the scientific ethos. If a theoretical physicist were to listen in on a professional conversation about sociology and history, he might conclude that a skeptical historian in the tradition of Croce or Colling-wood is in many ways more scientific than is his positivistic colleague in history or his neighbor in sociology – not because his standards of investigation are more precise or his conclusions more amenable to verification, but because his approach to data allows for a margin of indeterminacy and uncertainty and takes for granted that the subjective condition of the observer is an objective fact about the research setting itself. Our physicist might very well want to give the historian credit for understanding something that sociologists sometimes overlook – that any research finding is a datum about the investigator as well as a datum about the subject at hand.

This brings us back to the subject of *discipline*. Whatever else the term may mean, a discipline is a set of ideas shared among a community of scholars as to what constitutes a proper order of evidence, a proper method of investigation, a proper standard of criticism. These notions, presumably, do not have any special authority beyond the fact that they happen to make sense to the men who hold them, and to this extent a discipline must be understood as a normative order, a system of belief, a cultural product.

One of the important functions of a discipline is to represent stand-ards of performance against which scholars can evaluate their own research, a process that often goes under the heading of 'developing objectivity' or 'being scientific'. In many respects this way of phrasing the issue can be highly misleading. Any individual in a research setting brings with him from the different corners of his mind a potential for distortion and bias – inclinations that are related to his own private life and experience, his social class position and ethnic background, and so on. When we talk about making someone 'more objective', we are generally talking about submerging his private subjectivities into the subjectivities of a larger collectivity – shifting the moral center of gravity, as it were, from a private individual to a wider group.

For example, it is standard procedure in several of the social sciences to rely on a panel of judges whenever a researcher's impartiality is called into question, and then to be reassured when those judges agree. What happens, of course, is that the biases of one researcher have been washed away by the biases of several judges – experts, perhaps, and shrewd observers, but representatives of the same general sector of the moral order from which the researcher himself has ordinarily come. When the grayest elders of a tribe testify that polyandry is a law of nature, we call it culture; when the leading spokesmen of a religious movement insist that some article of creed is based on revelation, we call it ideology; but when five or six sociologists agree that the behaviour of a subject falls into a particular category, we call it science. This can put the sociologist in a curious position: while he may be the first to argue that the things 'everyone knows' are often a result of cultural conditioning, he is sometimes slow to realize that professional agreement on a method of procedure or a set of findings may amount to the same thing.

A discipline, then, reflects the best sense a community of scholars can make of the way they work and the best rules they can fashion for handling the data they view as their responsibility. That there may be room in these arrangements for bias of one sort or another should go without saying: the problem for a mature profession is to arrange its affairs as reasonably as it can *knowing this to be the case*. And this can prove to be a highly sensitive matter because a discipline – like any human group – is always struggling against the tendency of some of its members to settle for a seemingly simple and lasting solution to the ambiguity of its position. On the one hand, there is the very real danger that a discipline will dissolve into a kind of mindless antinomianism where everyone does his own thing and listens only to the sounds of his own voice. On the other hand, there is the equally real danger that a discipline will harden into a brittle orthodoxy where ritual rules and formulae long outlast the logic responsible for their invention.

Historians have been struggling with both of these inclinations for a number of years, but to one sociologist looking in from the outside (and perhaps with an outsider's readiness to idealize) it would seem that the academic atmosphere in which history is studied often reflects an easier balance between the two. At his best, a person who works with historical documents comes to accept as a working principle the fact that the eyes with which he sees have all the defects of the age in which he lives, and that other eyes will see things differently as a matter of course; yet at the same time he accepts the conventional lore of his discipline as a provisional source of wisdom, a base from which to operate. He manages to resist the attractive notion that every man is his own historian, responsible only to his own convictions and impulses; and he manages to resist the equally attractive notion that history is a discipline governed by natural laws of inquiry.

Sociology in the United States has generally leaned in the more positivistic of those directions, developing a form of scientism that no longer seems to resemble the natural science models from which it derived. There have been unmistakable signs in recent years, however, of a swing in the opposite direction – toward a species of radical skepticism in which persons distrust their own intelligence and all the established apparatus of sociology for fear of the various class and racial and ideological biases that might be hidden within them. We may hope that historical experience and historical consciousness can help us to find a responsible stance somewhere between the two extremes.

2. The achievement need and economic growth

DAVID C. McCLELLAND

ENGLAND FROM TUDOR TIMES TO THE
INDUSTRIAL REVOLUTION

The economic history of Great Britain is of special interest for several reasons. For one thing it provides the longest and most intensively studied record of economic development available for any society. In fact, the record is long enough so that one ought to be able to detect more than one wave of growth of the sort already investigated in Ancient Greece and Spain. Furthermore, England was at the very center of the Industrial Revolution which ushered in the modern most impressive phase of economic growth. It should therefore be of special interest to see what was happening to the level of achievement motivation in England in the eighteenth century. Finally, English literature is available for coding from 1400 on, so that it should be possible to push the assessment of n Achievement level back well before the first major wave of economic growth. In doing so, we may be able to detect the actual *rise* in achievement motivation which presumably occurred both in the Greek and Spanish cases but which the data do not actually show. In both instances n Achievement starts out high and drops off steadily.

Presumably if we had been able to measure it earlier, the n Achievement level would have been lower, but one of the lessons a student of human behavior learns early is to take nothing for granted. An alternative explanation of the Greek and Spanish findings is that n Achievement decline precedes economic growth, since all we have actually measured is such a decline and we do not know whether the initial point is high or low relative to what it had been earlier. It may always be

David C. McClelland (1961) from Chapter 4 in *The Achieving Society*, (New York, D. Van Nostrand) pp. 133–149.

difficult to measure the earliest levels of presumably low *n* Achievement, for the simple reason that if a culture is really low in *n* Achievement, it may in fact not produce enough literature to be scored. Nevertheless it becomes of the greatest importance to demonstrate if possible that *rises* in *n* Achievement level precede waves of economic growth in a way that was not possible in the Greek or Spanish case so that such an alternative interpretation of the data may be more decisively eliminated. The length of the literary record in England and the care with which it has been assembled and dated provide us with better opportunities for detecting rises as well as declines in *n* Achievement level.

Therefore Bradburn and Berlew[1] who made the study, set out to get a continuous record of *n* Achievement level in England from around 1400 in half century periods up through the beginning of the Industrial Revolution (around 1830). In other words, they wanted to start well before England began to stir under the Tudor kings, back in the days when it was still largely pasture and woodland, when 'from Blacon Point to Hillbree a squirrel may jump from tree to tree,' and to carry the record continuously up through the time when England was largely a concentration of great industrial cities that became the workshops and commercial capitals of the world. [. . . .] They succeeded in finding forty to fifty authors and 150 pages of comparable text to represent each time period (usually a half century). The literary material used was of three general kinds: drama, accounts of sea voyages, and street ballads. The choice of these particular literary forms was again dictated by the fact that they represented popular imaginative literature through the time period under investigation rather than the production of only an 'off beat' literary or élitist minority.

Only authors whose productive years fell largely within the limits of a given time period were included. Under these restrictions it proved possible to get adequate samples for all three literary types for six time periods beginning with 1501–1575 and ending with 1776–1830. In the case of drama it was possible to get an earlier sample also representing the fifteenth century. (See Table 2·1.) Among the better known plays used in part for coding were the following for each of the time periods:

1400–1500

1. Anonymous: *Everyman*

[1] N. M. Bradburn and D. E. Berlew, 'Need for achievement and English industrial growth', *Economic Development and Cultural Change*, **10**, no. 1 (1961), pp. 8–20.

2. Anonymous: *Noah's Ark. A Newcastle Play*
3. Medwall, Henry: *Fulgens and Lucres*

1501–1575

1. Robert Wever: *Lusty Juventus*
2. John Skelton: *Magnificence*
3. Richard Edwards: *Damon and Pythias*

1576–1625

1. Christopher Marlowe: *Tamburlaine*, First Part
2. William Shakespeare: *King Richard II*
3. Ben Jonson: *The Alchemist*

1626–1675

1. George Digby: *Elvira*
2. John Milton: *Samson Agonistes*
3. James Shirley: *Gamester*

1676–1725

1. Thomas Southerne: *The Fate of Capua*
2. William Congreve: *The Way of the World*
3. Joseph Addison: *Cato*

1726–1775

1. David Garrick: *The Guardian*
2. Samuel Johnson: *Irene: A Tragedy*
3. Oliver Goldsmith: *She Stoops to Conquer*

1776–1830

1. William Wordsworth: *The Borderers*
2. Richard Sheridan: *The Critic; or, A Tragedy Unrehearsed*
3. Percy Bysshe Shelley: *Prometheus Unbound*

The coding of the samples for *n* Achievement was done by one of the investigators who did not know what time period a work represented or for the most part who wrote it. Furthermore, the investigator, who made the literary selections knew nothing about the economic data which had been collected, to minimize the possibility of bias entering into his selection of the materials to be scored. Actually such bias is particularly unlikely to have entered into the selection of street ballads, since in this instance large numbers of short selections were coded wholesale with the single criterion for selection being that they were accurately dated. Both coders were highly experienced, [. . .] but to check on their reliability both of them scored one-third of the total sample of selections. The correlation coefficient between their two estimates of *n* Achievement present in the same material was ·93 and periodic checks with shorter

TABLE 2·1 *Number of authors and frequency of achievement imagery by type of literature from the fifteenth to nineteenth centuries in England*

Time period	Sample size per period:	Literary form			
		Drama 2,240 lines	Sea voyages 2,500 lines	Street ballads 1,308 lines	Totals 6,048 lines
1400–1500	Authors	14			
	Achievement images per 100 lines	4·60			
1501–1575	Authors	14	11	20	45
	Achievement images per 100 lines	6·16	2·76	6·34	4·79
1576–1625	Authors	14	10	18	42
	Achievement images per 100 lines	4·20	3·04	9·25	4·81
1626–1675	Authors	14	9	27	50
	Achievement images per 100 lines	2·50	2·64	4·59	3·01
1676–1725	Authors	14	10	27	51
	Achievement images per 100 lines	2·28	2·08	5·96	2·99
1726–1775	Authors	14	10	25	49
	Achievement images per 100 lines	3·48	3·92	6·12	4·23
1776–1830	Authors	14	10	34	58
	Achievement images per 100 lines	2·67	6·24	11·24	6·00

(from Bradburn and Berlew, 1961.)

samples throughout the scoring showed that their agreement reliability coefficient never dropped below ·92. The results of their scoring, presented as usual in terms of average number of achievement images per hundred lines, are presented in Table 2·1 and Fig. 2·1. They show a high point at the beginning of the period of investigation, a drop in *n* Achievement to a low point between 1626 and 1725, followed by another sharp rise thereafter. The meaning of these changes can best be under-

stood after a discussion of how a measure of rate of economic development in Britain was derived.

The problem of getting a quantitative estimate of economic development in Britain was especially complicated by the fact that growth was
more or less continuous from 1600 on. That is, unlike the waves of
development in Ancient Greece or Medieval Spain, England has shown
no marked or prolonged drop in *absolute* level of economic activity or
prosperity since around 1600. So the problem becomes [. . .] one of
comparing *relative rates* of growth, to discover times when the English
economy was growing more rapidly or more slowly than at other times.
Deane[2] has collected some national income estimates beginning with
Gregory King's figures in 1688, but they do not go back early enough
nor are they continuous or accurate enough to use. Furthermore,
Bradburn and Berlew decided that since the problem was to compare
rates of growth, rather than the absolute levels of development that
might be represented in national income figures, it was only necessary
to find a quantitative series [. . .] which could be regarded as representative of what was happening in the economy as a whole. They
examined several such series and found that coal import figures at
London collected by Nef[3] and Jevons[4] in general followed quite closely
whatever other evidence was available on changes in rate of economic
growth. The reason appears to be that coal then, like electricity now,
provided the power for many key economic activities, both commercial and domestic. The only question that might be raised would
have to do with the earliest period for which coal figures are available,
from around 1585 to 1650, since it might be contended that coal at that
time was still largely for domestic rather than commercial use. Coal had
been burned as domestic fuel for several centuries earlier, but it did not
come into wide use until early in the sixteenth century when brick
chimneys were invented that would cheaply and efficiently draw up
the 'noxious fumes' that had formerly made it unpopular. Still by the
end of the century, or by 1585 when the figures begin, it was used quite
generally, not only for domestic fuel but for the dressing of meat,
washing, brewing, and dyeing.[5]

[2] P. Deane, 'The implications of early national income estimates for the measurement of long-term economic growth in the United Kingdom', *Economic
Development and Cultural Change*, 4 (1955), pp. 3–38.
[3] J. V. Nef, *The Rise of the British Coal Industry* (London, Routledge & Son,
1932).
[4] W. S. Jevons, *The Coal Question* (London, Macmillan, 1906).
[5] W. S. Woytinsky and E. S. Woytinsky, *World Population and Production* (New
York, Twentieth Century Fund, 1953).

But the figures are only for one method of entry of coal into one city. How can they represent adequately what was going on in the country as a whole? Two considerations may help explain why they do. London was during all this period (roughly 1600–1800), perhaps even more than later when the Industrial Midland developed, the hub and commercial center of the country. What happened in London was a good barometer of what was happening all over the country. Furthermore, the port figures are so important because London was not near coal fields and had to get its coal primarily by sea up until the middle of the nineteenth century when railroads came into wide use. Fortunately this is after the period under consideration.

Granted for the moment that the coal import figures provide probably as accurate an index as is available of the level of economic activity in England over this time period, how can they be used to get estimates of rate of growth? The normal procedure economists use is to express the gain from one time period to the next as a percentage of the level at the first time period. The objections to such a procedure have already been outlined. [. . .] Suffice it to say again here that such a method tends to inflate enormously the percentage gains at the early stages of growth when the initial levels are very low. For example, in the present instance the percentage gain in coal imports for the first 20- to 30-year time period in the series is 363 per cent, a figure considerably higher than the highest percentage gain ever recorded in a similar time period, even at the height of the Industrial Revolution in the early nineteenth century when coal imports were leaping upwards by millions of tons rather than thousands as in the earliest time period. The best and simplest solution to such problems appears to be to use a regression analysis. [. . .] One can estimate on the basis of the general trend relating level of coal imports to gains in imports, what the gain for a given time period should be and then see whether the actual gain was more or less than expected.

The exact method by which this was done by Bradburn and Berlew[6] for the coal import figures is as follows. The starting point was taken to be the first year for which figures are available, namely 1585–1586. Next, they decided to get estimates of coal imports for every third of a century thereafter to get enough points to plot a reasonably stable regression line. Rather than use the figure for any given year, such as 1618, 1651, etc., they averaged all figures available for the third of a century in question to get an approximation of imports *over* that period.

[6] Bradburn and Berlew, *op. cit.*

Such averages were used for two reasons: figures were often not available for a particular year needed and also yearly figures sometimes show much fluctuation due to short-range changes in the condition of business which are not of interest in a long-range study of trends. So the figures available for years between 1605 and 1637 were averaged to get an estimate for around 1618–1620, those between 1634 and 1667 to get an estimate for around 1650, and so on. Then gains in roughly equal time periods of approximately 33 to 35 years could be obtained simply by subtracting each level from the preceding one (i.e., the level for 1618–1620 subtracted from the level for 1585–1586, etc.).

Inspection showed that if level is plotted against subsequent gain in logarithmic terms, the relationship is clearly linear and very close ($r = \cdot 82$ for the 8 time periods under consideration). In other words the gain (in log units) is higher the higher the initial level (also in log units). The regression formula for the straight line relationship (log gain $= \cdot 671$ log level $+ 1 \cdot 6389$) predicts what the gain should be from one time period to the next. Then this predicted value can be compared with the obtained value and the deviation expressed in standard score units [. . .] to see how fast the economy was expanding or contracting in terms of its average performance over this time period. The standard score values obtained in this way by Bradburn and Berlew are plotted in Fig. 2·1 at mid-points in the intervals over which the rate of gain took place. That is, they plotted the gain between 1585 and 1618–1620 at 1600, simply because it had to be plotted at some point and the mid-point seemed more representative than the end point for a rate of gain taking place over the whole period. Actually if the plotting were done at the end points, no differences in the interpretation of the relationship between n Achievement and economic changes would be necessary.

Although the estimates are admittedly crude, they nevertheless show three rather well-defined phases in the economic growth of England to the Industrial Revolution. The first period, centering in the years 1600–1690, is one of moderate overachievement (mean standard score for the first three estimates of gain $= + \cdot 33$). This is followed by a period of stagnation or underachievement centering in the years 1700–1780 (mean standard score for the three estimates of gain in this time period $= - 1 \cdot 11$). Finally, by 1800 the third phase of phenomenal economic growth culminating in the Industrial Revolution is already well under way (mean standard score for the two estimates of gains in this time period $= + 1 \cdot 17$).

Now the question is: how well do these estimates of the three phases in economic growth in Britain agree with historical accounts and with the hypothesis that *n* Achievement levels should foreshadow such changes at an earlier date? Figure 2·1 plots for easy visual comparison the motivational scores for a 50-year earlier time period along with the economic gain figures. Obviously the fit between the two curves is fairly close, the main point being that the motivational changes *precede*

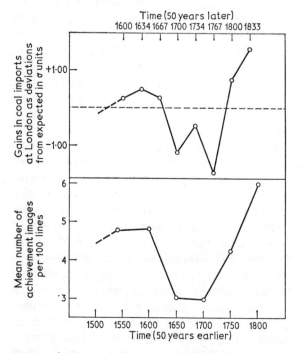

FIG 2·1 Average *n* Achievement levels in English literature (1550–1800) compared with rates of gain in coal imports at London fifty years later

the economic ones by 30–50 years. Let us consider in detail the evidence at each stage in development.

First, the figures show an above-average rate of economic development at the first point in time when an estimate is really possible, namely, around 1600. The most likely possibility is that the earlier rate of development was average. So a line has been drawn pointing downwards to indicate that the rise to the 'overachievement' represented by the estimate for 1600 occurred most probably in the last half of the sixteenth century. Does other evidence support such an inference? Bindoff states that the fifteenth century in England represented a period of economic decline – 'The area of land under cultivation instead of continuing to expand underwent a contraction. . . . Its industrial and commercial life exhibits the same tendency towards stagnation.'[7] Subsequently, however, during the reigns of the Tudor kings Henry VII and Henry VIII, England pulled herself together and showed a great burst of energy in the last half of the sixteenth century, symbolized by the exploits of Drake and Hawkins on the sea and the decisive defeat of the Spanish Armada in 1588. 'In the sixties and early seventies England had shaken herself free of that excessive dependence upon the Netherlands' market which had earlier exposed her economy to such severe crisis. Her merchants had opened up new markets, in Europe, Asia, and Africa, which they served with a wide range of goods. By about 1575 the nation began to reap the reward, and the next ten years, which saw Antwerp go down to irreparable ruin, were by contrast a boom period for English trade, and through trade for her industry and agriculture.'[8] The growth of trade and the expansive mood of the times are nicely illustrated by the foundation in 1599 of 'the most famous of the English trading corporations, the East India Company. . . . Thus there was planted, in the last year of the Tudor century, the seed of trade and dominion far exceeding the wildest flights of Tudor fantasy.'[9] There is little doubt that economic historians would agree with the estimates in Fig. 2·1, which show that England was advancing very rapidly economically around the turn of the seventeenth century. The figures indicate that the rate continued above average until well toward the end of the seventeenth century. While we have been concerned strictly with economic data, it is perhaps worth noting that Kroeber's figures[10] also show the whole of the seventeenth century to have been remarkable in England for its production of men eminent in literature, music and science. The scientist figures are of particular interest because of the contention by Weber, Merton[11] and others that interests in business and in science tend to occur together. Certainly together they produced the technological revolution in England a century later. If one accepts the argument that they are two aspects of the same type

[7] S. T. Bindoff, *Tudor England* (Harmondsworth, Penguin Books, 1950) p. 13.
[8] *ibid.*, p. 285.   [9] *ibid.*, p. 288.
[10] A. L. Kroeber, *Configurations of Culture Growth* (Berkeley, University of California Press, 1944).
[11] R. K. Merton, *Social Theory and Social Structure* (Glencoe, Illinois, Free Press, 1949).

of culture growth, then Kroeber's figures provide independent confirmation of the 'above-average' rate of growth in this culture area in the seventeenth century.

Was the economic peak preceded by a peak in n Achievement? The over-all estimate of n Achievement level, as shown in Fig. 2·1, is high in the period 1500–1575, though not higher than in the succeeding 50-year period. The simplest summary of the data is that n Achievement level was high from 1500 through 1625 and that this high level definitely appeared *before* the rapid economic growth that extended from 1600–1675. However, the figures for plays (Table 2·1) are especially interesting because they go back 50 to 75 years earlier, into the fifteenth century. They show that so far as this literary form is concerned, n Achievement level was lower earlier in the mid-fifteenth century (mean = 4·60) than it was later, around 1525 (mean = 6·16), confirming our hypothesis that our over-all measure starts (1540) at a high point in the n Achievement curve. The difference in the mean scores for the first two time periods in the drama curve is unfortunately not statistically significant ($p < \cdot 15$, pd). Nevertheless, the result is an interesting and potentially important confirmation of the theoretical expectation, not tested in Greece or Spain, that n Achievement has to *rise* to the high point at which it appears at the beginning of the phases of economic growth that have been chosen for study.

It is interesting to note, also, that the other two literary forms – accounts of sea voyages and street ballads—also show a rise in n Achievement but at a later period (1576–1625 instead of 1501–1575). If the p values for each of the rises considered separately are combined, using one-tailed significance tests throughout because all the trends are in the expected direction, the tendency for n Achievement level to rise from the first to the second period for which the literary forms are available is fairly dependable statistically speaking ($p < \cdot 05$).[12] At least this result fairly effectively disposes of the notion that n Achievement level is always highest in the earliest period of a literary form. Why it should rise at somewhat different historical time periods in the different types of literary forms is an interesting question. It is tempting to speculate that literary forms represented the thoughts and aspirations of different social classes in England in the sixteenth century, which showed a rise in n Achievement at somewhat different time periods. Perhaps, for

[12] The t's were combined by finding chi-square equivalents for the p values for the obtained t tests, summing the chi-squares, and obtaining the p value for the combined chi-square with three degrees of freedom.

example, the plays represented the feelings of the London population or of the more educated classes. The street ballads and accounts of sea voyages, on the other hand, may have represented the aspirations of the common people or the people from the smaller towns outside London. Then one could argue that the wave of n Achievement hit the better-educated city people first and then spread out to the provinces and to the less educated. But such speculations will have to be left to closer students of English history in the sixteenth century.

Do qualitative data support the finding that n Achievement level was high in England between 1500 and 1625? To begin with, it is certainly in accord with the best historical judgment that a wave of expansive energy reached England a century or more after it had reached its highest point in Spain. [. . .] Spain's level of n Achievement had dropped off significantly by the middle of the sixteenth century when England's was at a high point. The fact that Spain's absolute level was still higher than England's means nothing because absolute levels depend on the types of literature scored in the two countries which were not comparable. Neither epic poems nor history were scored in England, both of which in general give a very high level of n Achievement. Here [. . .] we find again that a country at a low point in n Achievement (Spain) suffers a major defeat at the hands of a country high in n Achievement (England) during the battle with the Spanish Armada (1588).

Even more interesting, in the light of the presumed connection between Protestantism and n Achievement, is the fact that the period 1500–1625 is precisely the time when Protestantism and eventually Puritanism was growing most rapidly in strength and numbers both in England and Scotland. In mid-century John Knox led the Calvinist revolution to a successful outcome, with the help of the English, in Scotland. In England the century began under the leadership of a king, Henry VIII, who certainly in his youth set an example of high n Achievement for his people. 'He could bend a bow with the best forester in the realm, and when complimented on his archery by the French ambassador could reply, "It was good for a Frenchman." His colossal suit of tilting armor in the Tower reminds us that once he flashed through the lists like Lancelot, laying low his adversaries and calling for more. He was a champion at tennis and a mighty hunter. . . . Among other accomplishments this Admirable Crichton was no mean musician, and played well on all known instruments.'[13] Henry, while orthodox

[13] G. M. Trevelyan, *History of England* (London, Longmans, 1926), p. 292.

enough himself in the beginning in religious matters, encouraged the 'new learning' brought over from Renaissance circles in Europe. Eventually he broke with Rome over the question of his remarriage, but certainly the rupture would not have lasted without the ground swell of support in public opinion led by the scholars he had encouraged and two great religious reformers – Cranmer, who translated the Prayer Book into English, and Latimer 'the soul of the popular movement' who 'by his rough, homely sermons, set the standard of that English pulpit oratory which, together with the Bible and the Prayer Book, effected the conversion of the people to Protestantism in the course of the next hundred years.'[14] The basis for the Protestant Reformation had been laid decades before by Wycliffe's translation of the Bible into English, but the popular movement which had failed then gained decisive momentum during the very years when our evidence shows that n Achievement level in England was high. So far as this period in history is concerned, the rise of Protestantism and n Achievement are closely connected, as they should be if our interpretation of Weber's hypothesis in psychological terms is correct.

To turn to the next decisive phase in the development of the British economy, the coal import data show a definite period of slower economic development roughly from 1700 to 1790. Do historians agree that this was a period of relative economic stagnation in England? Unfortunately they do not. While most of them would have agreed that the nation was developing slowly then as compared to her very rapid development subsequently in the Industrial Revolution, Deane's national income figures (1955) show a slow but steady rise in national income *per capita* between 1700–1770 and a slight decline thereafter which persisted through the early stages of the Industrial Revolution. Must we then conclude that England was developing rapidly early in the eighteenth century and slowly thereafter, instead of the reverse as the data in Fig. 2·1 show?

On the face of it to call the Industrial Revolution in England a period of relative economic decline seems absurd. The difficulty arises from using national income *per capita* as a measure of economic development. As Colin Clark also concludes on the basis of his estimates, 'the first half of the nineteenth century, with all the tremendous changes brought about, only just succeeded in maintaining real income per head constant.'[15]

---

[14] *ibid.*, p. 313.
[15] C. Clark, *The Conditions of Economic Progress*, 3rd ed. (London, Macmillan, 1957), p. 218.

It is the 'tremendous changes', the 'speeding up' of economic activity, that we need a measure of and that economists, at least part of the time, really have in mind when they speak of economic development. [. . .] Therefore we can hardly regard Deane's national income figures as a decisive contradiction of the inferences based on the coal figures that the English economy was developing more slowly between 1700–1770 than it had earlier or would later.

Deane[16] also presents figures on trade volume which increased steadily throughout the eighteenth century, though the rate of increase cannot be compared with the rate of increase in the seventeenth century to judge which is faster or slower. However, in one key direction British overseas trade languished in the first half of the eighteenth century – in respect to her trade with her American colony. In absolute pound volume it showed no consistent increase between 1690–1745, yet during this time period the number of colonists in America was increasing fourfold, from around 250,000 persons to about one million.[17] Certainly British traders were not taking advantage of the greatly increased market. On a per head basis, trade with the American colonies fell from around two pounds per head per year in 1690 to around half a pound per head per year in 1745. Yet American trade was valued by the English. 'I state to you', said Chatham, 'the importance of America; it is a double market: a market of consumption and a market of supply.'[18] And trade with the Colonies could increase rapidly as the sudden spurt in volume after 1745 clearly demonstrated. The inference seems clear: English businessmen were not as enterprising in the first half of the eighteenth century as they had been earlier or would be later.

It is extremely hazardous to draw inferences about economic life from what happens in other spheres of human activity, yet it is perhaps worth mentioning that the first half of the eighteenth century in England might well be described by some such term as 'stagnation' or 'consolidation' in many fields of endeavor. Politically, Walpole was primarily interested in peace and compromise, in letting sleeping dogs lie.[19] The universities and the Royal Navy languished. Kroeber notes 'a definite dip in the first half of the eighteenth century in the production of eminent men

[16] P. Deane, 'The industrial revolution and economic growth: the evidence of early British national income estimates', *Economic Development and Cultural Change*, 5 (1957), pp. 159–74.
[17] C. W. Wright, *Economic History of the United States* (New York, McGraw-Hill, 1949), p. 128.
[18] Trevelyan, *op. cit.*, p. 444.
[19] *ibid.*, p. 504.

of science in England, and other eminent men as well.'[20] He identifies 'two growths, one from 1600 to 1700, culminating in Newton; the other from 1750 to the present. . . . The interval of slump was real. The single figure of note in the interregnum was a Scotchman. The emphasis of the time was on "politeness"; which, earlier developed in France than in England, and perhaps contributed to the premature ending of the great Descartes – Fermat growth. . . . That the interregnum was profound though short is indicated also by the miscellaneous origins of the participants when British science began producing again after 1750.'[21] The one really outstanding achievement during this time was the firm establishment of parliamentary rule and the codification of English law, culminating in Blackstone's famous Commentaries. But other evidence[22] strongly suggests that interests in law, in codification of the traditional, is antithetical to interests in exploiting the new fields represented both by science and business. In general, then, aside from Deane's national income figures which we have questioned on other grounds, the historical evidence does support the slump in economic development clearly shown in the coal import figures in Fig. 2.1.

To turn now to the n Achievement data, there is no question but that the economic slump characterizing the first half of the eighteenth century was preceded by a fall in n Achievement level beginning in the period 1625–1675 and continuing through the next 50 years to 1725. The drop appears in all three forms of literary samples. The simplest statistical comparison is between the level for 1500–1625 versus the level for 1626–1725. T tests were computed for the comparison for each of the three types of literature separately, and their p values combined by the chi-square technique. The results show that the chances of the drop arising from sampling fluctuations are less than one in a hundred, i.e., the drop in n Achievement is marked and statistically highly significant. What produced it is really not a question for detailed examination here, but it may be noted in passing that these were years of great internal stress and civil war in Britain, of struggles between kings and Parliament as to who should rule. Apparently the generally unsettled conditions of ordinary life affected the motives and the values of the people at the time more than it did England's economy, which continued to thrive throughout the seventeenth century, a finding

[20] Kroeber, *op. cit.*, p. 148.
[21] *ibid.*, p. 149.
[22] R. H. Knapp and H. B. Goodrich, *Origins of American Scientists* (Chicago, Chicago University Press, 1952).

which may come as a surprise to some historians who look to more direct
and immediate connections between political and economic developments. If our argument is correct, the political instability of the seventeenth century did affect the economy not at the time, but a generation
or two later and then only indirectly by affecting the motives and aspirations of people.

Fortunately the third phase in the development of the English economy is not likely to be questioned seriously by anyone except those who
are trapped by their belief that national income *per capita* is the best
measure of economic development. A marked increase in the rate of
growth began near the end of the eighteenth century and continued on
through the Industrial Revolution. The coal import figures in Fig. 2.1
show that the gains from around 1770 to 1833 were well above average
and reached a magnitude several times as great as the earlier spurt in
Elizabethan times. Between the mid-eighteenth and mid-nineteenth
centuries the British economy was transformed 'in a way which no
country had ever before known'.[23] The chief agent of change was the
rapid growth in technology brought about by the marriage of science
and industry. The last third of the eighteenth century saw the practical
application of many technological improvements which made greatly
increased productivity possible – the spinning 'jenny', the power
loom, Watt's steam engine, new applications of chemistry to industry,
improved methods of producing pig iron, and the use of iron wire rope
for winding up coal.[24]

Did a rise in *n* Achievement level precede this striking economic
development? Once again the answer must be in the affirmative. All
three types of literature showed a rise in *n* Achievement between 1700
and 1750. The simplest statistical comparison again is to check the low
point in *n* Achievement from 1625–1725 with the level in the succeeding
century, 1725–1825. All three measures of *n* Achievement show a rise
from one to the other of these time periods and the probability of such
increases occurring by chance is less than one in a hundred using the
combined chi-square technique as in previous comparisons. Accounts
of sea voyages and street ballads both show a continuous and marked
rise on up to 1800, foreshadowing the continued and spectacular
economic development in the first half of the nineteenth century. On
the other hand the plays show a rise followed by a small but insignificant

[23] G. M. Meier and R. E. Baldwin, *Economic Development* (New York, Wiley,
1957), p. 149.
[24] *ibid.*, pp. 152–3.

drop around 1800 which might be attributed either to sampling error or to the fact that plays at this time may have represented less adequately the motivations of the men who were remaking England than they were in Elizabethan times.

THE WESLEYAN REVIVAL, n ACHIEVEMENT, AND ECONOMIC GROWTH

Once again there is an opportunity to check the connection between n Achievement and the rise of Protestantism. Was the increase in n Achievement between 1700 and 1750 accompanied by a Protestant revival? Certainly yes. It was precisely during this period beginning in 1729 at Oxford that John Wesley sparked the religious revival that culminated in the foundation of the Nonconformist Methodist Church. Trevelyan notes that 'the dissenting bodies of the Bunyan tradition which had been founded in the heat and zeal of the Cromwellian era' had tended to become more respectable and less enthusiastic (roughly from 1680–1730). The zeal of the first Methodists like John Wesley and George Whitefield 'was opposed in every respect to the character-istic faults and merits of the eighteenth century attitude of mind'[25] and put new life in the dissenting bodies. Furthermore, Methodism was influential precisely among those commercial and industrial classes that spearheaded the Industrial Revolution. History appears to have repeated itself. Once again in the first half of the eighteenth century as in the first half of the sixteenth century a strong Protestant movement coin-cides with a high n Achievement level and both are followed in a genera-tion or so by a greatly increased rate of economic growth.

Our interpretation of Weber's hypothesis [. . .] has two specific implications for developments in England at this time: (1) the higher n Achievement reflected in the literary samples was more heavily concentrated in the Nonconformist Protestant group and (2) the Non-conformist group, because of its higher n Achievement, was more responsible for the increased entrepreneurial activity that sparked the Industrial Revolution from around 1770 on. Direct quantitative evi-dence on the first hypothesis is not available as yet, although it could be obtained by comparing, for example, the n Achievement levels in Nonconformist vs. Anglican sermons or in other personal documents produced by key individuals of the two religious persuasions. But indirect evidence strongly supports the hypothesis. The twin keynotes

[25] Trevelyan, *op. cit.*, p. 519.

of Methodism were stress on constant personal communion with God and on Christian perfection in this life. The one promotes self-reliance in establishing and maintaining continuous contact with God and the other, high standards of excellence in judging one's own conduct. These happen also to be the key elements in the formation of *n* Achievement.

Both are nicely expressed in a verse from one of the well-known hymns of Charles Wesley.

> Heavenly Adam, Life divine
> Change my nature into thine
> Move and spread throughout my soul
> Activate and fill the whole.

The singer is, in effect, making a direct personal approach to God to help him be more perfect. And the perfection of the individual's relationship to God is 'known by its fruits', by right conduct. Wesley's insistence on the importance of Christian perfection was so strong that it got him into serious trouble with the established church: 'Christians are saved in this world from all sin, from all unrighteousness, that they are now in such a sense perfect, as not to commit sin.' Whatever its political or theological implications, such an uncompromising stress on excellence (as the very name Methodist implies) seems almost certain to have acted to promote the development of achievement motivation in Methodist children. [. . .] And the picture was similar in other Non-conformist bodies in England in the eighteenth century. It is one of the ironies of history that while the religious revivalists were almost exclusively concerned with man's relationship to God, they defined it in such a way that it tended to promote a trait of character – high *n* Achievement – that led in turn very often to marked business success. Wesley himself was puzzled and somewhat alarmed by the fact that Methodists tended to grow rich since he also believed that it was harder for a rich man to get into Heaven than for a 'camel to pass through the needle's eye'.[26]

[26] The Wesleyan revival was probably not the only source of a higher level of *n* Achievement. Ryerson, in a historical study of medical advice on child-rearing, has shown that the mid-eighteenth century represented a 'really startling point of change' in respect to a new stress on freedom in all physical activities stemming in part from the spirit of Rousseau. Such stress (including as it did much emphasis on self-reliant achievement) should certainly have stimulated the development of *n* Achievement *.c.f.* A. Ryerson ,'An investigation of child-rearing practices: advice given to laymen, 1545–1900', unpublished doctoral dissertation, Harvard University Graduate School of Education, 1960.

Evidence for the second hypothesis – that Nonconformists sparked the Industrial Revolution in England – is more direct. Historians and economists have long accepted the point without much question, illustrating it with a number of striking examples like the Quakers in the iron industry, but only recently has Hagen[27] collected the figures which permit a systematic test of the hypothesis. Relevant data are

TABLE 2·2 *Birthplace and religious affiliation of British innovators in the Industrial Revolution 1725–1850 (After Hagen, 1962)*

	Population estimates (around 1800)	Number of innovators	p
Birthplace			
England and Wales	9,187,000	55	
Scotland	1,652,000	18	
Per cent Scottish	15·2%	24·6%	<·05
Unknown or other		9	
Religious affiliation			
Anglican	—	27	
Unknown	—	27	
Nonconformist	650,000	28	
Per cent Nonconformist	6·0%	34·1%	<·001

summarized in Table 2·2 which shows the origins of innovating entrepreneurs in the Industrial Revolution. Hagen took all the names of such entrepreneurs mentioned by T. S. Ashton in his book *The Industrial Revolution*[28] and tried to track down their nationality and religious affiliation. The advantage of such a technique is that it starts with a presumably unbiased sample of industrial innovators and then attempts to see whether they are drawn in greater numbers from different segments of the population than would be expected on the basis of the proportion of that segment to the whole. The breakdown by birthplace is of interest here because the established church of Scotland was more Protestant in Weber's Calvinistic sense than the established church of England. And it is true that the percentage of known Scotchmen among the innovating group is significantly higher than it should be based on the estimate of the per cent of Scotchmen in the total British population.

[27] E. E. Hagen, *On the Theory of Social Change: How Economic Growth Begins* (Cambridge, Mass., Massachusetts Institute of Technology, 1962).
[28] T. S. Ashton, *The Industrial Revolution* (London, Oxford University Press, 1948).

However, the finding loses some of its force when it is noted that four of the eighteen Scotchmen were actually Anglicans. If they are eliminated, the difference in percentages becomes insignificant and it is doubtful that a case can be made for Calvinism being a more effective breeder of industrial entrepreneurs than other forms of Protestantism, at least so far as this comparison is concerned.

The situation is quite different so far as the Nonconformist bodies are concerned. They formed at the very most around 1800 6 to 8 per cent of the total population of England, Wales and Scotland, yet they produced at least a third of the innovators in the sample, a difference over the expected per cent which is highly significant statistically. Unfortunately it is not possible to compare very precisely the yield of the Nonconformist and established churches in numbers of innovators because no figures are available on what proportion of the population belonged in any real sense to the Anglican church. If one argues that everyone who was not a dissenter was an Anglican, then of course the yield of the Nonconformist bodies was much greater than that of the established church, but it is doubtful if being an Anglican meant very much religiously to a considerable percentage of the population. That is, an unknown percentage of the population ought really to be considered not religious, rather than included with the Anglican population. But even if one assumes that only half of the population belonged to the Anglican faith in any real sense, it can be seen from Table 2·2 that this 50 per cent of the population produced a significantly smaller percentage of the industrial entrepreneurs than it should have on a proportional basis. The connection of the particular form of Protestantism common to the dissenting bodies (Methodism, Quakerism, Unitarianism, etc.) with the innovating leadership of the Industrial Revolution seems firmly established. The presumptive reasons for the connection – a higher n Achievement level among the dissenting groups – has not been directly checked but is strongly supported by an analysis of the nature of religious revivals like Methodism in the eighteenth century and by inferences based on contemporary evidence [. . .].

In summary, Bradburn and Berlew's findings provide three separate confirmations of our basic hypothesis in the course of English economic development between 1600–1800. A rise or at least a high level of n Achievement in the sixteenth century preceded the first wave of economic growth in the early seventeenth century; a fall in n Achievement concentrated in the years 1650–1700 preceded the economic stagnation of the early eighteenth century; and a decisive rise in n Achievement beginning around the middle of the eighteenth century preceded the spectacular economic growth of the Industrial Revolution. The curves when juxtaposed so as to eliminate time lag, look very similar (Fig. 2·1). Furthermore, both the sixteenth and eighteenth century increases in n Achievement level were accompanied by strong popular Protestant movements within the church, and the fall in n Achievement corresponds to a time when Protestantism in England was not very active but was becoming 'respectable'. Finally, there is even some evidence that the rise in n Achievement at the end of the eighteenth century was significantly higher as it should have been than the rise in the sixteenth century which had preceded the first – and lesser – wave of economic growth. For the scores based on street ballads and accounts of sea voyages, the mean n Achievement in 1800 is significantly higher than it was at its previous high point between 1500–1625 ($p < ·05$ and $< ·02$ respectively).

The picture is complicated a little bit by the fact that the n Achievement in drama around 1800 is significantly lower ($p < ·02$) than it was at its high point earlier. Combining the p's to get an over-all estimate of whether the second peak in n Achievement is higher than the first is not very meaningful under the circumstances, though on balance it would suggest that the greater average height of the second peak would not often have arisen by chance ($p < ·15$, if a one-tailed test is permissible). Thus our hypothesis would certainly have to predict that since the second wave of industrial growth beginning around 1770 was considerably larger than the first one, the level of n Achievement preceding it should also be higher than the level of n Achievement preceding the first economic spurt. Rather than combine the results in this way, it is probably more meaningful to argue that plays written between 1775–1830 were less representative of the aspirations of the middle and lower classes than they had been in Shakespeare's time and that they were almost certainly less representative than the street ballads and the accounts of sea voyages were. Such a line of reasoning would lead to the inference that the second wave of n Achievement was stronger in the larger segment of the population represented by the lower middle classes than it had been in the sixteenth century. Even if the plays at both time periods are accepted as representing the interests of the 'better' classes equally well, we are still left with the suggestion of class differences in the effects of the two 'waves' of n Achievement: during the first one, the effect was greater in the 'better' classes (represented by the 'drama' figures) and during the second it was greater in the much larger middle and lower classes (represented in the figures for 'sea ballads' and 'letters'). Such a hypothesis must be considered highly tentative until it is confirmed by further evidence, but the main argument of Bradburn and Berlew's study seems fairly well established. Major stages in the rates of English economic development between 1600–1800 were foreshadowed and presumably determined at least in part by corresponding developments in n Achievement levels, as reflected in imaginative literature.

3.1 Resource allocation and Growth in early nineteenth-century British education

E. G. WEST

This article is of the kind which attempts to apply recently developed economic theory to past events. To the extent that this procedure tries out the new theory in the context of old data it is primarily an exercise in economics; in so far as it leads to a fresh classification of the facts, or throws up further questions which prompt us to unearth lesser-known material, it inevitably impinges upon history proper. The result, it is to be hoped, will be of reciprocal benefit to both subjects.

Upon popular impressions of nineteenth-century education the conventional historian has so far clearly had the predominant influence. Economists certainly seem implicitly to have accepted the historical opinion that over a century ago there was particularly severe educational underinvestment. If pressed on the relevant criteria for recognizing 'severe underinvestment', however, the economist is likely to draw upon analytical tools that have only recently been designed, in the attempt to answer such questions. The question of whether *any* good or service is 'undersupplied' on the market is nowadays usually set within the modern welfare – economics argument about 'external

This article has developed from an earlier and much shorter paper: 'Educational external economies in nineteenth-century Britain', presented to the 4th Congress of the International Economic History Association at Bloomington, Indiana, 1968.

I wish to acknowledge the benefit of helpful comments from my colleague Sean Glynn, who patiently read two versions of the manuscript. Acknowledgements are also due to the University of Kent Economic History Graduate Seminar Group and to P. J. Flavell and other members of the University Library staff.

E. G. West (1970) *The Economic History Review*, 2nd ser., XXIII, (Welwyn Garden City), pp. 68–95.

diseconomies (or economies)'. This argument consists of the tautology that private market organization fails to produce results that satisfy the necessary conditions for 'Pareto optimality' when 'Pareto-relevant' externalities remain in private equilibrium. (Pareto optimality is a situation where no further change in the allocation of resources could make anyone better off without harming some other person in the economy.) From this proposition economists develop the more empirical one that in the presence of such externalities, collectivization *could* so modify the results as to reach the desired Pareto welfare optimum.

Significant externalities exist when the costs (or benefits) of private transactions do not take into account spill-over costs (or benefits) to other individuals who do not participate in the transactions in question.[1] Because, for example, I do (or do not) have myself inoculated for my own safety, my decision determines the extent to which I shall be a potential danger to others. Again, because I do (do not) paint my house to maintain the economic value of my investment, my decision will have significant effects upon my more aesthetically sensitive neighbours. In the sphere of education, my decision whether to buy schooling for my child might affect the lives of others in terms of a wide assortment of influences ranging from the securing of public order to economic growth and prosperity. In more formal terms an externality relates to an activity which enters two or more persons' preference function simultaneously in varying degrees and in a positive or negative direction.

It is such reasoning about externalities which often gives economists a *presumption* that serious deficiencies *may* occur in the amount spent on education, deficiencies which might be corrected by collectivization and therefore legislation. It would be improper for the empirical social scientists to reject or accept such a hypothesis *a priori*; it is their task to test it, i.e. to measure the degree of its validity in particular cases. In doing so, however, they should bear in mind not only that collectivization *could* suitably modify results but also the less familiar but equally indisputable proposition that, given an initial presence of externalities in political equilibrium, the market *could* also work in the direction of social optimum. Our inheritance, from immediately preceding generations, of much municipal government activity may have blinded us to this ever-present possibility and coloured some of our views of pre-municipal times. On reflexion we can reasonably expect that in varying degrees:

[1] Such interdependencies, together with inability to appropriate them via suitable compensation on the market, are the most relevant for policy purposes.

If a municipal government does not exist for the performance of such functions, private citizens will, independently, hire guards and night watchmen, vaccinate their dogs against rabies, install fire protection devices, plant flowers in the spring, keep boulevards clear of snow in winter, send their children to school. . . .[2]

Expressed in another way we may observe that nearly all instances of consumption expenditure have external effects. The fact that most people in Western countries feed themselves adequately makes them resistant to disease and therefore presents external benefits (or involves lower external costs) to their neighbours. Externalities obviously provide a necessary but not a sufficient condition for intervention. We do not collectivize 'feeding' on these (externality) grounds and make it universally compulsory and 'free', since clearly no government action is called for if 'sufficient' feeding can be expected to occur from private actions even if these actions are associated with external benefits.

The economist's presumption in favour of intervention, in other words, relates not to all externalities but only to those that are 'Pareto-relevant', i.e. those in which there persist *marginal* gains to third parties which outweigh costs (which fall on the same third parties).[3] Where, in equilibrium, the marginal costs are positive, however, so will marginal external economies and diseconomies be positive.[4] Recent economic analysis [5] has brought out the fact that even a perfect Paretian world of optimal resource allocation (including investment allocation for growth) will be one which looks 'untidy' and 'unappealing'; for many externalities will still exist in such a world. Even the society with optimal resource allocation will, in other words, still feature positive amounts of congestion, noise, smell, smoke, health-risk, ugliness, and ignorance. The Britain of the nineteenth century was, as everyone knows, littered with such external effects. The historian's mere act of documenting them, nevertheless, does not prove past resource misallocation.

[2] James M. Buchanan and Gordon Tullock, 'Public and private interaction under reciprocal externality', in *The Public Economy of Urban Communities*, ed. J. Margolis (Washington, Johns Hopkins, 1965), pp. 52–73.
[3] For the formal definition of 'Pareto-relevant' externalities see J. M. Buchanan and W. C. Stubblebine, 'Externality', *Economica* XXIX (1962), pp. 371–84. For a brief verbal exposition of the idea see E. G. West, *Education and the State* (London, Instit. Econ. Affairs, 2nd ed., 1971), ch. 15.
[4] For instance, a community may subsidize factories to reduce the smoke from their chimneys up to the point where the positive marginal cost to the taxpayer is just balanced by the (still positive) marginal benefits of smoke reduction. In equilibrium smoke nuisance will be reduced, but not to zero.
[5] Buchanan and Stubblebine, *op. cit.*, pp. 380–1.

It is clear that an empirical study of early nineteenth-century education which aims to relate itself to this analysis should attempt to pave the way for assessing, in general terms, the degree to which private purchase of education resulted in jointly supplied external benefits and the degree to which such benefits were positive at the margin or were increasing or decreasing during the progress of the Industrial Revolution. Further points are implicit in the same analysis. First, even when the externalities are Pareto-relevant, marketization may be superior to collectivization, or vice versa, in working towards optima. Both methods involve costs and there is no *a priori* reason to expect that one method is at all times superior to the other. Next, the 'collectivity' which benefits through collectivization does not necessarily coincide with national boundaries. It could embrace mainly one region, one local industrial settlement, or one private or 'public' group within the widest political boundary.[6] Moreover, if collectivization appears to be the appropriate method, theoretically at least this does not necessarily imply coercion and therefore conflict with the use of a criterion of welfare which emphasizes 'choice'.[7] Such a Paretian change, promising benefits for most and the absence of harm to the rest, can at least in a 'perfect' political process be predicted to enjoy unanimous support.[8] Furthermore, since Pareto-relevant externalities often call for only marginal extensions, it commonly follows that *partial* subsidies alone will often suffice. If for instance society is interested in one particular child having 20 per cent more education than his parents are privately giving or would privately give him, then a 100 per cent subsidy (or 'free' education) is not called for.[9] Moreover, the necessary revenues

---

[6] J. M. Buchanan, *The Demand and Supply of Public Goods* (Chicago, Rand, 1968), chs. 4, 5 and 9.

[7] Included in modern public-finance theory there is a 'merit good' approach which does not take individual preferences as given but attempts to change them. Section III below (pp. 81–91) examines this approach in detail.

[8] The unanimity requirement, however, raises the most difficult part of the whole public goods problem. See the articles by P. Samuelson and R. A. Musgrave in *Public Economics*, ed. J. Margolis (Macmillan, London, 1969).

[9] Buchanan, *op. cit.*, insists that education is a *consumption* externality and that each separate family's activity must be considered as a separate public service. Ideally this calls for separate or discriminating treatment of each individual family from a 'Pareto-guided' government. See also West, *op. cit.*, chs. 13 and 15. Some argue, however, that in the case of education it may be that 100 per cent public production is essential to the quality of the product because 'social integration' can be achieved only via a free state-school system. For a thorough discussion of this question in the twentieth-century setting see the contributions by M. Blaug and E. G. West in *Education: A Framework for Choice* (London, Instit. Econ. Affairs, 1967) and W. Hettich, 'Mixed public and private financing

needed to finance the subsidies should not come from taxes on families which have the effect of reducing their private educational expenditure.[10] In the final analysis too we must take account of the external disceconomies associated with any real world 'solution' by legislation, diseconomies which are embedded in the political process itself. If, for instance, the fiscal mechanism depends on other than lump-sum taxes, external diseconomies in the form of excess burdens will arise.[11] When these burdens reach a critical limit collectivization ceases to be desirable. Finally, we should bear in mind the recent work in economic theory which suggests that the replacement of a mixture of private fee-paying, government aid, and charity in education by a system of an *all-exclusive* government-provided system will actually reduce the quantity of resources in education – the opposite result that is desired if underinvestment is initially diagnosed.[12]

In the modern search for optimum or 'target' growth-rates economists find themselves ranged between two positions. At one extreme are those who implicitly use the 'merit good' approach[13] and apply norms which are external or non-individualistic in the sense that 'imposed choice' is involved; at the other end are those who employ criteria which emphasize that, in order to be relevant, increases in output should always be related to individual consumer preferences.

---

of education', together with the comment by M. V. Pauly, *American Economic Review*, LIX (1969), pp. 210–14. This question is less relevant here since the predominant function of education in the nineteenth century was not 'social integration' but the preparation for electoral responsibility, personal morality, and religious respect.

[10] M. V. Pauly, 'Mixed public and private financing of education: efficiency and feasibility', *Amer. Econ. Rev.* LVII (1967), p. 120, argues that even if parents are not taxed the prospect of any public subsidy will reduce private expenditure below the size that families would have reached without it (i.e. there are 'reciprocal externalities' between private and public expenditure).

[11] This is a classic proposition in the modern theory of public finance. See e.g. R. A. Musgrave, *The Theory of Public Finance* (New York, McGraw-Hill, 1959), ch. 7. Excess burden inefficiencies together with 'allocational inefficiencies' constitute probably the most serious policy problem associated with the modern theory of public goods – at least in its application to the real world where simple majority voting rules are used. With less than unanimity voting arrangements, group choices as to the level of public goods provision (e.g. the size of the educational subsidy) will not meet the preference of those (outvoted) individuals who prefer more and those who prefer less than the actual amount decided upon. See Buchanan, *op. cit.*, p. 185.

[12] W. Stubblebine, 'Institutional elements in the financing of education', *Southern Economic Journal*, XXXII (1965); E. G. West, *Education, Economics and the Politician*, Hobart Paper 42 (1967).

[13] See below, Section III.

Those who occupy intermediate positions do not reject individual choice outright but give it some certain minimum weight.[14] Many will discuss the need for some appropriate balance between some kind of government-manipulated 'national' growth-rate and one that would occur 'naturally' or spontaneously through decentralized individual decisions. In early nineteenth-century England, however, there was no attempt by governments to obtain centrally devised economic growth targets and none of the detailed statistics that usually accompany such attempts. So there is no option but to study the achieved expansion of the period in terms of the second definition of growth. In other words we have to record as 'growth' that increase in output of goods and services (one of which was education) that individuals chose, a choice which was of course exercised within the constraints of their separate incomes and resources.

Conventional statistics in modern countries, incidentally, cannot properly adapt themselves to both definitions of growth. While command economies, for instance, use statistics of expansion of industrial and educational outputs, the latter may be quite unrelated to individual citizen preference. Where this is so the assessment of growth would be much inflated compared with the second definition; for on this criterion 'unwanted production is not production at all'.[15] In free or relatively free market situations of the nineteenth-century sort, on the other hand, the relationship between the second definition of growth and the development of industrialization can be expected to be closer. It is, indeed, the intention of this article to examine the degree to which, in such an environment, choice, industrialization, and output can generally expand together. We shall study education's inducement to growth and the converse, i.e. how far the industrial expansion which characterized the British economy in the late eighteenth and early nineteenth centuries brought with it substantial widening of choice, and therefore growth, in education itself.

In many works on nineteenth-century education it is often not made clear that what the author is primarily concerned to record is not so much the development of education as the growth of the centralized political control of it. Since it is easy for the unwary reader to confuse the two, the impression is frequently established without demonstration that 'education did not really start' until it was 'organized', until it

---

[14] P. J. D. Wiles, *The Political Economy of Communism* (Oxford, Blackwell, 1962), p. 216.
[15] The phrase is that used by Prof. Wiles, *ibid.*

became 'public', that is until a particular nineteenth- or twentieth-century Act of Parliament was passed. This error seems to be much more deep-seated in the subject of education than in others.[16] No one believes, for instance, that because it is only now in the twentieth century that legislative attempts are being made to weld transport into 'one co-ordinated system of public transport' that transport did not seriously exist or make any progress in the nineteenth century. So long as histories of education continue to be written predominantly in terms of the chronological sequence of legislation, many readers must certainly be forgiven for deriving the impression of an implicit presumption that no substantial progress could have occurred without it and that the major achievements actually stemmed from it. In the absence of formulations of these two particular hypotheses in suitably testable, or refutable, form the more fastidious will however surely be left unsatisfied.

Clearly there is serious methodological inadequacy in the customary procedure of simply conducting a chronological survey of experience and then making a summary judgement upon it without making explicit the link between the two. History could of course be better written if for every society with a particular institution we wish to study there was under a separate 'microscope' another society with no such institution to act as a statistical control. It would be useful to compare, for instance, the progress of one society which imposed educational legislation with that of another which did not, but which was identical in all other respects. The true effects of the school legislation could thus be better identified. Similarly, we could better observe the reciprocal effects between industrialism and education. Unfortunately the real occurrence of events has rarely such goodwill towards the scholar: for rarely are societies in real life so neatly distinguished. We must, nevertheless,

<hr/>

[16] See, for example, G. M. Trevelyan, *British History in the Nineteenth Century* (London, Longman, 1922), pp. 354–5, who emphasizes the crucial attainment in 1870 of a 'system' of education. Also G. R. Porter, *The Progress of the Nation* (London, Methuen, 1912); C. Birchenough, *History of Elementary Education in England and Wales* (London, Univ. Tut. Press, 1920), p. 123; and S. J. Curtis, *History of Education in Great Britain* (London, Univ. Tut. Press, 1965), p. 275, make estimates of children who 'were not provided for' in the nineteenth century without clearly specifying that they meant not provided for in the public sector of education . For further details see West, *Education and the State*, p. 148. More recently Lawrence Stone, 'Literacy and education in England, 1640–1900', *Past & Present*, XLII (1969), p. 127, asserted without much argument that: 'The major advances in elementary education in Scotland seem to have taken place in the late seventeenth and eighteenth centuries, when a national education system was set up by legislative action. '

do our best with such opportunities as present themselves. Here, we shall try to trace the effects of legislation by making before-and-after comparisons and by comparing those parts of the country that had statutory coverage (Scotland and parts of England affected by industrial legislation) with those that did not. We shall also examine the impact of industrialism upon 'non-legislated' education by comparing the developing conditions in the new manufacturing centres with those in the non-industrial areas.

The first part of the article examines the growth of education in Scotland during the Industrial Revolution, and the influence of both parochial legislation and the new industrialism. The second consists of a similar survey of early nineteenth-century English education, bearing in mind that Scotland had 'promotional' legislation while England, apart from some localized industrial legislation, did not. In an attempt to arrange this material in the perspective of the modern theory of public goods (externalities), this section also attempts a measure of the share of education in the early nineteenth-century national income and a comparison with present-day shares. Finally, in the context of the 'merit good' theory of 'imposed choice', the third section examines the emerging content, quality, and efficiency of English education and the particular methods and motives of contemporary leaders in attempting to control it from the 1830s onwards.

I

The educational impact of the Industrial Revolution upon the Scottish system of parochial schooling may be detected directly or indirectly from evidence contained in the 'Digest of the Parochial Returns made to the Select Committee, appointed to enquire into the Education of the Poor' in 1818. Elaborate information is also available in a report by a committee appointed by the General Assembly to investigate conditions in the 1820s.[17] From the commencement of the Scottish compulsory parochial school system in 1696 down to 1803, nothing much further had been done by law to alter the conditions that were laid down in the original statute. Further legislation in 1803 made some small increases in the salaries of teachers; and some new regulations were introduced

---

[17] S. C. *Education of the Poor*, Parl. Papers, 1818, III (hereafter '1818 Digest'). An account of both the reports is to be found in *Edinburgh Review*, XCI (1827), pp. 107–32. There is some brief reference to some of this information in G. Balfour, *The Educational Systems of Great Britain and Ireland* (Oxford, 1898).

for the government of schools and schoolmasters. If we assume that the statutory parochial schools accounted for the bulk of Scottish educational provision in the middle of the eighteenth century a serious decline in their share of total pupils educated had taken place by 1818 (see Table 3.1).

TABLE 3·1 *Schooling in Scotland, 1818*

	Pupils	Schools
Parochial schools	54,161	942
Private (unendowed) schools	106,627	2,222

Source: 1818 Digest.

These figures would seem to show that the population 'explosion' of the late eighteenth century had proved far too much of a strain for the system to carry, since by 1818 'non-legislated' private schools were bearing the main burden. The figures exclude the Sunday schools, Dame schools, and schools for the education of the rich. It is worth noting that very little of this education was free; nearly all the working-class parents paid fees whether they used the parochial schools or the more numerous private establishments.[18]

The view that educational growth during the Industrial Revolution in Scotland depended *primarily* upon statutory provision seems already to be challenged by these accounts. Still more is this so when we find that it was in the growing towns, where industrialism was establishing itself, that the growth and predominance of private schools for the working class in 1818 were most striking. In the county of Lanark, including Glasgow, while there were 56 parochial schools with 3,437 children in 1818, the private-school figures were about six times bigger: 307 schools with 18,270 pupils.[19]

[18] Thus to take randomly the first item from the 1818 Digest report on the county of Lanark, we find: 'Avondale: The parochial school, containing from 120 to 140 children, of whom 12 are taught gratis . . . the [master's] salary is £22 4s. 5d. besides a school-room, house and garden, and emoluments and fees amounting to £91 per annum . . .'

Similarly with the county of Fife the first parish recorded reads: 'Abbotshall: The parochial school, consisting of 80 children; the master's salary is £22 4s 5d besides the £5 per annum, payable out of an estate . . . and his emoluments amount to £25 and fees to £45 making in the whole £97 4s 5d per annum.' 1818 Digest, pp. 1345, 1385.

[19] *Edinburgh Review*, XLVI (1827), p. 113. In Glasgow the unendowed schools taught nine times as many students as the endowed. 1818 Digest, p. 1387.

Pointing out that it was in the new industrial areas that the private schools were flourishing most, the *Edinburgh Review* of 1827 observed:

> It is there that education is the most necessary and *the most easy to be got*; and yet these are the very places which are most excluded from the benefit of the parochial system. This, indeed, is the necessary result of the growth of the people in places for which there is, by law, only one teacher appointed. Whenever we look either at the digest of 1818, or at the recent returns, for a view of the state of education in great towns, we almost invariably find a blank at the place where the parish schools ought to be mentioned. There are none: or rather, the solitary one provided by law forms such an atom, as scarcely to be visible, or worth mentioning[20] [my italics].

In many of the non-industrial areas, meanwhile, the reports revealed stagnation and poverty. In 1822 a society at Inverness was instituted for the express purpose of 'educating the poor in the Highlands' and proceeded to measure the educational needs in those areas.[21] The society found that about one-third of the whole population was more than two miles, 'and many thousands more than five miles, distant from the nearest schools'. Half the population was unable to read. In the Hebrides and other western parts of Inverness and Ross, 70 per cent could not read. The Highlands population was 416,000. Of this, the children of school age numbered 52,000. Only 8,550 scholars were found to be at school.[22] Despite the parochial schools legislation, the society concluded, 'we are not much better furnished with the means of education than our predecessors in the last century; and the results of their tuition have only proved its deplorable inadequacy'. The failure of the Scots people in the non-industrial areas to do better for themselves than their neighbours in the towns was in effect attributed by these reports to the latter's superior income.

Despite these facts it seems to have been largely because of the circumstance that Scotland had specific legislation that historians have

---

[20] *Edinburgh Review*, XLVI (1827), p. 112.

[21] The results were published in *Moral Statistics of the Highlands and Islands of Scotland; compiled from Returns received by the Inverness Society for the Education of the Poor in the Highlands* (Inverness, 1826).

[22] The contemporary classification of children of school age to include those between five and fifteen years was unrealistic and resulted in an overestimate of children who did not receive a schooling (see below, p. 71, n. 49). Despite this qualification, however, the Highlands were clearly inferior to the industrial centres in educational provision.

traditionally given her the predominant credit for educational provision.[23] Legislation, however, is a many-sided activity. Primarily it can do one or more of four things in education: first, make it compulsory; second, provide partial and discriminate subsidies; third, make it 'free' (full subsidy); fourth, organize it into a 'nationalized' system. Modern writers who place Scotland in favourable contrast to England are sometimes too hasty in their reporting of the former's statutory coverage. Lawrence Stone, for instance, arguing explicitly that 'the major driving force for popular education has been the direct intervention of the state to provide tax-supported free schools and to enforce legislation compelling parents to send the children to them',[24] continues with the statement that among the countries which initiated these moves before the nineteenth century was Scotland, 'which acted in 1646 and 1696'. In contrast, the English state 'was peculiarly slow to move . . . Compulsion was not introduced until 1881 and non-payment until 1891'. The facts are, however, that Scotland did not introduce compulsion and non-payment (free schooling) until about the same time as England did. Compulsion in Scotland came in 1872 and 'free' schooling in 1891.[25] The main achievement of Scottish legislation in the first half of the nineteenth century was to supply educational subsidies to the benefit of about one-third of the total school population (i.e. to that minority which happened to use parochial schools). Even this favoured section still had to contribute a significant part of the educational costs through school fees.

The belief that legislation in Scotland had much more substantial results is nevertheless widely held and has a long history. In Victorian times the influential authority of the social statistician Sir Robert Giffen set its seal upon the idea. In his inaugural address as President of the Royal Statistical Society in 1883 he stated:

> The children of the masses are, in fact, now [with the 1870 Forster legislation] obtaining a good education all round, while fifty years ago the masses had either no education at all or a comparatively poor one.

[23] D. W. Roberts, *An Outline of the Economic History of England* (London, Longman, 1962), p. 200, observes: 'In contrast with this appalling state, conditions in Scotland were greatly superior, due principally to the fact that an act had been passed there as early as 1694 requiring schools to be established in every parish.' See also Trevelyan, *op. cit.*, p. 355, for an assertion that England 'lagged far behind Scotland'; Curtis, *op. cit.*, ch. XIV.

[24] Stone, *op. cit.*, p. 96.

[25] Balfour, *op. cit.*, pp. 138–43.

... If Scotland has gained so much, what must it have been in England, where there was no national system fifty years ago at all?[26]

It should be noticed that with continuous growth of *per capita* income any society will normally be able to observe at any point that fifty years previously education was, to use Giffen's words, 'a comparatively poor one'. This will be true of societies with public or private systems of education. More important, however, we should next test Giffen's type of view by comparing official figures of English and Scottish schooling in the immediate post-Napoleonic period. The proportion of the total population in Scotland that was receiving schooling in 1818 was about one in twelve while in England it was about one in fourteen.[27] Henry Brougham told the House of Lords in 1835 that by that year, according to figures produced by government investigation into education in England sponsored by Lord Kerry, there was little difference between the two countries.[28] In view of the subsequent exposure of error in the English figures (in the direction of significant underestimate), the existence of any substantial *quantitative* difference between Scotland and England in the 1830s or 1820s seems questionable (see below, pp. 67–9). Meanwhile, one broad similarity is clear: the majority of the Scottish schools, as in England, were unendowed and unsubsidized private establishments at which fees were being paid by large sections of the poor.

Interpreted in one way, Giffen's statement just concedes the possibility that there could have been equality in the quantity of education between the two countries; but only with the proviso that the English education must have been 'a comparatively poor one'. Judgement of the quality of education, however, is a much more complex task. Though further discussion of this must be deferred (below, Section 111), it may nevertheless be worth noting meanwhile that the Argyll Final Report on Scottish education in 1867 came to much the same conclusion about quantity and quality as had the Newcastle Report for England and Wales published in 1861.[29] In the year of the English Education Act of 1870, when comparative literacy statistics were just beginning to be made available, the proportion of Scottish males recorded as literate

---

[26] Sir Robert Giffen, *Economic Enquiries and Studies* (1890), p. 231.

[27] P.P. 1819, IX (c.) p. 1450; see also Curtis, *op. cit.* pp. 220–1.

[28] Hansard, *Parliamentary Debates*, House of Lords, 21 May 1835.

[29] Balfour, *op. cit.*, p. 136. It should be pointed out, however, that English education had the beginnings of a 'system' after 1833 when government subsidies began.

by the Registrars General was 90 per cent; that of England and Wales was 80 per cent.[30] Literacy, of course, measures only one dimension of the quality of education. It is clear at the same time that Scotland enjoyed an advantage on this score; nevertheless the superiority in this respect was marginal and not as substantial as Giffen's statement intimated. Moreover, to attribute even this lead to the Scottish legislation we need further arguments; for we have seen that the predominant number of Scottish children, in the large towns at least, received their schooling not from parochial schools but from competitive private fee-paying establishments. The question therefore arises: How far should the main credit for the superior progress in literacy be attributed not to the parochial schools but to the more widespread and more rapidly growing private schools?

Further arguments for the parochial schools are of course possible, but it is obvious that they require much more careful presentation and careful research. There is certainly an economic presumption that there would be a higher *per capita* educational expenditure in an aided system, such as Scotland's, which obtained its educational subsidies from taxes raised on property values, than in one which, as in England after 1833, provided them from a general and regressive tax system dependent especially upon taxes on food and tobacco. It is also permissible to argue that the parochial schools set the tone and the example. This in turn could have built up a common 'national ethos' in which high value was placed upon popular instruction. At the same time, however, it might be arguable that such a lead stemmed from the influence of the church or from 'national character' and not in the first place from the legislation. It is not likely, moreover, that the 'legislated' schools were always the main pace-setters; competition from the private establishments could well have had salutary effects upon the parochial establishments themselves, and it would be interesting to have further detailed studies on this point.

We conclude that writers seem to have accepted too readily the view that Scotland enjoyed *substantially* superior investment and progress in education compared with England, and the opinion that legislation was the most important agent in the former country and the most crucial missing link in the latter. We must of course probe much deeper into the facts of English education in England and Wales in the early nineteenth century to obtain a more precise conclusion.

[30] Stone, *op. cit.*, p. 120.

II

The 'Pareto-relevant' externalities in terms of which economists consider 'underinvestment' in education relate strictly to each separate family and are likely to differ in each individual case. Generally, it would be helpful to know the extent to which people were purchasing education 'naturally' (like, e.g., food), and the extent to which such purchases were increasing with income growth. So we shall attempt first to discover whether or not, in quantitative terms, the Industrial Revolution brought with it educational growth (*a*) in England and Wales as a whole and (*b*) in the industrial towns; next, to examine the facts of educational finance and estimate roughly the share of education in the national output in 1833; and finally to consider the special reasons why contemporaries believed that there was very serious underexpenditure on education (in our terms a high degree of Pareto-relevant externalities).

In 1818 the report of the Select Parliamentary Committee to inquire into the Education of the Lower Orders illustrated growth in the demand for education in these words:[31]

> There is the most unquestionable evidence that the anxiety of the poor for education *continues not only unabated but daily increasing*; that it extends to every part of the country, and is to be found equally prevalent in those smaller towns and country districts, where no means of gratifying it are provided by the charitable efforts of the richer classes [italics supplied].

The growing thirst for knowledge among poor families and indeed the degree to which education was competing with food as a claim upon family income were noted in the *Edinburgh Review* of February 1813:[32]

> Even around London, in a circle of fifty miles, which is far from the most instructed and virtuous part of the kingdom, there is hardly a village that has not something of a school; and not many children of either sex who are not taught, more or less, reading and writing. We have met with families in which, for weeks together, not an article of sustenance but potatoes had been used; yet for every child the hard-earned sum was provided to send them to school.

[31] *Third Report from the Select Committee on the Education of the Lower Orders*, P.P. 1818 (426), IV, p. 56.
[32] *Edinburgh Review*, XXI (1813), p. 216.

Every piece of statistical evidence on education between 1800 and 1840 points to significant growth. The first attempted comprehensive official statistics on schooling came with Henry Brougham's Select Committee report in 1820.[33] This revealed that in 1818 about one in fourteen or fifteen of the population was being schooled. This considerable improvement since the beginning of the century was attributable partly to the energy of ecclesiastical groups, but more importantly, as we shall see, to the willingness of parents to pay fees, which indeed in most cases at this time covered the whole of the cost. In 1828 Brougham in his private capacity followed up this initial estimate with a 5 per cent sample survey of his own, using the same sources (the parochial clergy) as before. His findings indicated that the number of children in schools had doubled in ten years.[34] The natural increase in population over this time would of course mean that the *per capita* growth-rate of schooling was less than the total rate. The total population increase over this period, however, was only about one-fifth. Moreover the age-structure did not vary significantly.[35] Another possibility which would qualify Brougham's findings is that the accuracy of local enumeration of schools could have improved in 1828 compared with 1818. Such an improvement, however, would have had to have been considerable to have accounted for *all* this appreciable growth. Among other items that seem consistent with significant educational growth is the observation that there was a noticeable surge in literacy rates after 1780.[36]

The Government began its programme of subsidies to education in 1833. It was something of a blind start, however, because it had no official figures of the overall extent of schooling. The results of the survey of the whole of England, which it authorized under a motion by Lord Kerry in the same year, were not available until 1835. When the Kerry statistics did at last appear[37] they went quite a way in supporting

[33] P.P. 1820 (151) XII, pp. 341, 349.
[34] Speech in the House of Lords, 21 May 1835.
[35] The population grew between 1821 and 1831 from 12 to 14 million. The age-structure was as follows:

Age group	1821	1831	1841
0-19	48·9%	48·2%	47·1%

The percentages for 1821 and 1841 are derived from the census figures. The 1831 percentage is taken from an estimate in James P. Huzel's 'Malthus, the Poor Law, and population in early nineteenth-century England', *Economic History Review*, 2nd ser. XXII (1969).
[36] Stone, *op. cit.*, p. 98.
[37] H.C. Paper 62, 1835, XLI–XLIII.

Brougham's private estimate of the rate of growth. The numbers in schools had increased from 748,000 in 1818 to 1,294,000 in 1833 'without any interposition of the Government or public authorities'.[38] It is interesting to notice how such a picture of the great spread of unendowed, fee-paying, private schooling for working families seems to have matched the Scottish experience.

The 1833 Kerry statistics have been widely reported in educational histories as unreliable. While some such works do not refer to the source of the criticism, others disclose it to be the Manchester Statistical Society.[39] What is rarely mentioned is that the complaint of this society against the Kerry statistics was that the true educational provision was significantly *under*estimated. Concerning the township of Manchester, at least, this criticism was indeed serious. According to the Manchester Statistical Society, which was one of the first bodies to undertake intensive local investigations, the total error made by the Kerry Report in this one town alone amounted to an underestimate of 8,646 scholars – mainly day scholars. This was a 27 per cent error when compared with the total figure of 32,166 day, evening, and Sunday scholars.[40] The understatement was much more serious when related to the population of day scholars. There were omitted in the Kerry Report about half the day schools and one-sixth of the Sunday schools. The underestimate of day scholars must have been at least $33\frac{1}{3}$ per cent.

Manchester was no exception compared with other manufacturing towns in the matter of official understatement.[41] The more the Kerry figures are adjusted upwards for error the more impressive would the growth-rate seem to be. For this to be fully accurate, however, we need evidence that errors in the 1818 investigation were not equally big. If the latter is demonstrated the more we need to revise our opinions of educational conditions in the earlier part of the Industrial Revolution

[38] Brougham, House of Lords, 21 May 1835.
[39] Curtis, *op. cit.*, p. 232, simply observes 'it was well known that the statistics given in the report were unreliable'; Birchenough, *op. cit.* pp. 71–2, merely states that it was the Manchester Statistical Society which 'proved the data of the Kerry Parliamentary Return to be untrustworthy'. Similarly Frank Smith, *A History of English Elementary Education* (Univ. of London Press, 1931), p. 151.
[40] *Report of a Committee of the Manchester Statistical Society on the State of Education in the Borough of Manchester in 1834* (2nd ed., 1837), pp. 2–4. Manchester Borough contained nine townships of which Manchester town was the largest with about 70 per cent of the borough population. The school figures for Manchester *town* appear on p. 43 of the Manchester Statistical Society Report for 1834.
[41] See below, p. 75.

and to consider the possibility that quantitative equality with Scotland came much earlier. Meanwhile, even ignoring the underestimates of the 1833 returns, the findings revealed striking development. In the 1851 Census (Special Report on Education) it was acknowledged that, in retrospect, a 'vast extension of Education' had been accomplished between 1818 and 1833. 'The population had increased by nearly 24 per cent, while during the same interval the number of Day scholars had increased by 89 per cent.'[42] The Census report concluded thus without taking into account the underestimate of the Kerry returns which it acknowledged to be about 10 per cent for the country as a whole. In all this development Sunday schools should not be forgotten. These establishments played a very special part in English education and not least in the promotion of literacy. Their growth even exceeded that of the day schools. Indeed between 1818 and 1833 they increased by 225 per cent or over double the growth-rate of the day schools.[43]

TABLE 3·2. *Schools in Manchester in 1834**

	Total	In or before 1820	Established 1821–30	1830–4	Not ascertained
Day (95% of which supported by parental fees)	549	95	163	284	7
Evening (supported by payments of the scholar)	83	12	25	45	1

* *Manchester Statistical Society Report on Manchester, 1834*, Table 1, p. 31 It must be noticed that the figures in this table refer only to school 'births'; school 'deaths' might qualify the picture.

To what extent did the rising manufacturing and commercial towns of the Industrial Revolution share in this national education growth? Here we have to rely mainly on the reports of the newly emerging local statistical societies. The Manchester Statistical Society was the earliest and most influential of them. The establishment dates of the 549 day schools and 83 evening schools reported by this body in 1834 suggest indeed a veritable school 'explosion' in Manchester in the first four years of the 1830s.

It is in the early 1830s, interestingly enough, that legislation could

[42] *Census of Great Britain, 1851, Education, England and Wales, Report and Tables* (1854), p. xvii.
[43] *ibid. Report.*

have begun to have some effect. The Factory Act of 1833, which is usually acknowledged to be the first one that was effectively policed, controlled the hours of textile workers of between 9 and 18 years. Children of between 9 and 13 years had to provide evidence that they had attended school part time in the previous week. No child was allowed to be employed who was 8 years old or under. There are five observations, however, that weaken the argument that this legislation was a substantial factor in the growth of Manchester day schools at this time. First, the legislation applied only to textile workers. Second, there is no evidence to suggest that before 1833 the number of children employees of 8 years and under was large.[44] Third, the evidence of part-time teaching that the 9 to 13-year-olds had to produce related only to a schooling of 'at least two hours per day in the preceding week'.[45] Fourth, the educational clauses did not come into full operation until well after 1833. One authority dates their virtual commencement from 1836.[46] Fifth, other towns that were not so dependent on textiles experienced similar rapid growth of schools in the 1830s. In Bristol, for instance, it was found that of the day and evening schools, apart from 33 schools whose establishment dates were not ascertained, 65 were established in or before 1820; 98 from 1820 to 1830 inclusive; and 316 from 1830 to 1840. The Statistical Society of Bristol, reporting these facts, commented:

> The great increase within the last 10 years cannot fail to be remarked, and as no less than 285 out of the 316 schools opened in this period are schools supported wholly by the payments of the children, it is a proof that the business of the schoolmaster has not been made worse by the agitation and inquiry which the subject of education has of late years undergone.[47]

Another indication of educational growth given in the local statistical reports was the testimony of inter-generation differences. A detailed house-to-house survey of the Lancashire cotton and mining township

[44] In the textile town of Pendleton in 1838, 37 out of 2,466 children under ten years (i.e. $1\frac{1}{2}\%$) were found at work (see below, n. 48).
[45] Curtis, *op. cit.*, p. 229.
[46] Alfred A. Fry, 'Report of the Inspectors of Factories on the effects of the educational provisions of the Factories Act', *Journal of the Statistical Society of London*, II (1839), p. 176. Smith, *op. cit.*, p. 143, quotes a witness to a select committee in 1834, who stated that in Manchester the educational clauses were 'a dead letter'.
[47] *Jnl. Stat. Soc. London*, IV (1841), p. 253.

of Pendleton in 1838 [48] showed that the current generation was receiving more education than its predecessors: 'not more than 2 to 3 per cent ... of the juvenile population are at present left entirely destitute of instruction, whilst of the surviving adult population 8 per cent represent their education to have been totally neglected.' [49] Similarly at Hull a survey of 1839 [50] showed that whereas out of 14,526 ascertained cases of *adults* 417 had never been at a day school (i.e. 2·8 per cent), only 47 out of 3,039 ascertained cases of *minors* between the ages of 15 and 21 had never been at school, a proportion of 1·5 per cent (the number of cases not ascertained was 759).

Growth figures of this sort are certainly not as dramatic as those of school increases. However, they at least conflict with the impressions of writers such as Trevelyan,[51] the Hammonds,[52] and Altick[53] who believed that during the Industrial Revolution educational retrogression, or at best stagnation, prevailed especially in the industrial towns.

So far as the rural areas are concerned the report on *Employment of Women and Children in Agriculture: Special Assistant Poor Law Commissioners Report*, in 1843, provides a general assessment. 'Boys', it was reported, 'begin to be regularly employed in farm work as early as 7 in some few instances, but generally at 9 or 10.' [54] There was much interruption of schooling because of the demands of the planting and harvest seasons. Sometimes, 'where a labourer has a large family, a farmer will be induced to take a child at the earliest possible age to relieve the

---

[48] Pendleton is a borough of Salford. It was surveyed by the Manchester Statistical Society. The report appears in *Jnl. Stat. Soc. London*, II (1839), pp. 65–83.

[49] *ibid.*, p. 74. These figures at first sight conflict with the Society's report that in Manchester in 1834 one-third of the children between 5 and 15 were not at school. The Society found in its Pendleton Report that most children left school at around 10 years. At this rate the proportion without any schooling would be very much less than one-third in Manchester and could well have been 2·3 per cent as in Pendleton. The 1833 government return was also seriously misleading in its estimate of children 'without schooling' since it also used a base of 5 to 15 years. This serious sort of ambiguity in nineteenth-century education statistics is examined in West, *Education and the State*, pp. 145–6, and in the Report of the Statistical Society of Bristol in *Jnl. Stat. Soc. London*, IV (1841), pp. 252–3.

[50] *Jnl. Stat. Soc. London*, IV (1841).

[51] Trevelyan, *op. cit.*, p. 354.

[52] J. L. and B. Hammond, *The Rise of Modern Industry* (London, Methuen, 1937), pp. 229–31.

[53] Richard Altick, *The English Common Reader* (Chicago, The University of Chicago Press, 1957), p. 84.

[54] P.P. 1843 (510) XII, p. 28.

father, and prevent his being driven to the poor-house'.[55] Clearly such
evidence does not suggest that in general the position was better than
in the towns. Some further and possibly relevant pieces of evidence on
comparative achievements in different areas come from the Registrar
General's reports on literacy. In his first Annual Report of 1839 he
observed that 88 per cent of the grooms in London were able to sign
their names on marriage compared with the national average of 67
per cent. The report for the year 1845 contains comparative literacy
attainments in the counties. The northern counties of Westmorland,
Cumberland, Northumberland, Durham, and Yorkshire had the highest
rates.[56]

The towns of course offered a much bigger variety of educational
opportunities beyond formal schooling. This point has been well
expressed by Frank Smith:

> Education is never synonymous with schooling; and the farther
> back we go the more important does this distinction become. In
> consequence, we can never measure the educational provision of the
> past by merely recording the numbers of schools and scholars; many
> children who never went to school got a sound education in other
> ways.[57]

In addition to some enlightened educational projects in the nineteenth-century factories[58] there was much stimulus from the new
voluntary educational establishments, such as evening schools for young
workers. Dr James Kay told a government Select Committee in 1838:

> I think it would be found on inquiry that in the manufacturing
> towns in the north the number of classes of mutual evening schools
> instruction existing, and the number of persons attending schools
> of mechanics institutions, above the age of 13, are very much greater
> than in towns in any other part of the country.[59]

The reliance upon Sunday schools was particularly heavy; in Manchester, Kay observed: 'The Report of the Statistical Society shows

[55] P.P. 1843 (510) XII, p. 28.
[56] Seventh Annual Report of the Registrar General, P.P. 1846 (727) XIX,
p. 245.
[57] Smith, *op. cit.*, p. 36.
[58] See Michael Sanderson, 'Education and the factory in industrial Lancashire,
1780–1840', *Econ. Hist. Rev* .2nd ser. XX (1967).
[59] *Report of the Select Committee on Education of the Poorer Classes*, H.C. Paper
589, pp. 1837–8, VII (hereafter 'The 1838 Select Committee Report').

that the education provided for the poorer classes in Sunday schools is considerably more extensive than in the day schools.'[60]

When we turn to particular local reports of the statistical societies we find one which, as it stands, does not particularly favour the towns. This is the report by the Manchester Statistical Society on the county of Rutland. The following table shows a bigger proportion of schooling compared with the Lancashire towns.[61]

TABLE 3·3

	Rutland in 1838	Liverpool in 1835–6	Manchester and Salford in 1834–5	York in 1836	Hull in 1839
Proportion of the total population of day and evening scholars between five and 15 years of age	12·13%	10·67%	8·51%	14·22%	13·12%

First, it must be noted that the Rutland figures, published in 1839, were based on an estimated population in 1838 of 20,000. The Census of 1841 reported a population of 21,340 which compares with 19,385 in 1831. The 1838 figure therefore must have been nearer 21,000 and this reduces the Rutland percentage of scholars to about 11·5. Next, even at their face value these figures still do not suggest the very stark contrast between educational provision in the growing towns of the Industrial Revolution and that of other areas such as is suggested in the writings of Trevelyan, Altick, and the Hammonds.

Rutland had many more endowed and charity schools. Comparing the proportion of the population educated in the different areas out of the charitable funds and endowments, it was found that it was 2·45 per cent of the population in Manchester and 8·26 per cent in Rutland. If we are studying the contribution of the new industry to the growth of education we should compare conditions in the same area over time. We have already seen evidence of inter-generation improvements in the towns, as well as evidence suggesting the very rapid growth of schools in Manchester and Bristol especially in the 1830s, growth that was not much aided by endowments or charity. Unfortunately we do not have

[60] *ibid.* para. 67. In the Manchester Statistical Committee's investigations Manchester was found to be superior to York and Rutland in the number and efficiency of the Sunday schools.
[61] Taken from the 'Manchester Statistical Society's Report on Hull', reproduced in *Jnl. Stat. Soc. London*, IV (1841), pp. 158, 159.

comparative indications of the reduction of the numbers entirely destitute of schooling in Rutland. Figures showing the dates of establishment of schools in Rutland [62] do not suggest the same pace of growth as in Manchester or Bristol. Moreover, the statistical superiority of Rutland was in terms of day schools. Manchester was found to have substantially more and better Sunday schools than average. [63] Furthermore, we must remember that over one-sixth of the family heads in Manchester were Irish. In such cases, measures of net growth in education from 1800 should be considered in the context of the educational conditions in the country of origin. [64]

The fact that growth in privately purchased education in general has been demonstrated to the above extent does not of course demonstrate that public finance was not seriously required. Educational assistance to families with below-average incomes may well be indicated even if average families do not need it. But we have not even established that modal family education expenditure was Pareto-optimum. Indeed we cannot assess this until we have some notion as to the 'correct' share of resources that 'should have' been employed. Such a figure has never, so far as is known, been derived or suggested. For the moment the best we can do is to attempt a rough estimate of the share of school education in the national income of the 1830s. It will be instructive then to compare it with the twentieth-century equivalent. Aggregate expenditure for one year, 1833, will be calculated and then related to national income estimates for the period. Since some degree of error will apply to each of the three relevant variables – aggregate school population, average fee, and length of the school year – the most suitable approach is to provide a range of estimates based on a corresponding range of assumptions.

The aggregate school population (day and infant schools) according to the 1833 government (Kerry) return was 1,276,947. [65] The local statistical societies, however, reported serious underestimates when they

[62] 'Report of the Manchester Statistical Society on the State of Education in Rutland', reproduced in *Jnl. Stat. Soc. London*, II (1839), Table II, p. 307.
[63] In 1834 as many as 22,000 minors were taught writing in the evenings in Manchester Sunday schools during the week. *Manchester Statistical Society Report on Manchester*, 1834, Table VI, p. 39.
[64] Dr Kay told the 1838 Select Committee that it was not immediately practicable to impose on manufacturers the rule that there should be no employment without some education 'on account of the immigration of the Irish, which the constant development of the cotton manufacture has stimulated, and by which it has been fed'. (para. 95).
[65] H.C. Paper 62, 1835, XLI–XLIII.

made their own checks shortly afterwards. The Manchester Statistical Society reported between a third and a half underestimate of day scholars. For the borough of Salford in 1835[66] it found that the Kerry returns had under-reported by 82 day schools and 3,440 day scholars, which amounted roughly to an underestimate of 50 per cent. A report on the town of Bury[67] for the same year also found serious underestimate in the Kerry figures. In Hulme,[68] containing a population of 9,609, the government return under-reported about one-third of schools and scholars (14 schools and 864 scholars). In Liverpool the omissions amounted to as many as 15,500 scholars, 'and though some few duplicate returns were made, there seems to be no doubt but that the omissions largely preponderated'.[69] A Birmingham report in 1838 showed a 50 per cent deficiency in the 1833 returns.[70]

We must decide, therefore, what degree of error to apply to the aggregate national figure in Lord Kerry's parliamentary returns. The 1851 Census report on education stated (without explanation) that for the whole country these returns were probably deficient by about 10 per cent. This observation seems to relate to total schooling, that is to the combined figure of day schools and Sunday schools. The underestimate of day schools was found by the local statistical societies to be a much bigger proportion than that of Sunday schools. We conclude that the national underestimate for day schools was probably at least 20 per cent and could have been as much as $33\frac{1}{3}$ per cent. On the 20 per cent adjustment the day-school population figure for England and Wales in 1833 would have been 1,596,184; on the $33\frac{1}{3}$ per cent adjustment it would have been 1,915,420.

The biggest part of the cost of day schooling in this period was covered neither by the church nor by philanthropy, but from direct payments (fees) from working families. The Bristol Statistical Society in 1841 found that a very big majority of its schools and scholars received no support whatsoever except from the parents. To these 446 schools

[66] *Report of the Manchester Statistical Society on the State of Education in the Borough of Salford in 1835* (1836), p. 5.
[67] *Report of the Manchester Statistical Society on the State of Education in Bury in 1835* (1836).
[68] *Manchester Statistical Society Report on Manchester, 1834*, p. 4.
[69] *Census of Great Britain, 1851, England and Wales, Education Report* (1854), p. xvii.
[70] 'Report on the state of education in Birmingham', by the Birmingham Statistical Society, reproduced in *Jnl. Stat. Soc. London*, III (1840) p. 27. The population increase between 1833 and 1838 would account for a small part of the difference.

the parents were paying £32,000 annually. In the 42 schools 'assisted by subscription' parents were annually paying £2,500. Only 24 schools were free and endowed. The Bristol Statistical Society reported: 'in the city of Bristol alone, with a population not exceeding 120,000 persons, a much larger sum is annually paid [by parents] for the purposes of education, than is contributed by the State towards the instruction of the five or six millions of children in the United Kingdom.' [71] (Even as late as 1869 parental payments in such towns as Leeds totalled half as much again as government grants.)

According to the Manchester Statistical Society 80 per cent of the school-children's education in Manchester was paid for entirely by parental fees.

TABLE 3·4. *Statement of the mode in which schools [in Manchester in 1834]* are supported*

	No. of schools	Total no. of scholars
Free	13	2,170
Not free 1. In which part of the expense is borne by the scholars	15	2,106
2. In which the whole expense is borne by the scholars	607	15,843
Totals	635	20,119

* *Manchester Statistical Society Report on Manchester, 1834*, Table II.

The government return for 1833 showed that 73 per cent of the day scholars paid fees; in 58 per cent of cases the parental fees covered the entire cost.[72] (See Table 3·5.)

The best method of approach to our problem of computing aggregate expenditure is to multiply the fees by the number of scholar-attendances. To this figure we can add estimates for the 'free' schooling. The school fees in the common day schools in Manchester varied from 3*d* to 1*s* 6*d* per week. The average weekly fee at common schools for

[71] 'Statistics of Education in Bristol', by a Committee of the Statistical Society of Bristol, *Jnl. Stat. Soc. London*, IV (1841), p. 255. The government's annual subsidy to education in England and Wales in 1841 was £30,000.
[72] There has been much erroneous reporting on this subject. Thus the 1851 Census (Education Report) observed: 'Up to this period [1833] the whole of what had been accomplished in the work of popular education was the fruit of private liberality incited mainly by religious zeal' (p. xvii). Similarly Curtis, *op. cit.*, p. 224, gives the impression that 'philanthropy' was the chief educational support prior to 1833. Clearly private purchase by working-class families was the main agency.

boys was $8\frac{1}{2}d$ and for girls $10\frac{1}{4}d$; the average at Dame schools was $4d$.[73] In the 'superior' private schools, which contained about 3,000 or 15 per cent of the pupils, the average weekly payment could have been about $2s$.[74] There are grounds for believing that these figures were reasonably representative of the whole country.[75] Assuming that entirely 'free'

TABLE 3·5. *Statistics of school population and school finance: government return, 1833**

Maintenance of schools	Infant schools scholars	Percentage share of total	Daily schools scholars	Percentage share of total
Endowment (no fees – free)	1,450	2%	152,314	13%
Subscription (no fees – free)	13,081	12%	165,436	14%
Payments (entirely) from scholars (fees)	40,721	46%	691,728	58%
Subscription and payments from scholars (fees)	33,753	38%	178,464	15%
Totals	89,005		1,187,942	

* *Summary of Education Returns, England and Wales, 1833*, H.C. Paper 62 [1835], percentage columns added.

(endowed and subscription) schools gave an education which was worth at least as much as the average fee-paying establishment, and remembering that of the fee-payers 21 per cent had a schooling that was privately subsidized from other sources, we shall suppose that the average weekly cost throughout the country was in the middle of the above fee quotations at $9d$ per week.[76]

[73] *Manchester Statistical Society Report on Manchester*, 1834, Table III, p. 33. Unweighted averages; weighted averages are similar, $8·2d$, $10·3d$, and $4d$. respectively.

[74] The report of the Manchester Statistical Society on education in Salford in 1835 reported that the terms of the superior private schools varied from $10s$ $6d$ to £5 $5s$ per quarter.

[75] In the Manchester Statistical Society's report on the county of Rutland in 1838 the fees were about $1d$ less. The Birmingham Statistical Society's report for 1838 showed the same level of charges as Manchester. Figures reported by the Statistical Society of London for 1837 (see *Jnl. Stat. Soc. London*, Dec. 1838) show higher charges for three Westminster Parishes.

	Dame	Common day	Middling
Average weekly fee	6d	$10\frac{1}{4}d$	boys 1s 3d girls 1s

Superior schools charged an average of £1 $10s$ per quarter or $1s$ $6d$ per week.

[76] Several of the free schools of course gave an education of an economic value considerably in excess of $9d$ per week. The Manchester Free Grammar School, for instance, educated 200 boys and was supported by an income of £4,000 per annum. Chetham's Hospital, or Blue-Coat school, with 80 boarders, and several other generously endowed schools, similarly provided an education worth much more than $9d$.

The next variable to consider is the length of the school year. On our reading of the evidence it is most doubtful that the number of weeks in the year when schools were officially closed for holidays would have been bigger than today. In view of the need to keep up their earnings many proprietors had every incentive to keep open as long as possible. Let us assume that the average working time was 42 weeks in the year. The next problem is to adjust for absences. Although the 1833 returns are not helpful in this respect the 1851 Census report found that the number of children attending on any particular day in private schools which were dependent entirely on fees was 91 per cent of the school roll and in public schools (i.e. schools receiving any subsidy from any source) the number in attendance was 79 per cent.[77] We shall assume 80 per cent attendance – roughly the lower of these estimates for 1851. Such a figure is reasonably consistent with the 1838 report on Pendleton which classified one-third of the students as 'irregular'. Defining the 'irregular' group in Pendleton as attending on average for only one-half of the school weeks (i.e. 21 weeks or 105 days) the average attendance for the whole school population would be about 80 per cent.[78]

At this rate out of the 42 weeks of available day schooling the average scholar would attend for 34 weeks. The average weekly cost of 9d can now be converted into an annual cost per pupil of £1 5s 6d.[79] Our lowest estimate of scholars in 1833 derived from the Kerry returns was 1,596,184, say 1,600,000. This would mean that resources devoted to day schooling would have been of the value of approximately £2,040,000. Using our higher estimate of 1,915,420 (say 1,900,000) scholars in 1833 the aggregate educational value for the year would have been £2,422,500.

Any serious estimate of total educational resources used in 1833 must

[77] 1851 Census (Education Report), pp. xxx–xxxxi.
[78] The Report for Hull in 1838 showed that only one fifth of the scholars were irregular. Some idea about average attendance can be obtained from the Manchester Statistical Society's estimate that common school teachers earned between 16s and 17s a week and that on average they had 32 pupils on their books and the typical fee was 9d per week. Misleading impressions about attendance are given in some school reports which complained that they could not keep some scholars for more than six months or so. Many scholars could well have transferred to other establishments so that their yearly school attendance could have been compensated.
[79] This estimate would seem to be rather on the low side in the light of the Bristol Statistical Society's conclusion (see above, p. 76) that parents were contributing £34,000 for schooling in Bristol with a total population of not more than 120,000 and a school population which we estimate to have been between 15,000 and 18,000.

take some account of important nineteenth-century institutions, other than day schools, for the education of children. Probably the most important of such institutions was the Sunday school. There were roughly the same number of scholars in Sunday schools as in day schools (after correcting for errors in the 1833 return). Nearly all the Sunday schools taught reading and a large number taught writing. The Kerry return described these institutions as being financed primarily by voluntary subscriptions.[80] Assuming we can regard attendance at these schools on Sundays as the equivalent of one day's attendance at a day school, then our estimate of aggregate resources devoted to schooling should be increased by one-fifth.[81] This would increase our valuation of total resources devoted to schooling from £2·42 million to £2·9 million and our lowest estimate from £2·04 million to £2·45 million.

In addition, in some areas there seems to have been considerable educational provisions for young workers between 10 and 15 years old in factories. Dr M. Sanderson observes that down to 1833 there were signs of 'considerable advance in the direct participation of the factory owner in education'.[82] He gives examples of small 'factory colonies' in 'obscure fell districts' where 'paternalistic' mill proprietors were establishing schools in or close to the factories.[83] Examples are given by Sanderson of education-minded firms in Preston, Rochdale, Horwich, Bolton, Oldham, Didsbury, Caton, and Galgate. In Bury, for instance, a firm with 23 apprentices had a schoolmaster 'whose sole occupation was to instruct the children in reading during working hours'. The addition of such activity to our estimates of annual total educational resources in 1833 (which so far ranges from £2·45 million to £2·9

[80] H.C. 62, 1835, XLI, XLIII.
[81] The nineteenth-century Sunday school movement has no substantial counterpart today.
[82] Sanderson, *op. cit.*, p. 267.
[83] The extent to which such activity was 'philanthropic' is debatable. Dr Sanderson argues that this pattern of education 'was an ideal way of exerting the social control of the firm over its workers and of raising up young labourers in obedience if not in scientific skill'. Such 'paternalism', Prof. Gary Becker has shown (*Human Capital*, Chicago: Nat. Bur. Econ. Res., 1964), 'may simply be a way of investing in the health and welfare of employees in underdeveloped countries'. Prof. Becker demonstrates that there are bigger incentives for firms to make educational investments in their employees the more specific is their productivity to the particular firm and the bigger its monopsony power. Sanderson's one pioneering factory settlement in 'an obscure fell distrist' could well illustrate this case. Where the employees also profited from such educative investment we have instances of what are called reciprocal externalities which the private market internalizes.

million) presents the most difficult problem since we have no means of measuring it accurately. It would not seem unreasonable to us, however, to reach a tentative conclusion that total resources were just above or just below £3 million.

The gross national income of Great Britain in 1831 has been estimated at £340 million.[84] By 1833 it was probably £362 million.[85] To obtain the figure for England and Wales we have to subtract the share of Scotland. If we do this on a *pro rata* population basis we arrive at £310 million. Comparing this with our estimate of around £3 million on lower education, it seems clear that the latter accounted for not much more or less than 1 per cent of *net* national income.[86]

Great caution is obviously needed in comparing such early national income estimates with those of the twentieth century. Nevertheless, it is interesting to observe that between 1920 and 1945 the share of day schooling (primary and secondary) in the United Kingdom was also around 1 per cent of the U.K. net national income.[87] The share for 1965 had increased to 2 per cent. If we take the category of children below 11 years, then the 1833 share of the national income was about 0·8 per cent.[88] This was a higher share than in most years of the twentieth century. The following table summarizes the main results.

TABLE 3·6 *Percentage of net national income spent on day schooling, 1833–1965*

	1833	1920	1965
Children all ages	1·00% (approx.)	0·70%	2·00%
Children below 11 years	0·80% (approx.)	0·58%	0·86%

It is this type of evidence that has relevance for any attempted assessments of nineteenth-century educational 'underinvestment' that are

[84] B. R. Mitchell and Phyllis Deane, *Abstract of British Historical Statistics* (Cambridge, 1962), p. 366.
[85] Mitchell's and Deane's national income estimate for 1841 is £452 million. We have derived the 1833 figure on the assumption of a straight-line increase between 1831 and 1841.
[86] We have no exact figure for net national income in 1833; but clearly it would have been less than the gross national income of £310 million.
[87] John Vaizey and John Sheenan, *Resources for Education* (London, Allen and Unwin, 1967), Tables IX and X. The figures we have extracted relate exclusively to primary and secondary education, i.e. they exclude such things as meals and milk and inspection. They indicate approximate rates of 0·7 per cent for 1920, 1 per cent for 1945, and up to 1·25 per cent in the intervening years.
[88] We base this estimate on the report of the student ages in the Pendleton Report for 1838 (see above, p. 71. n. 48).

based on the criteria of Pareto-relevant externalities. Such evidence is similarly significant with respect to questions about the probability that governments will, or can, redirect and expand resources in the direction of objectives postulated in welfare economics. In the 1830s there is no doubt that many advisers were exceptionally sanguine about such quantitative expansion and reallocation. What equally exercised their minds, however, was the simultaneous prospect of making 'desirable' changes in the *quality* of existing provision. Modern historians will also at this point raise questions as to the quality of the pre-1833 educational achievements. Relying upon the reports of early nineteenth-century select committees, they may well insist that in many cases school conditions were so bad that the quantity of what can rightfully be described as 'education' was significantly less than our figures have indicated. The final section examines this problem in some detail.

III

The modern theory of public goods (externalities), on which we have so far based our approach, is built on the assumption that all goods, public and private, should be supplied in line with individual preferences. Any need for public policy arises only in those cases where there has been a failure of the market to allocate resources in accordance with these preferences. Collective provision that is 'justified' on these grounds is not coercive since all stand to benefit. Modern literature on public finance, however, contains another concept, that of 'merit goods,' which is outside this 'consumer sovereignty' welfare tradition.[89] According to the 'merit good' theory, preferences of individuals are no longer taken as given but indeed are the main object of interference by 'society'. This 'theory of imposed choice' strictly implies the predominance not of the wishes of society but of those of a small 'informed group' within it. Prof. Musgrave, the originator of the idea, explains: 'the critic feels that preference should be imposed within certain limits by a chosen élite, be it because its members are better educated, possess greater innate wisdom, or belong to a particular party or sect'.[90] He also attempts to reconcile the theory of 'merit goods' with the

[89] Musgrave, *The Theory of Public Finance*. See also John G. Head, 'On merit goods', *Finanzarchiv*, XXV (1966).
[90] *Public Economics*, ed .J. Margolis (1969), pp. 143–4. Prof. Musgrave uses the terms 'society' and 'chosen *élite*' interchangeably.

non-authoritarian welfare tradition. Firstly, it is suggested that prosperous people may suffer disutility from seeing the low standards of
consumption of their poor neighbours:[91] the provision of a specific
subsidy to reduce the inequalities of the consumption of necessities
thus meets the preferences of the rich *and* benefits the poor at the same
time. This implies a voluntary redistribution of income from rich to
poor. This version clearly does not find support in our empirical study.
In the nineteenth century educational subsidies (after 1833) were
derived from regressive taxation.[92] Secondly, there is the suggestion
that rational choice requires full knowledge of the alternatives and that
the *temporary* use of imposed choice is justified in the learning process.
'Thus, what appears to be imposed choice may be compatible, in the
longer run, with the objective of intelligent free choice.'[93] Strictly the
imposed choice could refer to quantity or quality of a particular good.
In education it is today usually the need for an increase in quantity
(often from zero levels) that is implied. Prof. Musgrave, echoing
J. S. Mill, observes: 'The advantages of education are more evident to
the informed than the uninformed, thus justifying compulsion in the
allocation of resources.'[94]

On our evidence the masses of people in the 1830s already did appreciate the advantages of education; it was mainly lack of income which
prevented their having more; with the passage of time increasing incomes were generally leading to increased private demand for schooling.[95] The 'chosen élites' which advised governments were concerned
especially about the quality of the instruction that the new tide of education was bringing forth. It was this quality that they especially wanted
to change; education to them was a 'merit want', particularly in this
sense. The nineteenth-century denominational elements in the 'chosen
élites', for instance, complained to governments that religion was
increasingly being neglected in the new 'educational mix'. The Utilitarians objected that free choice was leading to the fostering of tech-

---

[91] Musgrave, *ibid.*, p. 143; and *Fiscal Systems* (New Haven, Conn., Yale Univ.
Press, 1968), p. 12.
[92] Progressive taxation was not introduced until the twentieth century. Taxes on
food and tobacco alone accounted for well over half the government revenue in
the 1840s and 1850s. S. Northcote, *Twenty Years of Financial Policy* (1862).
[93] Musgrave, in *Public Economics*, ed. Margolis, p. 143.
[94] *idem*, *The Theory of Public Finance*, p. 14.
[95] The report on Hull in 1838 observed (p. 161): 'With few exceptions the
working classes in Hull seem to have a just appreciation of the value of education, as well as those parents who have been deprived of the advantages of
instruction, as those who have been more favourably circumstanced,'

nically inefficient schools. It was the Utilitarians particularly who argued for a 'temporary interference' with public choice on the grounds that ultimately the public could be better informed and their preferences no longer distorted.

Such a theory of 'temporary imposed choice' is of course testable by evidence. If the paternalism turns out to be 'longer than temporary' the 'merit good' is no longer reconcilable with the traditional consumer sovereignty assumption. On the other hand if, after a period of 'forced tasting', the public actively rejects the product that the 'informed group' has imposed, then it is strongly arguable that the latter was not after all well informed about 'true' public preferences. The same conclusion applies if the élite fail ever to produce the superior service because experience suggests that it is a Utopian ideal well beyond the limitations of available resources. Corresponding to 'market failure' we would now have a case of 'government failure'.

The activities of the predominant advisory élite groups in education in the 1830s can now be examined in the light of these various meanings and implications of the 'merit good' approach.

In the late 1830s a Select Committee on Education of the Poorer Classes was set up 'to consider the means of providing useful Education for Children of the Poorer Classes in large Towns throughout England and Wales'. It included Sir Robert Peel, Lord Ashley, and Mr Gladstone, and the chief witness was Dr James Philip Kay.[96]

Having brushed aside much of the quantitative evidence, the committee was impressed by many of the pessimistic qualitative details provided by the local statistical societies. In examining these strictures in the twentieth century we must keep a sense of perspective. The relevant choice, to repeat, is not between the real and some ideal but between alternative real institutional arrangements attainable within given finite resources at any one time. The practitioners of a 'nirvana' approach,[97] on discovering discrepancies between the ideal and the real, simply deduce automatically and without argument that the real is inefficient. Those who use the 'comparative institution' approach, on the contrary, assess the 'lesser of evils' among alternative possible institutional arrangements within the recognized national income restraints. Clearly no 'ideal' has yet been reached in twentieth-century education, characterized as it is in many parts by over-crowding,

[96] See above, p. 72 n. 59.
[97] Harold Demsetz, 'Information and inefficiency: another viewpoint', *Journal of Law and Economics*, XII (1969), p. 1.

teacher-shortage, and overstretched or inferior buildings. The defence
that a particular institutional set-up will 'one day' approach the ideal
can be applied to all alternative arrangements as separate declarations
of faith by the champions of each system in turn.

Consider the Manchester Statistical Society's detailed complaints.
First, they condemned pupil–teacher ratios as too high. In fact they were
better than today's.[98] Next, irregular attendances were emphasized. To
a large extent these have been taken into account in our quantitative
estimate.[99] There is little doubt that lack of continuity of education was
a serious defect for many children. Absenteeism, however, stemmed
mainly from precarious incomes. In the society's report on Pendleton
of 1838, for instance, half of the irregularity was attributed to poverty.
Much of the rest concerned loss of parents, nursing at home, etc. which
are also closely related to poverty. Irregularity, therefore, was not
usually the fault of the schools or of the families.

Lack of 'character-training' and 'proper religious instruction' was
probably the strongest criticism made by those who advised governments. The society objected that in the common schools, 'Religious
instruction is seldom attended to beyond the rehearsal of 'a catechism',
and moral education, real cultivation of the mind and improvement of
character, are totally neglected.'[100] Twentieth-century historians may
or may not have views as to the effect of Bible knowledge, religious
discipline, and recognition of one's 'proper station in life' upon the
fulfilment of ultimate and undistorted individual preferences. Whatever
their own opinion, those of them who seek to measure the relationship
between education and economic development will be interested in the
degree to which the early official concepts of 'efficiency' in education
meant primarily a schooling which scored high marks in divinity and
morality. Some of the schools were often written off by the statistical
societies as worthless largely on account of failure in these respects. Yet
the increase of secular education and the new emphasis on the 'three
Rs' was provided by the schools in clear and direct response to parental
wishes.[101] By this time the Establishment was clearly fighting some-

[98] The number of common day scholars to a teacher averaged 26·8 in the 1830's
in the six towns, Bury, Salford, Liverpool, Manchester, York, and Birmingham
(*Jnl. Stat. Soc. London*, III (1840), 33). In 1967 there were 29·7 pupils per
teacher in English primary schools – the nearest twentieth-century equivalent to
the nineteenth-century common day schools.

[99] See above, p. 78.

[100] *Manchester Statistical Society Report on Manchester, 1834*, p. 10.

[101] Today there is general agreement that religious and 'moral' education is still
one of the least satisfactory parts of British education. The founder members

thing of a rearguard action against the new expression of popular educational preferences. Not that there was a serious decline in the demand for religious instruction, but in the parents' opinion the teeming Sunday schools catered for that quite well; on week-days families were demanding education in more 'practical' matters.[102]

In the 1830s, interestingly enough, the religious Establishments, now on the defensive, were joined by new and unexpected partners, the Utilitarians. In the heyday of enthusiastic Benthamite blueprints for the reform of society it was argued that the 'greatest happiness' could be achieved only after middle-class Utilitarian leaders had exercised temporary empire over the minds of men. In the words of Roebuck when (successfully) presenting his Education Bill to Parliament in 1833, 'The people at present are far too ignorant to render themselves happy.'[103]

The anxiety of the Utilitarians to obtain pedagogic influence was aptly reflected in Dr James Philip Kay's replies to the 1838 Select Committee's questions. Kay, the fellow spirit of Bentham's other disciple Chadwick, had been appointed on Nassau Senior's recommendation as an assistant Poor Law Commissioner. At this time keenly occupied with the building of large experimental Benthamite school establishments in pauper settlements, he was eager to spread what he was convinced to be their advantages to the mass public and to see them supersede the smaller private establishments which free choice was fostering. While Bentham himself was anti-religion, Benthamites often saw their main chance through alliances with the clergy and its spokesmen. Kay's answers[104] to the 1838 Select Committee as chief witness certainly demonstrated the strategic appeal of the religious aspects of education to his contemporary peers. The committee, simply wanting to know how much education existed in the towns, asked via (the

---

of the Manchester Statistical Society, and the 1838 Select Committee, would undoubtedly be at least as critical of today's 'religious instruction'.

[102] For an account of the way in which pressures for the 'three Rs' led to the suppression of the traditional-type education in Nottinghamshire, see J. D. Chambers, *Nottinghamshire in the Eighteenth Century* (London, Frank Cass, 1966), pp. 308–9.

[103] Hansard, *Parl. Debates*, X, cols. 139–66, 30 July 1833. The sentence well represents the central message in James Mill's essays 'Education' in the *Encyclopaedia Britannica*. Roebuck was one of Bentham's protégés. Bentham spoke of him to John Bowring: 'But I have a new tame puss. I will make Roebuck my puss for his article on Canada; and many a mouse will he catch.' J. Bentham, *Collected Works* (1843), XI, p. 81.

[104] Kay was a churchman. See Smith, *op. cit.*, p. 178.

devout) Mr Gladstone the direct and apparently innocent question: 'Can you form an estimate of the amount of deficiency in the means of education in any given district, say for instance, the district of Manchester?' Promptly diverting attention to quality and away from quantitative facts (which contained much potential surprise for those prepared to probe), Dr Kay replied: 'If by education I am to understand what I have previously described, sound religious instruction, correct moral training, and a sufficient extent of secular knowledge suited to their station in life, I should scarcely say that it exists within the limits of my observation.'

Chairman: 'You think it is not afforded by any schools at present efficiently?'

Dr Kay: 'Not efficiently.'[105]

It was this kind of 'evidence' which led to the committee's conclusion that half of the schooling in the towns was of little use.[106]

Kay, a utilitarian enthusiast for new large-scale school methods, had an almost doctrinaire dislike of small schools and a preference for the large national (charity) schools run by the National Society (sponsored by the church) and the Lancasterian schools supervised by the British and Foreign School Society. In reaching its conclusions as to the quality and quantity of schooling, the 1838 Committee relied heavily on Kay's evidence and that of the Manchester Statistical Society, of which Kay was treasurer and a founder member.

Since poverty was the main reason for the failure of many to have a longer schooling, that is as long as their twelfth or thirteenth year, the direct government policy that suggested itself was specific subsidies to the benefit of the families most in need. This could be done by official intermediate agencies to assist selected family incomes and to help pay the school fees. Another method was to abolish fees and use the government funds to subsidize particular schools. Kay at first argued strongly that the payment of fees for working-class education should be con-

---

[105] 1838 Select Committee Report, paras. 100 and 101.
[106] The conclusions of the influential Manchester Statistical Society's Report on Manchester in 1834, which seem to have been presented in increasing order of importance, finish with a comparison with German schools. While none of the latter was 'allowed to *exist*' which did not effectively teach religion, the report's last two sentences protest: 'in this town on the other hand, and generally throughout this country, the acquisition of Reading, Writing and Arithmetic seems to be considered as constituting the finished education of the children of the lower classes of the people . . . and that the real improvement of the character, instruction on moral and religious subjects, and all the more valuable *objects* of education, are totally neglected and forgotten' (p. 19).

tinued. He told Gladstone that when instruction was given gratuitously 'the parent surrenders the right of interfering as to the quality and extent of the instruction which shall be given to his child, and that in point of fact he places himself in that respect in the position of a pauper, who is to be treated according to the will of others, and not his own.'[107] Yet Kay stressed to the committee that the education 'markets' were not producing sufficiently economical units of schooling because of the lack of appreciation, by parents and others, of certain economies of scale and better methods of instruction that were available in the particular large-scale schools of which he and his fellow Benthamites approved. He thus found himself advocating 'temporary imposed choice'.

Given a 'temporary' local education rate and some centralized direction, especially of teacher training, Kay claimed that he could obtain better use of resources than already prevailed. His system made use of pupil teachers and was geared to one superior trained teacher presiding in the gallery of a vast establishment, reminiscent of Bentham's Panopticon.[108] People would acknowledge the virtue of his scheme, argued Kay, given some experience with it.[109] It would be implemented through the larger organizations such as the National schools and the Lancasterian schools which were already receiving the existing parliamentary subsidies. Kay had in mind the squeezing out of the small schools which would receive no subsidies but pay taxes; subsidies would be (and eventually under directives of the Treasury Board were) made preferentially to big schools.[110] There were 4,000 boys in Manchester paying fees

[107] 1838 Select Committee Report, para. 81.
[108] Kay emphasized to the committee his view that the teaching of children in the environment of large morning assemblies had especially a most important moral and religious influence upon them: 'The gallery is particularly suited to convey instruction, in which the sympathy of a large number can be brought to bear on the feelings of the rest, and therefore it appears to me to be singularly well adapted to convey moral and religious instruction.' *1833 Select Committee Report*, para. 35.
[109] Kay obviously impressed the Whig element in Parliament, for the next year he was appointed first secretary of the newly formed Committee of Council on Education. The Committee under Kay's supervision channelled most of the public funds through the National Society and the British and Foreign Schools Society. Pupils in the national schools were all obliged to receive instruction in the liturgy and catechism of the established church. In the Lancasterian schools of the second society, the Bible was read but no denominational teaching allowed.
[110] Under the subsequent administration small private schools were typically deprived of the new public support since preference was given to schools intended to accommodate at least 400 scholars. The grants were confined to school buildings and were subject to the condition of half the cost being met by voluntary contributions. Balfour, *op. cit.*, p. 4.

for their attendance at numerous (and much smaller) private day schools where, according to Kay, for qualitative reasons already examined, the standards were poor. At the 'superior' Lancasterian and national schools at which no fees were payable, there were 1,000 students.

Kay was asked by Mr Pusey, a member of the 1838 Select Committee: 'why parents give the preference to the worst kind of education for which they are obliged to pay, rather than to that education which you say is superior and which is afforded to them gratuitously?' Kay replied that there was a shortage of the free school places and there might be a large potential demand for such education; 'though I have not yet great confidence in the ability of the population to appreciate, *in the first instance*, the difference in the quality of instruction conveyed'[111] (my italics). The freedom of parents to choose through a fee-paying system was in Kay's view, for the moment at least, largely a hindrance to progress; for in his opinion they were choosing the wrong type of school. The implicit assumption was that the local (regressive) tax which he advocated would help to circumvent this problem because, in contrast to a direct fee, it would be a compulsory payment for publicly standardized service.

In terms of modern public-finance theory Kay was obviously treating education as a 'merit good', a concept which can be interpreted either as full authoritarianism or as 'temporary imposed choice' aimed at removing individual preference distortions. One of Kay's main contributions was the pioneering of teacher-training and the use of separate classes. The diversion of resources to these purposes may well have had beneficial consequences that were later generally acknowledged by consumers of education.[112] On the other hand the Lancasterian schools (which Kay championed before the 1838 Select Committee) soon became unpopular with many authorities. In its report on Salford in 1835 the Manchester Statistical Society complained they were apt to become too mechanical and to degenerate into the 'Parrot system'.[113] The monitorial schools, which especially enjoyed the public subsidies after 1833, came in the eyes of the inspectors in the 1840s to stand 'hopelessly

---

[111] *1838 Select Committee Report*, paras. 114 and 115.
[112] There is, however, no absolute consensus about the suitability of the products of the later Victorian training colleges that were set up. Dickens's Mr McChoakumchild in *Dombey and Son* was a notable caricature. Altick, *op. cit.*, p. 162, refers to some of the later training establishments as 'pedant factories'.
[113] *Report of the Manchester Statistical Society on the State of Education in Salford in 1835* (1836), p. 8.

condemned'.[114] In retrospect, the earlier reluctance of families to patronize these institutions suggests that parental preferences had not been as 'distorted' as the early utilitarian champions of the monitorial system had believed.

The most striking failure of the 'temporary imposed choice' variety of the 'merit good' approach in the nineteenth century was, on Kay's own criterion, the gradual erosion of parental fees as the central means of finance and the eventual permanent substitution of free schooling later in the century. On Kay's argument the parent eventually surrendered 'the right of interfering as to the quality and the extent' of his child's instruction when fees were abolished.[115] The argument that parents, later in the century, could not have afforded the fees does not (and did not) hold because where redistribution is needed to help poor parents, financial transfers to the families (conditional upon earmarked spending if necessary) instead of the reduction of prices to zero is (and was) an available alternative policy. Clearly, if after the period of imposed choice via taxes and free schooling, the parents' preferences ceased to be distorted, as Kay expected, the termination of this 'temporary' period would have required the removal of the taxes and the restoration of the fees. The fact that the opposite happened might suggest that the 'merit good' intervention was the full authoritarian kind after all, and one which is irreconcilable with the modern welfare tradition of individual preference.

For the 'temporary imposed choice' theory to hold, the 'imposed' period obviously must not be longer than the individual's lifetime. By the mid-century so many families were continuing resistance to the prescriptions of the 'informed élites' that the latter either forgot the 'temporariness' of their original task or, like Nassau Senior, had extended it to at least three or four more generations. In 1861 he argued that the middle classes might still look forward to the time when the labouring population may be safely entrusted with the education of their children: 'but no Protestant country believes that this time has come, and I see no reason to hope for it until generation after generation has been better and better educated'. By the latter part of the twentieth century, Senior continued, England might become 'what no country

---

[114] Balfour, *op. cit.*, p. 9. Kay himself did not approve of the traditional monitorial schemes since they put too much responsibility on very young monitors. He certainly believed in division of labour in his large establishments but it was based not on mutual instruction but on the class system and put more emphasis on teacher-training of older persons. His pupil-teachers were senior boys.
[115] See above, p. 87.

has ever yet become, an Utopia inhabited by a self-educated and well-educated labouring population'.[116]

It may be argued that in the nineteenth century education policy was *inevitably* authoritarian because at that time the franchise had not been extended. Respect for individual preferences, however, does not necessarily presuppose 'full democracy'. Indeed it is interesting that while the nineteenth-century leaders felt obliged to be almost apologetic in their insistence that control was only temporary, in the more enfranchised ('democratic') twentieth century the prevailing assumption is that control is permanent. Few educationists today suggest the restoration of fees.

The discussion at this point, of course, leads to issues wider than those that are relevant to this article. In conclusion, however, it can be suggested that the current situation might yet be explicable in terms which are consistent with the general corpus of welfare economics. To recapitulate, such economic theory postulates that 'market failure' occurs when individual preferences are not correctly respected by the private suppliers because competition is impeded by imperfect knowledge of the consumer or by monopolist activity. This is matched, however, by the case of 'political failure' when governments also do not respect individual preferences. The latter failure too can stem from imperfect communication between governments and voters, and/or from the monopolistic behaviour of education providers. In this environment government supply of what begins innocently enough as a 'merit good' (in the temporary sense) may become permanent because eventually it serves a particular interest group, in this case the education suppliers, that is education administrators, teachers, etc. who are more politically organized than the dispersed consumers. The 'merit good' in other words may ultimately cease to have merit for society but continue to have merit for special interest groups. There is no room here to test this hypothesis in detail; but it may be fruitful, among others, in explaining the precise mechanics of the evolution of our present educational system – a subject about which there is still much we do not understand.[117]

---

[116] Nassau Senior, *Suggestions on Popular Education* (1861), p. 5. Senior complained that many parents were of the opinion that the subsidized school was vulgar, 'or their boy had been punished there, or he is required to be clean, or to be regular, or the private school is half a street nearer, or is kept by a friend, or by someone who will submit his teaching to their dictation'.

[117] This hypothesis has been tested for New York State in the nineteenth century with some positive results: E. G. West, 'The political economy of American public school legislation', *Jnl. Law and Econ.* X (1967).

The main points which emerge from the present study are that if 'schools' are defined as those that were measured by the government bodies and local statistical societies, then their growth and extent in our period, especially in towns, were much more than is usually recognized; but judgement of their *qualitative* inferiority by the contemporary authorities was often based on criteria that today need fresh scrutiny. The physical condition of many schools was certainly 'bad' from a twentieth-century point of view; the difficulty is, however, that when seeking a balanced judgement we have to take into account that most other things – houses, hospitals, roads, clothing, feeding, etc. – were also 'bad' and 'under-supplied' from the twentieth-century point of view, simply because nineteenth-century national income *per capita* was lower than ours. The scarcity of resources at any one time is in a sense the major public 'bad' that societies inherit; making the best of each 'bad' situation by at least achieving something near to optimal resource allocation is a major 'public good'. Exactly how far carly nineteenth-century society was from an educational optimum remains of course an open question; but on our evidence the degree of deficiency was considerably less than is usually assumed.

3.2 Professor West on early nineteenth-century education

J. S. HURT

In his recent article,[1] Prof. West has shown a remarkable faith in the accuracy of the educational statistics that were collected in the first half of the nineteenth century. This faith was shared neither by those by whom they were compiled nor by those for whom they were produced. The reasons for this scepticism are not far to seek. The survey on the state of education in England and Wales, conducted in response to Lord Kerry's motion of 24 May 1833, was made by the overseers of the poor. These officials, in making a return for the purposes of implementing the 1832 Reform Act, had already given contemporary society adequate evidence of their incompetence. In the words of one observer: '[they] are quite as likely to fail in giving a correct account of the number of schools and of pupils in their respective districts, as in making an accurate return of the number of houses rated at £10 a year.' Little more, it was pointed out in all fairness, could be expected of 'men who (especially in the rural districts) have had but small advantages of education, and who are forced into office contrary to their inclination, and without any remuneration'.[2]

Moreover, this inquiry was conducted at a time of bitter rivalry between the main parties interested in education. The two leading

J. S. Hurt (1971) *The Economic History Review*, 2nd ser. XXIV, (Welwyn Garden City), pp. 624–32.
[1] E. G. West, 'Resource allocation and growth in early nineteenth-century British education', pp. 53–91 (present volume).
[2] F. Hill, *National Education: Its Present State and Prospects*, 2 vols. (1836), I, p. 11. See also *Return of the Parochial Assessment ... in each Township sending Representatives to Parliament*, Parl. Papers, 1831–2, XXXVI, pp. 333 ff.

religious societies, the Anglican National Society and the Nonconformist British and Foreign School Society, had only one interest in common. They were both resolutely opposed to the principle of state control. In every other respect, they were at loggerheads. Hence they fought out with each other, and with the state, a battle of statistics. As a consequence both societies, by 1839, claimed that they had a million and a half children in their schools.[3] Since it has been estimated that there were 3,024,000 children between the ages of three and twelve at this time,[4] the two societies had apparently cornered the market. Thus it was in a highly charged atmosphere that the overseer of the poor assisted by the schoolmaster, whose shortcomings will be discussed later, provided answers to the ambiguously worded query, 'The number of Scholars in each school?'[5]

The word 'school' is ambiguous for two reasons. Firstly, infants' schools, daily schools, and Sunday schools were counted separately if they had individual teachers, even though they formed part of the same building complex. The newly established Education Department continued this practice by counting infants', boys', and girls' schools separately if each had its own teacher. One yardstick by which the extent of the confusion caused by this practice can be assessed is provided by examining two successive reports of the Education Department. In the year ending 31 August 1868, the inspectorate visited 15,572 *schools or departments* in Great Britain. The following year they visited 9,563 *schools* containing 13,276 *departments*.[6]

Secondly, the word 'school' had a far wider meaning than it has today. A contemporary dictionary defines a 'school' as 'a house of discipline and instruction'.[7] The use of the word 'schooldame' given in the same dictionary is even more revealing – 'sending little children of two or

---

[3] *Report from the Select Committee on the Education of the Poorer Classes*, P.P. 1838, VII, H. Dunn (secretary, British and Foreign School Society), QQ. 395–6; *Hansard* (Commons), 3rd ser. XLV, p. 274, Lord John Russell, 12 Feb. 1839.

[4] This figure includes 420,000 in 'the upper and middle classes'. The criteria on which this judgement is based are contained in the *Report of the Schools' Inquiry Commission (Taunton Report)*, P.P., 1867–8, XXVIII, A, app. II, 'On the number of boys within scope of the Enquiry , pp. (6), (8); *Special Reports on Educational Subjects*, Vol. II, P.P. 1898, XXIV, 'Elementary education in England and Wales, 1833–70', p. 447, gives an estimate of the population in 1833.

[5] The questionnaire is reprinted in *Education Enquiry, Abstract of the Answers and Returns*, P.P. 1835, XLI, 4.

[6] *Report of the Education Dept*, 1868–9, P.P. 1868–9, XX, p. x; *ibid.* 1869–70, P.P. 1870 XXII, p. viii. My italics.

[7] S. Johnson, *A Dictionary of the English Language* (3rd ed., 1827).

three years of age to a school-dame, without any design of learning one letter, but only to keep them out of fire and water'.

Hence it was possible for there to have been an increasing number of children 'attending school' without there having been that 'increase of secular education and the new emphasis on the "three Rs" . . . provided by the schools in clear and direct response to parental wishes' which Prof. West claims to have been the case.[8] Whatever children were sent to 'school' for, it was not to satisfy a 'growing thirst for knowledge among poor families'.[9] Given a free choice, many parents opted for illiteracy.

The reports of the statistical societies leave no doubt on this point at all. The following quotations are taken from the reports that Prof. West has used. For reasons that remain obscure, he has chosen either to ignore these comments or to reject them.

> Many of the rooms which are called schools [in Newcastle-upon-Tyne], and are included as such in the foregoing tables, are merely receptacles for children that cannot be conveniently taken care of at home, and where instruction is scarcely even expected or wished for by the parents.

> [In Westminster] a very large proportion are sent *avowedly* 'to do nothing', the injunction from the parents being, that they are not to be 'worried with learning', and in some cases not even 'with needle-work'.

> [In Kingston-upon-Hull] the prevailing idea existed, too, that the scholars are sent to the dame schools merely to be out of the way.

> Both the mistresses and the parents seem to regard them [the dame schools of Bury] rather as asylums for mischievous and troublesome children, than as actual seminaries of instruction, which indeed the superintendents are seldom qualified to render them.[10]

---

[8] West, *op. cit.*, p. 84 (present vol).
[9] *ibid.*, p. 66.
[10] *Journal of the Statistical Society of London*, I (1839), 'Educational, criminal, and social statistics of Newcastle-upon-Tyne', p. 358; '3rd report on the state of education in Westminster', p. 452; *Jnl. Stat. Soc. London*, IV (1841), 'Kingston-upon-Hull', p. 158; *Report of a Committee of the Manchester Statistical Society on the State of Education in the Borough of Bury, Lancs, 1835* (1835), pp. 4–5.

Both the early nineteenth-century ambiguity in the use of the word 'school' and parental indifference to the teaching of the 'three Rs' can be demonstrated in another way. Two handicraft industries, those of straw-plaiting and lace-making, were conducted on a domestic basis in workplaces known as 'schools'. The most that Major J. G. Burns, an assistant commissioner to the Children's Employment Commission in the early 1840s, could say of the straw-plaiting schools of Buckinghamshire, Hertfordshire, and Bedfordshire was: 'In some few [schools] reading is taught once a day.' One keeper of a Hertfordshire plaiting-school told him: 'I teach my own children sewing and reading as well as plaiting, and have offered to teach the scholars who come to my school, but the parents care nothing for it, and plaiting alone is everything with them.'[11] Burns's verdict on the lace-making schools of Northamptonshire, Oxfordshire, Bedfordshire, and Buckinghamshire was similar: 'Reading is slightly taught at only a few of the schools.' Another area in which lace-making was practised by children in workshops that were described as 'schools' was Honiton, Devonshire.[12]

The unsatisfactory nature of many of the dame and common day schools can be demonstrated in another way, by examining the standard of living of their proprietors. The average wage weekly of schooldames in York was put at 'rather under four shillings a week'. This was stated to be less than 'the receipts of a child of twelve years of age, in the manufacturing districts'.[13] The report on York continued: 'England is the only country where parish paupers are considered competent to conduct the education of any portion of the rising generation.' Even this low income was by no means an assured one, for bad debts seem to have been a major occupational hazard. 'The average remuneration which the teachers receive, *or are owed*, weekly, is 9s 6d in the boys' schools, [common day schools in York], and 8s in girls' schools.'[14] In the county of Rutland, an average weekly charge of $3\frac{1}{4}d$ gave 50 schooldames with 678 scholars an income of less than 4s a week. Even this low level of income could be achieved only if there were no absentees or bad debts. Moreover, the calculation is based on the highest fees charged in each

[11] *Second Report of the Children's Employment Commission*, P.P. 1843, XIV, 'Report by Major J. G. Burns and statement of Mrs Watts of Hemel Hempstead', pp. A 10, a 50 (12, 66).
[12] *ibid.*, 'Report and evidence collected by Dr L. Stewart, pp. D6, d 27–33 (370, 391–7).
[13] *Report of a Committee of the Manchester Statistical Society on the State of Education in the City of York in 1836–7* (1837), p. 8.
[14] *ibid.*, p. 10. Original italics.

school for tuition in reading and needlework.[15] Lastly, the school proprietors of Bury were being left behind in the race for a higher standard of living. Their gross annual average receipts of £62 were 'a smaller sum than common industry would procure for them in many mechanical and manufacturing employments'.[16]

From the reports of the statistical societies of the 1830s and the *Report* of the Newcastle Commissioners, published in 1861, it is apparent that dame and common day schools were often set up by their proprietors as a desperate last resort. The precarious income they earned kept them out of the workhouse. Since little or no capital was required, these schools were ephemeral institutions. It is accordingly useless to look solely at the number of schools opened over a particular period. We need to know also the number that were closed over the same period. Thus the fact that 329 of the 632 day and evening schools, in Manchester in 1834, had been established since 1830 does not necessarily 'suggest indeed a veritable school "explosion" in Manchester in the first four years of the 1830s'.[17]

Fortunately, one report of the Manchester Statistical Society gives us some idea of the rate of turnover. When the township of Pendleton was surveyed in 1838, a comparison was made with the situation that had existed there two and a half years earlier. This is one of the few occasions, possibly the only one, on which two investigations were made in the same area over a short period of time. The Society reported:

> One superior girls' school has been discontinued since 1835, and of two new ones now in operation one has been raised from a common school since the last inquiry. Neither of the common boys' schools, recorded in the first inquiry, exists as such now ... The only common boys' school now is kept by a teacher of the [discontinued] charity school ... There were formerly five common schools for girls, one ... has risen to the rank of a superior school; the other four have ceased to exist, and the two now reported are new in the township. One of the dame schools is kept by the wife of the former teacher of a common boys' school, and it is not a little illustrative of the unsettled character of the people, that only one of the eight dames met with in 1835 is now keeping school in the township, and

[15] 'Report of a Committee of the Manchester Statistical Society on the state of education in the county of Rutland in the year 1838', *Jnl. Stat. Soc. London*, II (1839), pp. 307–8.
[16] *Report on Bury* (1835), p. 7.
[17] West, *op cit.*, p. 69 (present vol.)

she is not in her former abode. The remaining six dame schools are all new.[18]

In this particular instance, the number of new schools established over a two and a half-year period supports the 'explosive' theory. In fact, however, this was a period of overall decline. It might be thought that the rapid turnover in Manchester in the 1830s was an atypical case. Twenty years later, one assistant commissioner to the Newcastle Commission found the same phenomenon in the rural west country. J. Fraser reported:

> The majority of these private schools – I speak now of the whole district – are of very mushroom growth, by far the larger proportion of the existing ones have sprung up since the census of 1851; and the teachers of them have often no special fitness, . . . but have taken up the occupation in default or after the failure of other trades.[19]

Horace Mann, the compiler of the 1851 census on education, picking his way through the statistical minefield with great care, avoided reaching an 'explosive' conclusion. After showing that 22,214 of the 46,042 schools existing in 1851 had been established during the previous decade, he decided:

> As to *Private* day schools, indeed, the statement proves but little: since the frequent changes, to which these are subject, of proprietors and residences, makes it certain that the great majority of those established in the last ten years are merely substituted for others which existed under other masters and in other places. It displays however, rather strikingly the amount of private enterprise which positively now prevails; although it does not show to what extent, if any, such enterprise has been more active and productive in recent than in former times.[20]

Schoolkeeping, then, was a casual occupation that attracted the nomadic entrepreneur until something better turned up. It offered little more than an uncertain and precarious means of subsistence. The

[18] *Jnl. Stat. Soc. London*, II (1839), pp. 66–7, n. II.
[19] *Report of the Commissioners appointed to inquire into the State of Popular Education in England* (*Newcastle Report*), P.P. 1861, XXI, B, 'The Rev. J. Fraser's report on specimen agricultural districts in the counties of Dorset, Devon, Somerset, Hereford, and Worcester', p. 38.
[20] *Census of Great Britain, 1851, Education, England and Wales*, P.P. 1852–3, xc p. xx. Original italics.

keeper of the common day school, let alone the schooldame, failed to achieve the living standard of a competent clerk or artisan. As early as 1834, it had been thought that schoolmasters, well versed in the techniques of the basic subjects, would have to be paid at least £100 a year in London and other large cities to keep them in the classroom.[21]

To say that 'Some of the schools were often written off by the statistical societies as worthless largely on account of [their] failure in these respects [giving a schooling which scored high marks in divinity and morality]' is only part of the truth. The schools were condemned with equal severity by the societies for their failure to teach the 'three Rs' competently. As Dr Kay's remark to the 1838 Select Committee shows, he was as concerned with the scholastic shortcomings of the schools as with their deficiencies in moral training.[22]

There can thus be little doubt that the Manchester Statistical Society was justified in concluding, *inter alia*:

1 That the number of children returned as attending different schools, affords a very imperfect and fallacious criterion of the real state of education in any town or district where such returns are made.

2 That . . . the means of education at present existing in the borough of Manchester for the lower classes of the people, are extremely inadequate, and are in general very little fitted to secure any of the really valuable results of education to the children who attend them.

3 That of the children who attend the Dame schools, amounting to 4,722, and the greater part of whom are under five years of age, the vast majority receive no instruction which is at all deserving of the name, and derive little benefit from their attendance at school, but that of being kept out of harm during a few hours of the day. [and]

6 That of the children who attended the common day schools, amounting to nearly 7,000, the greater part receive an extremely poor education, scarcely meriting the name: . . .[23]

---

[21] *Report from the Select Committee on the State of Education*, P.P. 1834, QQ. 1075–6, 1318–9, 1596–8, 2547.
[22] West, *op cit.* pp. 84–6. (present vol.) Kay said: 'If by education I am to understand what I have previously described, sound religious instruction, correct moral training, *and a sufficient extent of secular knowledge suited to their station in life*, I should scarcely say that it exists within the limits of my observation.' My italics.
[23] *S.C. on Education in England and Wales*, P.P. 1835, VII, app. I, 'Report of the Manchester Statistical Society on Education', p. 105 (871).

By the late 1850s, the semantic ambiguities of the word 'school' had been resolved. 'Dame schools' were seen for what they really were, that is nurseries, and the 'schooldames' were seen as child-minders. 'Infant schools are public nurseries for the poor,' runs a marginal note in the *Newcastle Report*. '[Dame schools] are frequently little more than nurseries . . .'[24]

Equally questionable is the suggestion that Sunday schools normally provided an important source of secular education. The Rev. J. C. Wigram, secretary to the National Society in the 1830s, did not share this view. He condemned the practice of teaching writing in them as a 'desecration of the Lord's Day'.[25] In Salford, for instance, while reading was taught in all 31 Sunday schools – this does not mean that it was taught to all the pupils – writing was taught in only eight and arithmetic in five. None of those teaching the last two subjects was an Anglican institution.[26] The position in the county of Rutland was similar. Here the Manchester Statistical Society found: 'Sunday schools very rarely profess to give secular instruction.'[27] Thus the instruction in Sunday schools was almost entirely confined to that moral and religious instruction that Prof. West elsewhere argues was imposed on parents thereby depriving them of their freedom of choice.

On the other hand, moral and religious instruction was thought to confer the benefit of a 'Pareto-relevant externality'. During the 1830s the propertied classes feared the imminence of revolution. At a time when England lacked an effective police force, she turned to the schoolmaster and the workhouse master as substitutes. They were the twin agents by whom the labouring masses were to be reconciled to their unfortunate lot in a nascent capitalist and industrializing society. An education in the habits of religion and industry was seen as a means of safeguarding the existing social order. It had the further merit of providing a docile labour force for the new industries. On this basis some degree of collectivization was economically justified. Since the state gave only a partial subsidy, something approaching a position of 'Pareto optimality' may well have been achieved.[28]

[24] *Newcastle Report*, P.P. 1861, XXI, A, 28.
[25] J. C. Wigram, *Practical Hints on the Formation and Management of Sunday Schools* (1833), p. 43.
[26] *Report of the Manchester Statistical Society on the State of Education in the Borough of Salford, in 1835* (1836), p. 39.
[27] *Jnl. Stat. Soc. London*, II (1839), p. 304.
[28] Between 1839 and 1870, £5,285,862 9s 5¼d was provided for the building of public elementary schools in Great Britain. The state granted £1,556,819 3s 10½d and private promoters provided £3,729,043 5s 6¾d – Special

II

We must now turn from a qualitative to a quantitative analysis and consider more closely the accuracy of the statistics provided in the 1830s. Firstly, the evidence that has been quoted to show that 80 per cent of the school population was normally in regular attendance requires some comment. The statement that the Pendleton report classified one-third of the students as 'irregular' should be set in its original context.[29]

> In conversing with the parents and children on this subject [regularity of attendance], the agent found that out of 2,657 cases of minors, who either were then or who had been formerly at day or evening schools, he could learn nothing satisfactory respecting 716. Of the remaining 1,941, 665 were acknowledged to have been *very* irregular in their attendance; while, of 1,276, or two-thirds, a more favourable report was made.[30]

In other words, the parents concerned admitted that the attendance of only 1,276 out of 2,657 children was better than 'very irregular'.

Similarity Prof. West writes: 'The Report for Hull in 1838 showed that only one-fifth of the scholars were irregular.'[31] The survey on Hull, conducted between March and June 1839, concludes:

> Out of 5,345 children who were at school at the date of this inquiry, 307 cases occurred in which no satisfactory account could be obtained as to the regularity of attendance; and the attendance in 997 cases was admitted to be very irregular; so that in 4,001 [*sic*] cases alone can it fairly be assumed that the children were deriving from their attendance the whole of the benefit, little or great, [the report cautiously added] which the schools were capable of affording . . . Taking the whole of the minors who had been, or were at the time of the inquiry, at school, 6,427 were stated to have attended with

---

Reports, P.P. 1898, xxiv, p. 532. The total income of schools inspected for a grant under the Revised Code in the year ending 31 Aug. 1869 was £1,622,152 4s 0d, made up as follows: endowments £68,206 19s 10d, voluntary contributions £448,946 8s 0d, school pence (fees) £543,199 5s 5d, government grants £533,448 9s 9d, other sources £28,351 1s 0d – *Report of the Department*, P.P. 1870, XXII, Table II.

[29] West, *op. cit.*, p. 78 (present vol.).
[30] *Jnl. Stat. Soc. London*, II (1839), pp. 68–9. My italics.
[31] West, *op. cit.*, p. 78, n. 78 (present vol.).

regularity, and 2,668 irregularly; and in 850 cases no information could be obtained.[32]

Thus the suggestion that the attendance of four-fifths of the children of Hull was 'regular' – whatever that word meant in the early nineteenth century – is equally untenable.

Lastly Prof. West has been misled by the statement in the 1851 Census report that 'in private schools the number of children attending on any particular day is 91 per cent of the number belonging to such schools; while in the *public* schools the number in attendance is 79 per cent . . .' These figures are based on the returns made on the census day for schools, Monday, 31 March 1851. They refer not to any particular day, but at best to one particular day.[33] It is mainly on evidence such as this that the conclusion has been reached that the average attendance of children in the late 1830s was 80 per cent. If this indeed was the case, the English educational system soon deteriorated. Average attendance in public elementary schools did not top the 80 per cent level again until the school year 1893–4.[34]

Reference to the later and much better documented *Newcastle Report* reveals some of the difficulties and hazards involved in arriving at any clear picture of children's school-attendance habits. Naturally the commissioners wanted to find out for how long and with what regularity individual children attended school. Equally understandably, they were sufficiently aware of contemporary conditions to realize that the answer could not be found as children changed schools so frequently. In 1859, for example, 37·81 per cent of the children at school that year were thought to have attended that particular school for less than a year. Hence their conclusions were general. They reported that 76·1 per cent of the children on the registers in public day schools were in daily attendance. Somewhat inconsistently, they found that '63·7 per cent of the children attended 100 days and upwards [to a maximum of 220 days]'.[35] Daily attendance, however, did not necessarily mean full-time attendance. In explaining the exceptionally high percentage

[32] *Jnl. Stat. Soc. London*, IV (1841), p. 160.

[33] *1851 Census (Education Report)*, P.P. 1852–3, XC, pp. xxx-xxxi, original italics; Table A, p. cxxii, shows 1,119,216 attendances out of a possible 1,413,170 in public day schools and 635,596 out of 695,422 in private day schools on the census day.

[34] *Special Reports*, P.P. 1897, XXV, p. 50. Average attendance rose from 68·32 per cent in the year ending 31 Aug. 1871 to 81·61 per cent in the year ending 31 Aug. 1895.

[35] *Newcastle Report*, P.P. 1861, XXI, A. 172–3.

of 27·2 who attended for more than 200 days a year in Bradford and Rochdale, the commissioners wrote: 'The high percentage, above 200 days, in [Assistant Commissioner] Mr Winder's district is no doubt, attributable in this, as in a previous table, to the half-time system.'[36]

Apart from the ambiguities that are so easily masked by the sub-conscious application of twentieth-century value judgements to statements made in the nineteenth, the accuracy of the figures cited by the Newcastle Commissioners, even after their lengthy and careful investigation, is open to legitimate doubt. It is arguable that there are no trustworthy statistics of school attendance before the late 1860s. As we have already seen, managers and teachers alike in the voluntary schools had an incentive to exaggerate the numbers. Sectarian zeal provides only part of the explanation. Dishonesty and incompetence provide the balance.

The Education Department was well aware of what was happening. 'In the earliest stages of the proceedings of the Committee of Council', R. R. W. Lingen – Kay-Shuttleworth's successor as secretary – wrote in 1855, 'the greatest difficulty was experienced in obtaining even the simplest returns.' After pointing to a recent improvement, he added an illuminating comment on the way in which earlier school attendance figures had been obtained: 'No one would believe, who had not made the experiment, how great is the difference of the result, in averages and other particulars, when taken from general impressions, and when calculated from actual entries.'[37] Schoolmasters and school proprietors relied on their general impressions. Often it was all they had to go on. The Education Department did not require schools to keep registers until 1853. In that year, the capitation grant, an annual grant assessed mainly on attendance, was offered to schools in rural areas. Hence registers were required as evidence to justify the expenditure of public money. Three years later, the new grant was extended to urban areas as well.[38] Thus it was not until the late 1850s that the bulk of state-aided voluntary schools began to keep registers so that they could substantiate their claim for the annual capitation grant. Even then, only a minority of all children attending school were covered by these records. The Newcastle Commissioners calculated that, in mid-1858,

[36] *ibid.*, p. 652.
[37] *Circular Letter to Principals of Training Schools*, 5 Feb. 1855, P.P. 1856, XLVII, 13 (21).
[38] *Minutes of 2 April 1853* and *26 Jan. 1856*, P.P. 1854–5, XLI, p. 243; and P.P. 1857–8, XLVI, p. 154.

there were 2,213,694 children of the poorer classes on the books of day schools in England and Wales. Two years later, there were 917,255 on the books of schools in receipt of annual grants from the Education Department. During that same year, the capitation grant was allowed on 262,006 children in schools that claimed they had an average annual attendance of 625,126.[39]

Some idea of the inaccuracy of earlier records can be given. During the year 1 November 1850 to 31 October 1851, the year of the census, the state-aided voluntary schools claimed an average attendance of 250,214. Yet the inspectors on their long-heralded visits – the day of the year when one would have expected every child on the books to be in attendance – counted no more than 236,656 in the classrooms.[40] Clearly school managers and teachers alike conspired to inflate the numbers of their pupils. They had good reason. The quota of pupil-teachers allowed to each school, for whose tuition the teacher was paid on a *per capita* basis, depended on the 'average attendance' figure.

With the introduction of the capitation grant, the Department soon found that it was one thing to compel schoolmasters to keep registers; to ensure that they kept accurate registers was another. Yet if anyone should have been able to perform this simple task, that person was the two-year trained certificated teacher who had already spent five years in the classroom as a pupil-teacher. However, the papers written by second-year students in the training colleges for their final examinations held in December 1855 show how groundless was this supposition.

A perusal of the papers written by the women candidates showed that a common mistake was to calculate the daily average by adding up the morning and afternoon averages. Thus a child who attended both morning and afternoon sessions was counted as two children. However, a countervailing deflationary tendency was given by those who used 13, the quarterly divisor, instead of 4 for arriving at a monthly average.[41] The men made an equally bad showing. Only 5 per cent of their answers to a question on the keeping of registers were graded as 'good'. 'Yet the answers marked good . . . can only be called good', Lingen commented, 'by a very lenient construction.' Lastly, a further question requiring a straightforward calculation of averages showed that 25 per

[39] *Newcastle Report*, P.P. 1861, XXI, A, pp. 79, 83; *Report of the Committee, 1860–1*, P.P. 1861, XLIV, p. xxiv.
[40] *Minutes of the Committee*, P.P. 1852, XXXIX, p. 143 (479). These figures include children attending Roman Catholic schools in Scotland.
[41] *Circular Letter to Principals of Female Training Schools*, 21 Jan. 1856, P.P. 1856, XLVII, pp. 14–15 (22–3).

cent of the masters who were due to go into the schools in January 1856 would be unable to calculate the weekly average attendance in their schools.[42] There can be little doubt that the state of the registers remained unsatisfactory for some years. The introduction of the Revised Code in the early 1860s brought a spate of complaints from the inspectorate. Gradually schoolmasters began to keep their registers more competently and to hide any of their falsifications with greater competence. By the end of the 1860s the inspectorate were usually satisfied with the way in which the registers were being kept.

From what has been said above, it is manifestly clear that the returns of the 1830s are of little value to the historian. As contemporaries realized, they were of little use to them either. For this reason the omission of some dame and common day schools is of little importance. Such institutions were not 'schools'. They were no more than crèches. Estimates of 'regular attendance' at 'schools' made by semi-literate schooldames or by parents anxious to give the 'right' answer provide a precarious basis on which to build a model of educational activity in the 1830s and to argue that 'Every piece of statistical evidence on education between 1800 and 1840 points to significant growth.'[43]

[42] *Circular Letter to Principals of Male Training Schools*, 22 Feb. 1956, P.P. 1856, XLVII, pp. 17–18 (25–6).
[43] West, *op. cit.*, p. 67 (present vol.).

3.3 The interpretation of early nineteenth-century education statistics

E. G. WEST[1]

The critic who questions another writer's statistical sources can approach from three directions. First, he may adopt the 'nihilistic' position and contend that *all* statistical sources are unreliable. Second, he may use the 'my statistics (sources) are better than your statistics' approach. Third, he may concede that the sources are respectable but argue that one's interpretation of them is erroneous. The first approach ('nihilism') has strong implications. Having previously rejected all evidence on the state of nineteenth-century educational conditions, for instance, the 'nihilist' must himself remain agnostic; his attitude must be that things might have been 'bad' – but they may also have been 'good' – we just do not know. Few writers can restrain themselves thus far on the subject of nineteenth-century education. Dr Hurt is no exception.

His opening observations about the dangers of a writer having a 'remarkable faith in statistics' seem to herald the 'nihilistic' position. Ultimately, however, he adopts a combination of the second and third approaches. The second one is the first to reveal itself. Heroes as well as villains soon appear among the statistical sources to which Hurt refers. The predominant favourites on which he rests his case are: the Manchester Statistical Society (hereafter M.S.S.), the Statistical Society of London, Horace Mann, the 1851 Census Report, Dr James Kay, and the Report of the Select Committee on the State of Education 1834. The one major villain in Hurt's account is the government return for

E. G. West (1971) *The Economic History Review*, 2nd ser. XXIV (Welwyn Garden City), pp. 633–42.
[1] I wish to acknowledge the benefit of discussion in the Graduate Seminar in Economic History at Carleton University.

1833 (the Kerry Report, published in 1835). He makes no reference to my evidence on Scottish experience. His argument deals not with education as widely defined to embrace industrial schools, mechanics' institutes, on-the-job training, and so on, but only with formal schooling. The important general problems of economic methodology that were integral to the argument in my article are not discussed. Particularly surprising is the absence of reference to one specific hypothesis that I set out to test, the hypothesis (implicit in much of the literature) that educational conditions in the new manufacturing areas during the Industrial Revolution were worse than elsewhere.

The most astonishing aspect of Hurt's comment is the implication that 'his statistics are better than my statistics' in the sense that I have accepted uncritically the findings of the government return for 1833 (the Kerry Report). Not only did I criticize this document, but I did so with much more detailed examination and explanation than that provided by Hurt. His own verdict of unreliability seems to rest predominantly on the subjective opinion of a single (and not particularly well-known) contemporary commentator. There is in fact (as I showed) much more substantial evidence of error than this. In presenting this evidence I relied, curiously enough, upon the very sources that are Hurt's own favourites. Indeed his 'villains and heroes' are almost identical with mine. I made use, for instance, of Horace Mann's retrospective estimate of the degree of error in the Kerry Report.[2] Similarly I accepted the verdict of the M.S.S. (and by association Dr J. Kay) that the Kerry returns for Salford, Bury, Manchester, and Liverpool were serious underestimates. I also preferred the findings of such local statistical societies as those of London, Birmingham, and Bristol.[3] In criticizing me of all people for 'innocent' reliance on the Kerry Report, Hurt has clearly erected a straw man. His statistics are not better than my statistics. They are the same.

Hurt's third type of approach, the contention of erroneous interpretation of given sources, gives ground for more fruitful debate. As a preliminary, though, I must first clear away what appears to be an irrelevant issue. Whereas Hurt makes much of the distinction between

[2] E. G. West, 'Resource allocation and growth in early nineteenth century British education', p. 75 (present vol.). Mann's estimate is contained in the 1851 Census Report (Education).
[3] Despite the well-known objections to the 1833 returns which I detailed in my article, these figures still seem to be accepted without comment in current textbooks. See, for instance, Phyllis Deane, *The First Industrial Revolution* (Cambridge University Press, 1965), p. 150.

'schools' and 'scholars', my discussion was concerned exclusively with the number of scholars and aggregate expenditure on schooling. The basis upon which the total expenditure was estimated was the multiplication of the average individual fee by the numbers of scholars. The number of schools was not needed in this process.

The first relevant issue deserving further discussion is Hurt's suggestion that parents typically sent their children to school not to receive instruction but simply in effect to obtain the services of 'child-minding'. It is implied that I give an unbalanced account because of the omission of fuller references to the verbal testimonies in the reports of the statistical societies. My reply is that unbalanced impressions are much more likely to come from, and have come from, the practice that Hurt recommends. His own use of extracts is an eminent illustration. Consider his quotation from the Statistical Society of London's *Report on Westminster*: '. . . a very large proportion are sent [to school] *avowedly* "to do nothing", the injunction from the parents being, that they are not to be worried with learning . . .' Hurt does not tell his readers that these comments come from a small section of the report dealing with dame schools. These schools contained 759 scholars out of the total of 7,755 day scholars investigated (less than 10 per cent). Of the 759 scholars, 379 were under five years old. It should be remembered that in those days children were sent to dame schools sometimes as early as two years old. The under-fives in Britain today (and the under-sixes elsewhere) find hardly any provision in the public system. In the very few schools that do exist in this area today, we find concentration primarily upon social education and the avoidance of forcing upon three- and four-year-olds systematic instruction routines of reading and writing at an age when they are usually not ready for it. From the standpoint of many modern educationists that 'large proportion' of parents in the 1830s which requested that their three- and four-year-olds were not to be 'worried with learning' seems to have been expressing views that were in advance of their time. If the early Utilitarian investigators were disappointed that many parents undervalued 'instruction' in the cases of children between the ages of two and five years, their reports conceivably tell us of Victorian middle-class authoritarianism from which it seems parents and others have only recently been emancipated.[4]

[4] Referring to the 'Common and Middling Day Schools' which contained students predominantly in the age range of 5–14 years, the same Report on Westminster observed that 'the points on which most stress is laid are writing and arithmetic; the parents are more anxious, and make more enquiries about these than any other branch of their children's education; they are, in fact, the

Since Hurt's references to Hull and to Newcastle-upon-Tyne similarly referred to dame schools my reply to these is in the same vein. It should also be observed that in the account of the bad conditions in Newcastle the following observation appears on the next page to the one referred to by Hurt: 'It is necessary to understand that this account of the condition of the schools is confined to those situated in parts of the town inhabited by the lower classes.' Dr Hurt in other words is repeating a practice which has for a long time been common in conventional histories of education, the practice of quoting the most arresting and colourful instances without stating the full context and without giving the reader some guidance and perspective.

While the 'crèche function' of some (minority of) schools in the nineteenth century may be dismissed, as it usually is by historians such as Hurt, it is of considerable economic significance in its own right. For some time it has been attracting the attention of modern economists (and should now presumably alert that of economic historians). Prof. B. A. Weisbrod treats the child-minding function of twentieth-century schools as a substantial external economy.[5] Schools make it possible for parents, who would otherwise be supervising their children, to do other things. Weisbrod recently examined the case of the three and a half million mothers in the United States with children of six to eleven years of age. On the assumption that as few as one million of these mothers would not work except for the schools, and on the reasonable additional assumption that $2,000 were the earnings of each mother during the school year, the value of the 'child-minding' services of elementary schooling was estimated at about $2 billion per year, a significant portion indeed of the national income. If this recognition occurs in the twentieth century, the case for giving it some weight in the nineteenth century is now overdue. Even if one believes, like Hurt, that most nineteenth-century schools were primarily child-minding institutions, it does not remove the obligation to assess their economic significance and their implications for other kinds of education. The growth of the 'child-minding industry' must be duly measured and its place among other contributors to the growing nineteenth-century national output should be evaluated. Historians like Hurt should be identifying the converse case to that described by Weisbrod so that 'child-minding' and

---

only branches in which they are judges, and the teachers knowing this, are naturally induced to pay more attention to them' (p. 452).
[5] B. A. Weisbrod, 'Education and investment in human capital', *Journal of Political Economy*, LXX (1962), pt 2 (supplement), pp. 106–23.

'education' simply change places in emphasis. Child-minding can be viewed as the major product and education (especially social education) can be treated as the by-product. Child-minding must have allowed considerable amounts of education of other sorts. Young parents would have been enabled to undertake many types of investments in human capital such as that associated with on-the-job training within firms. This would be especially so where 'specific training' was concerned because in this case when improvements in worker-productivity are peculiar to particular firms the managements have an incentive to provide the training free. In these circumstances the full wages representing some reflexion of both present and anticipated future productivity would be earned immediately. These same wages could simultaneously have provided more than sufficient means for paying for child-minding or schooling services.

Consider next Hurt's argument that the quality of schooling was poor because school teachers were 'being left behind in the race for a higher standard of living' and that their annual incomes were 'a smaller sum than common industry would procure for them in many mechanical and manufacturing employments'.[6] The difficulty with this argument is that it seems to be asserted under all conditions at all times. It is certainly continuing to be made today. Yet the fact that employees in one service industry get less than employees in other industries does not imply that the value of the former is zero. Otherwise we should be receiving zero education today! Indeed the distinction between quantity and quality in discussions on education can be a misleading one. When competition prevails differences in quality of schooling can largely be resolved in terms of differences in the quantity of expenditure on inputs. If quality is strongly related, for instance, to the size of classes (teacher–pupil ratios) it can improve by an increase in quantity of expenditure on teachers. Where national income is steadily rising the quality of services provided at some previous time is usually bound to be lower than that of the present since real expenditure or inputs was less. Today 'quality' has improved because so has 'quantity'; education while still 'imperfect' is less 'imperfect' than previously. When educationists complain, as they always do, that the system is 'imperfect' they usually mean that they want more resources devoted to it. The conclusions of the M.S.S. which Mr Hurt quotes should be viewed in this perspective. The first was to the effect that 'the number of children returned as attending different schools, affords a very imperfect criterion

[6] See J. S. Hurt's article, p. 97 above.

of the real state of education . . .'[7] The second conclusion was that the means of education were 'extremely inadequate'. Hurt's third conclusion from the report of the M.S.S. has already been discussed. It is the complaint about dame schools often being nothing but child-minding institutions. The M.S.S. admitted that the majority of children in dame schools were under five but regretted that they received no 'instruction' and derived little benefit from their attendance at school, but that of being kept out of harm during a few hours of the day.

My observation that Sunday schools provided an important new agent in the promotion of literacy and especially of reading is next questioned by Hurt. He quotes from the M.S.S. findings on Rutland to the effect that 'Sunday Schools [in Rutland] very rarely professed to give "secular" instruction'. In my article I do not mention 'secular' instruction but stress simply the teaching of reading in Sunday schools. Dr Hurt agrees that in Salford all the 'schools' taught reading but observes that 'this does not mean that it was taught to all pupils'. But in the absence of any evidence that the proportion not so taught was large, this comment achieves little. Moreover, Hurt seems to have forgotten that I was testing the hypothesis that educational conditions in the Industrial Revolution 'frontier towns' were worse than elsewhere. I found that the latter were much better supplied with Sunday school instruction in reading and writing than non-industrial places. The M.S.S. did indeed report little secular instruction in the rural area of Rutland, as Hurt observes; the same body, however, when referring to the growing manufacturing town of Pendleton reported: 'we are justified in considering the Sunday Schools to be means of secular instruction . . .'[8] For Manchester it stated 'that the education provided for the poorer classes in Sunday schools is considerably more extensive than in the day schools'. The same authority also reported that as many as 22,000 minors were taught writing in the evenings in Manchester Sunday schools during the week. I must therefore firmly reject Hurt's conclusion that 'instruction in Sunday schools was almost entirely confined to that moral and religious instruction that Prof. West elsewhere argues was imposed on parents thereby depriving them of their freedom of choice'.

On the question of choice, I argued that attempts were made to impose a curriculum balance that did not meet family preferences, but I

[7] It is interesting that Dr Hurt's quotation from the 1835 edition contains the words 'and fallacious' after the expression 'very imperfect'. The adjective 'fallacious' does not appear in my own version which comes from the revised second edition published in 1837.

[8] *Jnl. Stat. Soc. London.* I (1839), p. 74.

gave evidence that parents were beginning to succeed in their demands that day schools put more emphasis on the teaching of the three Rs. One more illustration may be appropriate here and this time in relation to Sunday schools. Arguing that Sunday schools had a considerable influence on literacy, Prof. Harold Perkin recently observed that although the church was often reluctant to teach writing, it still took place. The vigour of parental initiative and enthusiasm for such teaching is well brought out by Perkin's example of a group of cotton operatives in Glossop, Derbyshire. Seeking instruction for their families and unable to persuade the existing Sunday schools to teach their children to write, they 'founded their own, and met, for lack of other accommodation, in the largest local public house'.[9] It should be observed finally that minors went to Sunday schools often until their late teens. The anxiety of parents for 'instruction' of children in these schools could have been quite consistent with an opposite attitude with respect to their three- and four-year-olds in dame schools.[10]

Hurt argues that in the early nineteenth century 'England' used education to make the working class more docile. When he explains that the motive was that the masses were to be 'reconciled to their unfortunate lot in a nascent capitalist and industrial society' he leaves no doubt about where he stands in the standard of living debate. But notice that his argument now implicitly concedes that significant quantities of education did exist. This is at odds with the rest of his article where he seems to be trying to counter this view. With respect to the internal logic of this new argument a serious question must be faced. If the working classes were passively receiving from their superiors 'conditioning' kinds of education in schools, how did such cultural and mental manipulation succeed when education was neither compulsory nor free? Perhaps all that is being suggested, however, is that the ruling classes expressed their motives wherever they could by complementing parental and ecclesiastical effort with subsidies. But if this was the interpretation we should expect to find bigger subsidies in the new 'proletariat' areas than in others. Yet the M.S.S. reported that 80 per cent of the schooling in Manchester was paid for entirely by parental fees, a much bigger proportion than in country areas such as Rutland and in cathedral cities such as York.[11]

[9] H. J. Perkin, 'The origins of the popular press', *History Today*, VII (1957), p. 428.
[10] See above, p. 109, n. 4.
[11] The Kerry Report gave a proportion of 58 per cent for the whole country. West, *loc. cit.* Table 3·5, p. 77.

Another question that occupies Dr Hurt is that of school attendance. My estimate of 80 per cent average attendance was based on Horace Mann's 1851 Census Report and M.S.S. reports on Pendleton and Hull, sources which Hurt himself respects. Placing my quotation from the Pendleton Report 'in its original context', as Hurt requests, does not alter its validity. I reproduced the report's classification of one-third of all known cases as 'irregular' in 1838. This particular year, as will be shown later, was one of severe depression. The agent found that with respect to 716 cases, 'he could learn nothing satisfactory'. Of the remaining 1,941 cases, 665 were acknowledged to have been 'very irregular' in their attendance.[12] Hurt has no grounds at all for throwing the 716 'unknowns' into the category of 'irregular'. If information had been available concerning these 'unknowns' it would possibly allocate some of them to the irregular class and others to the regular attenders; the bias would go either way. The same kind of comments can be made about Hurt's reference to attendance in Hull.

The 1851 Census Report stated that in private schools the number of children attending on any particular day was 91 per cent of the number belonging to such schools. Hurt objects that these figures 'refer not to any particular day, but at best to one particular day'. The authorities were clearly assuming that the census day was a typical one in the year. It is certainly open to Hurt to attempt to challenge this implication. If the census day (Monday, 31 March 1851) was not typical, however, the bias could have been either way; it could have overstated or *understated* the true average attendance. The required evidence to show non-typicality, and evidence to show a bias towards overstatement, are both missing in Hurt's criticism.

One can easily be given the impression of an excessive frequency with which children changed school from Hurt's example that about 38 per cent of the children at school in 1859 were thought to have attended that particular institution for less than a year. Perspective on this point is quickly obtained, however, when we remember that the average school life in those days was around five years. Typically a child would spend, say, one year in a dame school and four in a common school. It would

---

[12] Pendleton Report. *Jnl. Stat. Soc.* London, II (1839), p. 69. The agent found the better-off families more reluctant to give information. 'At the houses of the rich it was not always so easy to obtain even the few essential points necessary to complete, with accuracy, the tables of number and age; but from the poor, respect and civility were almost always experienced, and the opportunities afforded of verifying their statements, with few exceptions, proved their accuracy' (p. 73).

therefore be not unusual for over 50 per cent of the pupils in a dame school to consist of those who had attended for less than a year. With a typical common school, and an average school life of four years per pupil, one would expect that 25 per cent of the scholars on average would fall into the category of having attended for less than a year. Any bigger percentage could well be accounted for by two prevailing circumstances: (a) a mobile population associated with the new industrialism; (b) the exercise of choice in a competitive and expanding education market.

I stated that the figures in Table 1 of the M.S.S. Report on Manchester suggested 'explosive' growth between 1830 and 1834, since over half the schools existing in 1834 were established in those four years. I made the same kind of precautionary observation, however, that Horace Mann made in the 1851 Census (to which Hurt refers). In a note to the table I remarked: 'It must be noticed that the figures in this table refer only to school "births"; school "deaths" might qualify the picture.'[13] Hurt draws attention to the considerable school turnover between 1835 and 1838 in Pendleton. Notice, nevertheless, the Pendleton Report's opening comments:

> At this period of this enquiry (1838) there had been a continuance of nearly two years of dull trade, and many of the working classes had consequently suffered much distress, during the winter . . . To this circumstance, no doubt, may be in part attributed the falling off in the number of children attending the common and day schools, compared with the former Report.[14]

In any case my inquiry was less concerned with detecting variations within particular trade cycles than with longer-term trends. *Per capita* educational improvements over the period of a generation previous to the (depressed) year of 1838 were indicated in the Pendleton Report's comment: 'not more than 2 to 3 per cent . . . of the juvenile population are at present left entirely destitute of instruction, whilst of the surviving adult population 8% represent their education to have been totally neglected'.[15]

Most of the statistical society reports carried tables which stated the dates of establishment of schools investigated in one year. It is difficult

---

[13] West, p. 69 above, Table 3.2.
[14] Pendleton Report, p. 66.
[15] *ibid.*, p. 74. Of the 15 and under 21 age group who had some schooling, that is well over 90 per cent of the group, 76 per cent could read, 14 per cent were barely able to read, and 10 per cent could not read. *ibid.* Table VII, p. 80.

to understand the persistence of the practice if the turnover of schools (school births and deaths) was typically as substantial as Hurt suggests. Contemporary statisticians would surely have at least drawn attention to this point where it was important. Besides the apparently 'explosive' growth figures of Manchester similar ones appeared for Bristol. Out of 479 known cases in 1840, 316 schools had been established since 1830. The Statistical Society of Bristol commented: 'The great increase within the last 10 years cannot fail to be remarked.' It would have been curious if such statisticians did not check that the new schools were not largely replacing old ones so that there was no substantial net increase over the period. The precautionary remarks made by Horace Mann (to which Hurt refers) relate mainly to the growth of *completely* private schools, those receiving no philanthropic or government assistance whatever. The remainder of private schools which received *any degree* of support other than from the students' fees (which for convenience Mann described as 'public' schools) contained the bulk (two-thirds) of the total school population. With reference to these, Mann observed that 'the table seems to testify to the existence of much modern zeal, and proves that within the past ten years a very considerable number of *new* Schools must have been established or that old ones must have been enlarged.'[16]

The evidence with which Hurt supports his claim that the school managers and teachers conspired to inflate the numbers of their pupils in attendance is interesting but not sufficiently substantial seriously to qualify my general assumptions. Some aided voluntary schools in rural areas, Hurt explains, claimed an average attendance of 250,214 in 1851, the year of the census; the inspectors, on the other hand, counted no more than 236,656 in the classrooms. This is an error of about 5 per cent. It refers only to state-aided voluntary schools receiving *per capita* grants where some incentive to inflate could have existed. These schools accounted for only about one-eighth of the total school population reported in the census. The reported attendance in the non-public sector as a whole was 91 per cent. That of the public sector was 79 per cent. My selection of 80 per cent overall is thus a very conservative one and more than sufficient to take account of Hurt's adjustments. An alternative way of checking attendance figures which I made use of is the comparison of reported teachers' incomes with reported average fees paid. Hurt, however, makes no reference to it. It may be helpful to ask what adjustment would I have to make to my computation of

[16] *Census 1851, Education,* p. xx.

national expenditure on education even if I accepted Hurt's most 'pessimistic' conclusions on attendance, say an attendance rate of 50 per cent instead of 80 per cent? My estimate of percentage of national income devoted to elementary education in 1833 would be reduced from £3 million to £2 million, a figure which would still approximate to 0·66 per cent of the 1833 national income. This is still a significant ratio and roughly matches that given for the year 1920 (see my Table 3·6).

None of Hurt's comments can seriously qualify my statement that every important piece of statistical evidence on education between 1800 and 1830 points to significant growth. This conclusion does not rest on the predominant dependence upon the 1833 government return, a source that, to repeat, I criticize more comprehensively than does Hurt. My evidence was collected from a wide variety of bodies including that of Brougham's Select Committee Report of 1820 and Brougham's own private survey of 1828, upon both of which Hurt does not comment. Horace Mann, the compiler of the 1851 census on education who, according to Hurt, was adept at 'picking his way through the statistical minefield with great care', observed in the census report that between 1818 and 1833 the number of day scholars had increased by 89 per cent compared with a population increase of 24 per cent and that Sunday schools had increased by 225 per cent over the same period. This strong growth trend continued well into the 1860s. Between 1832 and 1861, whereas the population increased by 40 per cent, the number of day scholars grew by 68 per cent.[17] The membership of the Mechanics' Institutes rose from 7,000 in 1831 to 200,000 in 1860. Newspapers increased in circulation by 273 per cent; the number of letters sent by post increased by 600 per cent, and in addition cheap literature of all kinds was being purchased by the working classes in substantially increased quantities.

Hurt believes he has made serious inroads on such observation of substantial educational growth by the counter-proposition that in the growing number of formal institutions of education the bulk of the schools were 'no more than crèches'. This is ineffective, for five reasons. First, because the population of other schools besides dame schools, where the description could possibly apply, were increasing in still greater number; second, because dame schools accounted for never more than a minority in the national school population; third, because

---

[17] J. F. C. Harrison, *Learning and Living: 1790–1960* (Routledge & Kegan Paul, 1961), p. 217.

even dame schools provided *some* education in addition to the services of child-minding; fourth, because the growth of child-minding services allowed young parents to obtain employment which carried both general and specific training; and fifth, because education was increasing in non-formal institutions such as mechanics' institutes, factories, friendly societies, and so on. Even if Hurt's arguments on irregular attendance are accepted they are not a serious drawback to the conclusion that there was substantial growth of education. For he is obliged to show not so much that attendance was 'bad' in any given year as that attendance rates were getting worse with the growth of schools and their populations. This demonstration is not forthcoming.

My article was partly an attempt to apply recently developed economic theory to available historical data – a practice which is of peculiar importance for the separate discipline of *economic* history. The sections of modern economic theory that I concentrated upon were welfare economies and public finance theory. The new branch of economics known as human capital theory is of at least equal importance. The historical facts of education growth as I found them conformed eminently to the predictions of this theory as it has been expounded by Prof. Gary Becker.[18] According to his analysis in a competitive society investments in human capital can be predicted to be a function of working-life expectancy and the rate of interest. The period we have been considering provides a classical case where mortality and morbidity rates were both in secular decline and the trend of interest rates was also downward. According to the new analysis such combined circumstances give the maximum stimulus to education from private initiative, whether that initiative comes from employees or from employers. The growth of human capital can also be expected to occur more especially in those areas where its scarcity is more conspicuous. In our period these were clearly identified with the new industrial sectors. Here innovations and physical capital growth were both demanding supplies of complementary human capital.

The findings hitherto of conventional history would refute this analysis. The traditional view of historians has been that the Industrial Revolution was accompanied by educational failure. My assessment of the available data, which related to Scotland as well as to England, challenged this tradition. I did not find a smaller growth and level of formal educational activity in the Industrial Revolution towns than elsewhere. When the term 'education' is widened, as it should be, to

[18] Gary Becker, *Human Capital* (Chicago, 1964).

include non-formal varieties, my findings would indeed support the broad generalization that disproportionately more of it was appearing in the industrial areas. But on this issue of differential supply of education Dr Hurt is surprisingly silent. I am nevertheless grateful to him for having afforded an opportunity for further developing my theme by meeting some criticisms that I had previously anticipated but could not accomplish for lack of space. On the remaining (unanticipated) issues I trust the discussion has been fruitful and will provoke still more inquiry.

4 Railroads as an analogy to the space effort: some economic aspects

ROBERT WILLIAM FOGEL

INTRODUCTION[1]

Viewed as an investment, the central issue posed by the space effort is: Will the increase in national income made possible by the space programme exceed the increase in income that would be obtained if the same resources were invested in other activities? To answer this question one has to know the increment to national revenue that will follow from space activities in all future years. Given this information, the present value of the stream of returns can be computed and compared with the cost of the programme. If the present value of the returns exceeds the cost, then it should, from the purely economic view, be undertaken. If not, it should, on the same view, be abandoned. Of course, it is possible that political or military factors might dictate a course of action different from that implied by purely economic considerations. However, political and military issues are beyond the scope of this paper.

In order that a study of the influence of railroads on American economic growth may contribute to the evaluation of the investment decisions posed by the space effort, two conditions must be met. First, the analysis of railroads must focus on the incremental contribution of this innovation. Discussions merely of things the railroad did are of no use unless

Robert William Fogel (1966) *The Economic Journal*, LXXVI, (London), pp. 16–43.
[1] This paper was commissioned by the Committee on Space of the American Academy of Arts and Sciences. I have benefited from comments by Raymond Bauer, Albert Fishlow, Edward Furash, Bruce Mazlish and Peter Temin.

The paper draws on concepts and empirical findings developed in my book, *Railroads and American Economic Growth: Essays in Econometric History* (Baltimore, The Johns Hopkins Press, 1964). I am grateful to the Johns Hopkins Press for permitting me to make use of these findings.

we know whether these services represent more or less than would have been contributed by alternative investments. Second, one must be able to show how the effects of the space programme may conform to or deviate from the types of effects attributable to railroads both in magnitude and in quality. While this paper focuses primarily on the first of the aforementioned conditions, a concluding section will deal with some aspects of the second one.

From an economic point of view the central or primary feature of the railroad was its impact on the cost of inland transport. Obviously if the cost of rail service had exceeded the cost of equivalent service by alternative forms of transport over all routes and for all items railroads would not have been built and all of their derived consequences would have been absent. The derived consequences of railroads can be divided into two categories. The 'disembodied' consequences are those that followed from the saving in transport costs *per se*, and which would have been induced by any innovation that lowered transport costs by approximately the amount attributable to railroads. The 'embodied' consequences are those that are attributable to the specific form in which the railroads provided cheap transport services.

THE EFFECT OF RAILROADS ON THE AVAILABILITY OF RESOURCES

The change in the availability of resources is perhaps the most important of the disembodied effects of the railroad. Of course, all parts of the nation would have been physically penetrable, even in the absence of railroads. However, without this innovation the cost of transport to and from some areas might have been so great that, from an economic point of view, large sections of the land mass would have been nearly as isolated as the moon is from the earth. By reducing the cost of transport railroads increased the *economic accessibility* of various parts of the natural endowment of the United States. The question is: Which endowments were so affected and by how much?

Agricultural land

Agricultural land was the most valuable of the natural resources of the United States in 1890. It was also more widely dispersed than coal, iron ore, oil and other mineral deposits. Land in farms occupied one-third of the national territory in 1890. No state devoted less than 1% of the area within its borders to farming, and no single state contained more than

8% of the nation's total farm acreage.[2] In these circumstances one would expect to find that railroads were more essential in obtaining access to farm land than to other resources.

However, even in the case of farm land, certain factors suggest that the incremental contribution of railroads was limited. One of these is the experience of the half century following the ratification of the Constitution. The occupation not only of the territory east of the Appalachians but also that lying between the Appalachians and the Mississippi River was well under way before the coming of the railroad. As Kent T. Healy has pointed out, it was 'water transportation, available first on natural waterways and later on canals' which made possible the 'astonishing redistribution of population and economic activity' during the first four decades of the nineteenth century. By 1840, 'before a single railroad had penetrated that area from the coast, some 40 per cent of the nation's people lived west of New York, Pennsylvania and the coastal states of the South'.[3]

This western population was, of course, primarily engaged in agriculture. Two decades before the Civil War Ohio was the chief wheat-producing state of the nation. It, together with Michigan, Indiana and Illinois, accounted for 30% of the nation's total wheat crop. Moreover, with one out of every four of the bushels produced in these states sold in the East and South, it is clear that commercial agriculture was well under way in the Old Northwest long before the era of substantial railroad construction.[4] The geographic locus of corn production provides an even more striking demonstration of the same point. Although they contained a bare total of 228 miles of disconnected railroad track, Michigan, Ohio, Kentucky, Tennessee, Indiana, Illinois and Missouri produced 187 million bushels of corn in 1840 – half the nation's total.[5] As for cotton, the westward movement of this culture was virtually com-

---

[2] U.S. Bureau of the Census, *Eleventh Census of the United States: 1890, Report on the Statistics of Agriculture in the United States*, Vol. V (1895), p. 74; U.S. Bureau of the Census, *Statistical Abstract of the United States: 1963* (84th ed., Washington, D.C., 1963), p. 173.

[3] Kent T. Healy, 'American transportation before the war between the States', in *The Growth of the American Republic*, ed. Harold F. Williamson (New York, Prentice-Hall, 1944), p. 187.

[4] U.S. Bureau of the Census, *Sixth Census of the United States: 1840, Compendium* (1841), p. 358; Percy W. Bidwell and John I. Falconer, *History of Agriculture in the Northern United States, 1620–1860* (Washington, D.C., 1925), p. 329.

[5] *ibid.*, L. Klein, 'Railroads in the United States', *Journal of the Franklin Institute*, **30** (1840), p. 306.

pleted in 1850, by which time the geographic 'limits of the cotton belt were practically the same as they are at present [1900]'. Yet during the entire ante-bellum period the transport of cotton 'was conducted almost exclusively by means of water'. As late as 1860, about 90% of all cotton shipped to New Orleans arrived by boat or barge.[6]

The fact that the initial occupation of the trans-Appalachian lands was based almost exclusively on waterways is suggestive; but it by no means proves that waterways could have sustained later developments. The acreage of agricultural land in the North and South Central states under-went a four-fold expansion between 1850 and 1890.[7] It is therefore necessary to devise a method of determining how much of the land settled after the advent of railroads would have been settled in their absence.

Without railroads the high cost of wagon transport would have limited commercial agricultural production to areas of land lying within some unknown distance of navigable waterways. It is possible to use the theory of rent to establish these boundaries of feasible commercial agri-culture in a non-rail society. Rent is a measure of the amount by which the return to labour and capital on a given portion of land exceeds the return the same factors could earn if they were employed at the intensive or extensive margins. Therefore any plot of land capable of commanding a rent will be kept in productive activity. It follows that, even in the face of increased transport costs, a given area of farm land will remain in use as long as the increased costs incurred during a given time period do not exceed the original rental value of that land.

Given information on the quantity of goods shipped between farms and their markets, the distances from farms to rail and water shipping points, the distances from such shipping points to markets, and the wagon, rail and water rates, it is possible to compute the additional transport costs that would have been incurred if farmers had attempted to duplicate their actual shipping pattern without railroads. In such a situation shipping costs would have risen not because boat rates ex-ceeded rail rates but because it usually required more wagon transport to reach a boat than a rail shipping point. In other words, farms immediately adjacent to navigable waterways would have been least affected by the absence of rail service. The farther a farm was from a navigable water-

---

[6] 'The cotton trade of the United States and the world's cotton supply and trade', U.S. Bureau of Statistics (Treasury Department), *Monthly Summary of Commerce and Finance* (March, 1890), pp. 2551, 2563, 2564.
[7] *Eleventh Census, Agriculture*, pp. 92, 100.

way, the greater the amount of wagon transport it would have required. At some distance from waterways the additional wagon haul would have increased the cost of shipping from a farm by an amount exactly equal to the original rental value of the land. Such a farm would represent a point on the boundary of feasible commercial agriculture. Consequently, the full boundary can be established by finding all those points from which the increased cost of shipping by alternative means the quantities that were actually carried by railroads is equal to the original rental value of the land.

This approach, it should be noted, leads to an overstatement of the land falling beyond the 'true' feasible boundary. A computation based on the actual mix of products shipped does not allow for adjustments to a non-rail technology. In the absence of railroads the mix of agricultural products would have changed in response to the altered structure of transport rates. Such a response would have lowered shipping costs, and hence extended the boundary. The computation also ignores the effect on the level of prices of a cessation of agricultural production in areas beyond the feasible region. Given the relative inelasticity of the demand for agricultural products, the prices of such commodities would have risen in the absence of railroads. The rise in prices would have led to a more intensive exploitation of agriculture within the feasible region, thus raising land values. The rise in land values would have increased the burden of additional transport costs that could have been borne and shifted the boundary of feasible commercial agriculture farther away from water shipping points.[8]

The method outlined above has been used to establish the boundary of feasible commercial agriculture for 1890. In this year the relative advantage of railroads over alternative forms of transport was probably greatest. During the half century that preceded it, increases in productivity reduced the cost of railroad transport more rapidly than those of boats and wagons. The selected year also precedes the emergence of motor vehicles as an effective alternative. It thus appears likely that the incremental contribution of railroads to the accessibility of agricultural lands was at or near its apex in 1890.

Analysis of the relevant data indicates that in the absence of railroads the boundary of feasible commercial agriculture would have been located at an average of about 40 'airline' miles from navigable water-

---

[8] For a more detailed discussion of the theoretical issues involved in, and of the computational methods employed for, the establishment of the feasible boundary see Fogel, *Railroads*, Chap. III.

ways. Forty-mile boundaries, drawn around all natural waterways used for navigation in 1890 as well as all canals built prior to that date, brought less than half of the land mass of the United States into the feasible region.[9] However, as Table 4·1 indicates, the feasible region includes 76% of all agricultural land by value. The discrepancy is

TABLE 4·1 *Farm land lying beyond the feasible region of agriculture, 1890** (thousands of dollars)

Region†	(1) Value of farm land 1890	(2) Value of farm land beyond the feasible region 1890	(3) Col. 2 as a percentage of Col. 1	(4) Value of land beyond feasible region as a percentage of the value of all agricultural land
North Atlantic	1,092,281	5,637	0·5	0·07
South Atlantic	557,399	117,866	21·1	1·45
North Central	4,931,607	1,441,952	29·2	17·75
South Central	738,333	158,866	21·5	1·96
Mountain	129,655	123,016	94·9	1·51
Pacific	671,297	95,200	14·2	1·17
United States	8,120,572	1,942,537	23·9	23·91

* For sources and method of computation see Fogel, *Railroads*, Chapter III, especially Table 3·7.
† The states included in each of the regions are *North Atlantic:* Maine, New Hampshire, Vermont, Massachusetts, Rhode Island, Connecticut, New York, New Jersey, Pennsylvania. *South Atlantic:* Delaware, Maryland, District of Columbia, Virginia, West Virginia, North Carolina, South Carolina, Georgia, Florida. *North Central:* Ohio, Indiana, Illinois, Michigan, Wisconsin, Minnesota, Iowa, Missouri, North Dakota, South Dakota, Nebraska, Kansas. *South Central:* Kentucky, Tennessee, Alabama, Mississippi, Louisiana, Texas, Arkansas. *Mountain:* Montana, Wyoming, Colorado, New Mexico, Arizona, Utah, Nevada, Idaho. *Pacific:* Washington, Oregon, California.

explained by the fact that over one-third of the United States was located between the hundredth meridian and the Sierra Nevada Mountains. While this vast area fell almost entirely beyond the feasible range, it was of extremely limited usefulness for agricultural purposes. By value the area represented only 2% of all agricultural land in use in 1890.

Table 4·1 also shows that barely one-quarter of 1% of the lost agricul-

[9] A map of the area falling within the feasible region is given in Fogel, *Railroads*, Fig. 3.4.

tural land is located in the North Atlantic region, while only 6% is in the Mountain states. About 75% of the loss is concentrated in the North Central region. Indeed, more than half of all the land lost by value is located in just four states: Illinois, Iowa, Nebraska and Kansas. This finding does not support the frequently met contention that railroads were essential to the commercial exploitation of the prairies. The prairies were occupied at a time when the railroad had achieved clear technological superiority over canals. Consequently, the movement for canals that played so important a part in the development of Eastern states was aborted in the prairies. The fact that major loss of land was concentrated in a compact area suggests an entirely different conclusion: a relatively small extension of the canal system would have brought into the feasible region most of the productive land that Table 4.1 puts outside of it.

Indeed, it would have been possible to build in the North and South Central states a system of thirty-seven canals and feeders totalling 5,000 miles. These canals would have reduced the loss of agricultural land occasioned by the absence of railroads to just 7% of the national total. The system would have been technologically feasible and economically profitable. Built across the flat lands of the middle west, the average rise and fall per mile of the proposed waterways would have been less than that which prevailed on all canals successful enough to survive railroad competition through 1890. The water supply would have been more than ample. And in the absence of railroads, the social rate of return on the cost of constructing the system would have exceeded 45% per annum.[10]

The loss in agricultural land could have been further reduced by improvements in common roads. According to estimates published by the Office of Public Roads in 1895, regrading and resurfacing of public roads could have reduced the cost of wagon transportation by 50%. This implies that the boundary of feasible commercial agriculture would have fallen 80 miles from navigable waterways. Together with the proposed canals, road improvements would thus have reduced the loss of agricultural land to a mere 4% of the amount actually used in 1890.[11]

It thus appears that while railroads did increase the availability of agricultural land, their incremental contribution was – even at the apex of railroad influence – quite small.

[10] *ibid.*, pp. 92–100, 218.
[11] *ibid.*, p. 110.

Iron ore and coal

Unlike agricultural land, which in 1890 occupied nearly a million square miles of territory in over 2,000 counties in every state of the nation, the mining of iron ore was highly localised. The volume on mineral industries prepared for the Eleventh Census reported that the[12]

> 'ranges embraced in the Lake Superior region are none of them of great extent geographically, and if a circle was struck from a center in Lake Superior with a radius of 135 miles, all of the present iron-ore producing territory of that region would be embraced within one-half of the circle, and most of the deposits would be near the periphery. The output of this section in 1889 was 7,519,614 long tons. A parallelogram 60 miles in length and 20 miles in width would embrace all of the mines now producing in the Lake Champlain districts of northern New York, whose output in 1889 aggregated 779,850 long tons. A circle of 50 miles radius, embracing portions of eastern Alabama and western Georgia, included mines which in 1889 produced 1,545,066 long tons. A single locality, Cornwall, in Lebanon county, Pennsylvania, contributed 769,020 long tons in 1889. . . . In the areas named, which are only occupied to a limited extent by iron-ore mines, there were produced in 1889 a total of 10,613,550 long tons, or 73·11 per cent of the entire output of iron-ore for the United States.'

Each of these major iron-producing areas would have been economically accessible in the absence of railroads. Cornwall was within 5 miles of the Union Canal and could have had a direct connection with that waterway.[13] The Coosa River, which was actually made navigable as far east as Rome, Georgia, flowed past the main iron-ore deposits of eastern Alabama and western Georgia. The red hematite deposits of central Alabama could have been reached by a relatively short canal built northward from the Alabama River to Shades Creek on the Cahawba River.[14]

[12] U.S. Bureau of the Census, *Eleventh Census of the United States: 1890, Report on Mineral Industries*, p. 9.
[13] *Cram's Standard American Railway System Atlas, 1892* (New York, 1892), p. 51.
[14] *Eleventh Census, Mineral Industries*, p. 3; U.S. Bureau of Corporations, *Report of the Commissioner of Corporations on Transportation by Water in the United States*, 3 vols. (Washington, 1909–13), Vol. I, pp. 85–6; Thomas Dunlap (ed.), *Wiley's Iron Trade Manual* (New York, 1874), pp. 446–7; U.S. Geological Survey, *Water Supply Papers, No. 1384*.

As for the Lake Superior ores, their exploitation, beginning in 1854, preceded the construction of railroads in the northern parts of Michigan and Wisconsin. Five years later, although the region was still without railroad service, its mines accounted for over 4% of the national production of iron ore.[15] Here, too, the water supply and terrain would have permitted the construction of canals that directly linked the iron deposits of Michigan, Wisconsin and Minnesota with the Great Lakes. A canal built along the Menominee River to Florence, Wisconsin, would have traversed the iron-mining district of the Menominee range. A canal built along the Escanaba River to Ishpeming would have pierced the centre of the mining area in the Marquette range. Canals could also have been built along the Montreal River and to Vermillion Lake in Minnesota.[16]

Many of the smaller deposits of iron ore were also well located with respect to water transport. The main carbonate deposits of southern Ohio and northern Kentucky were located at the Ohio River; Tennessee's red hematite fields straddled the Tennessee River; and Pennsylvania had important iron ranges located along the Allegheny River, the Susquehanna River and various of the state's canals.[17] However, it is not necessary to consider all of the smaller deposits in detail. For if one subtracts from the total domestic production of ore in 1890 that part required for railroad iron, the residual is about equal to the ore production of the major fields singled out by the Eleventh Census.[18] Undoubtedly, in the absence of railroads, the iron consumption of boats

[15] Dunlap, *op. cit.*, p. 462; U.S. Bureau of the Census, *Eighth Census of the United States: 1860, Manufactures of the United States in 1860*, p. clxxvii; Frederic L. Paxson, 'The railroads of the "Old Northwest" before the Civil War', *Transactions of the Wisconsin Academy of Science, Arts and Letters*, XVII (1914), p. 266.
[16] *Eleventh Census, Mineral Industries*, p. 3; *Cram's Standard American Railway Atlas*, pp. 98, 154, 160; *Water Supply Papers, No 1387*.
[17] *Eleventh Census, Mineral Industries*, p. 3.
[18] Data in the *Eleventh Census* indicate that it required an average of about 2 tons of iron ore to produce 1 ton of rolled steel and iron. In the census year of 1890 some 2,092,000 tons of rails were produced. Thus, rails alone consumed about 4,200,000 tons of ore. Rail roads required an additional 1 ton of iron for every 2 tons used as rails. At this rate the total ore consumption of railroads in 1890 was 6,300,000 tons. However, railroads generated scrap which was the equivalent of 2,300,000 tons of ore. Hence the net ore consumption of railroads was about 4 million tons. Subtracting the last figure from domestic ore production leaves a residual of 10,400,000 tons, an amount which is slightly less than the output of the four main centres of production referred to by the Census. U.S. Census Bureau, *Eleventh Census of the United States: 1890, Report on Manufacturing Industries*, Part III, pp. 402, 410, 412, 417; *Eleventh Census, Mineral Industries*, p. 9; Fogel, *Railroads*, Table 4.8.

and other non-rail forms of transport would have risen. But it is unlikely that such an alternative demand would have accounted for more than a fraction of the ore consumed in the production of railroad iron.

The production of coal, like that of iron ore, was highly localised. Nine states accounted for about 90% of all coal shipped from mines in 1890. And within these states production was further localised in a relative handful of counties. Forty-six counties shipped 76,000,000 tons – 75% of all of the coal sent from mines in the nine states. Moreover, all of these counties were traversed by navigable rivers, canals actually constructed or the proposed canals discussed above. In this case, too, many of the smaller deposits were well located with respect to water transport.[19] Hence it seems likely that a non-rail society could have had low-cost access to all of the coal it required.

THE POSITION OF RAILROADS IN THE MARKET FOR MANUFACTURED PRODUCTS

While the railroad was the chief vehicle by which late-nineteenth-century society actually achieved access to natural resources, other mediums could have fulfilled essentially the same function. However, the low-cost services of these alternative forms of transport were embodied in different forms of equipment and structures than those characteristic of railroads. Hence it is still possible that railroads profoundly affected the course of economic growth because of the specific inputs, particularly of manufactured goods, required to produce railroad services.

Railroad input requirements could have affected the productivity of manufacturing in two ways. First, the railroad's incremental consumption of the output of various industries could have been so large that it moved these industries to a level of production that permitted significant economies of scale. Second, the railroads could have uniquely induced changes in the technology of manufacturing processes that affected the production not only of railroad goods but also of goods consumed by other sectors of the economy. This section examines the first line of possible influence. The next section deals with the nexus between railroads and technological innovation.

[19] *Eleventh Census, Mineral Industries*, pp. 347, 348, 355–417; Fogel, *Railroads*, Fig. A.1.

The ante-bellum *period*

Iron is frequently cited as the classic *ante-bellum* case of an industry raised to modern status by railroad purchases. Hofstadter, Miller and Aaron, for example, report that the railroad was 'by far the biggest user of iron in the 1850s' and that by 1860 'more than half the iron produced annually in the United States went into rails' and associated items.[20] Such statements, however, are not based on systematic measurements but on questionable inferences derived from isolated scraps of data. Casual procedures have led to the use of an index that grossly exaggerates the rail share, to the neglect of the rerolling process, and to a failure to consider the significance of the scrapping process.

Since the iron industry did not produce one homogeneous product, and since railroads consumed various types of iron, the usual problem of how to aggregate these products arises. A desirable procedure would be to aggregate by prices and to use

$$I_1 = \frac{\text{Value of domestically produced railroad iron}}{\text{Value of all final products of the iron industry}}$$

as an index of the proportion of the output of the American iron industry consumed by railroads. The numerator of I_1 is defined to exclude railroad iron purchased from abroad. The denominator is defined to exclude double counting. Unfortunately, the available data are not complete enough to permit the construction of this index. Even for the years following the Civil War, the breakdown of production by type of product is not detailed enough and prices of many individual products are not available.

As a consequence, writers dealing with the impact of railroads on the iron industry have resorted to indices based on the tonnage of iron production and consumption. A frequently used measure is

$$I_2 = \frac{\text{Tons of iron used in the construction and maintenance of railroads}}{\text{Tons of pig iron produced}}$$

The implicit assumption made in using I_2 is that $I_1 = I_2$. This assumption would be true if: (1) all railroad iron was purchased from domestic producers; (2) the amount of pig iron required to produce a ton of more highly manufactured iron was the same for all products; (3) only pig

[20] Richard Hofstadter, William Miller and Daniel Aaron, *The American Republic*, 2 vols. (Englewood Cliffs, 1959), Vol. I, p. 557.

iron was used to produce more highly manufactured iron; and (4) the values of the final products of the iron industry were proportionate to the amounts of pig iron used in their production.

In actual fact, all of these conditions were violated in such a way that I_2 is greater than I_1 by a substantial amount. A large part of railroad iron consumed through the seventies was purchased from abroad. During the 1850s foreign rails represented nearly two-thirds of all rail purchases; in 1871 they still accounted for 37% of purchases. The pig-iron requirement of a ton of rolled iron differed from that of cast iron and hammered iron. Pig iron was not the only form of crude iron used in the production of final products; scrap iron became an increasingly important part of total crude iron consumption in the years following 1850. Finally, the value of all final products was not directly proportional to the amount of pig iron required to produce them; the ratios of the price of a ton of steel and the price of a ton of hammered bar to the amount of pig used in their production exceeded the ratio of the price of a ton of rolled bar to its pig-iron content. Consequently, the use of I_2 as a measure of the share of output of the domestic iron industry consumed by railroads contains a considerable upward bias.

The neglect of the replacement process has also served to exaggerate the importance of railroads in the market for iron. Replacements became a major factor in rail consumption very early in the history of railroads. In fifteen of the thirty years following 1839 replacements represented more than 40% of total rail requirements; in five of these years replacements accounted for two-thirds of requirements. However, most replaced rails were scrapped. The availability of such scrap spurred the development of the rerolling of old rails. As early as 1849 one-fourth of all domestically produced rails were rerolled from discarded ones. By 1860 rerolling accounted for nearly 60% of domestic rail production.[21] Thus, although replacements rapidly became a substantial part of total rail consumption, replacement demand had little effect on the growth of blast furnaces. Replacements generated their own supply of crude iron. And scrapped rails that were not rerolled supplanted pig iron as an input in the production of other products.

When corrections are made for the biases of traditional indexes and when account is taken of the replacement process it turns out that the net addition to pig-iron production attributable to rails during 1840–60 amounted to less than 5% of the output of blast furnaces. The significance of railroads appears somewhat greater if account is taken of all

[21] Fogel, *Railroads*, p. 194.

forms of railroad consumption of iron from all sectors of the iron industry. On this basis railroads accounted for an average of 17% of total iron production during the two decades in question. While it is true that the railroad share rose to 25% in the final six years of the period, more germane is the fact that during the quinquennium ending in 1849 railroad consumption of domestic crude iron was just 10% of the total. Even if there had been no production of rails or railroad equipment whatsoever, the domestic crude iron consumed by the iron industry would have reached an average of 700,000 tons in the second quinquennium. The rise over the previous quinquennium would still have been 338,000 tons – an increase of 94% as opposed to the 99% rise that took place with the railroads. Clearly the new high level of production attained by the iron industry during 1845–49 did not depend on the railroad market.[22]

Furthermore, the demand for iron by industries other than railroads was more than adequate to permit a firm size capable of realising the economies of scale in the production of non-railroad iron that were actually achieved prior to 1860. The average capacity of blast furnaces prior to the Civil War was 4,800 tons; and the capacity of the largest furnace was under 10,000 tons. Similarly, except for rolling mills engaged exclusively in the rolling of rails, no firm appears to have produced more than 13,000 tons; but even if one assumes that the optimum firm capacity was 20,000 tons (the product of the largest rail firm in 1856 was 18,600 tons), the non-rail production of rolled iron at the time would have permitted seventeen firms of such size.[23]

Railroads occupied an even more modest position in the markets of other *ante-bellum* manufacturing industries. In the case of lumber, railroads purchased a minuscule share of total output – this despite the large quantities of wood consumed as fuel and in the construction of track. The paradox is partly explained by the fact that wood burned in the fire-boxes of railroad engines was not lumber. A similar consideration is involved in connection with the railroad's consumption of cross ties. Throughout the nineteenth century railroad men believed that ties hewn by axe would resist decay better than sawn ties. Consequently, lumber mills supplied ties amounting to only 450 million ft B.M. during the last two decades of the *ante-bellum* era. This was less than one-half of 1% of all lumber production. When the lumber required for car construction

[22] Fogel, *Railroads*, pp. 130–5, 199.
[23] American Iron and Steel Association, *Bulletin of the American Iron Association* (Philadelphia, 1856–58), pp. 58–63, 79, 103, 107, 155, 171, 173.

is included the figure rises by half a point to 0·96%. The modest position of railroads in the market for lumber products emphasises the scale of lumber consumption by other sectors of the economy.[24]

The share of the output of the transport equipment industry purchased by railroads is also surprising. From 1850 through 1860 some 26,300 miles of new track were laid. During the same time about 3,800 locomotives, 6,400 passenger and baggage cars, and 88,600 freight cars were constructed. Yet value added in the construction of railroad equipment in 1859 was only $12 million or 25·4% of value added by all transport equipment. The output of vehicles drawn by animals was still almost twice as great as the output of equipment for the celebrated iron horse.[25]

As for other types of machinery, railroads directly consumed less than 1%. Again, the situation does not change appreciably if indirect purchases at more remote levels of production are considered. When the share of machinery consumed by the lumber, iron and machine industries attributable to the railroad is added to that of transport equipment the railroad still accounts for only about 6% of machine production in 1859.[26]

The transport equipment, rolling-mill, blast-furnace, lumber and machinery industries were the main suppliers of the manufactured goods purchased by railroads. Using value added as a measure, railroads purchased slightly less than 11% of the combined output of the group in 1859. Since these industries accounted for 26% of all manufacturing in that year, railroad purchases from them amounted to a mere 2·8% of the total output of the manufacturing sector. Railroad purchases from all the other manufacturing industries raise the last figure to just 3·9%.[27] This amount hardly seems large enough to attribute the rapid growth of manufacturing during the last two *ante-bellum* decades to the requirements for building and for maintaining railway systems.

The post-Civil War era

Since the real capital stock of railroads increased at approximately the same rate as the real output of manufacturing, a detailed survey of changes in the position of the railroad in the market of most industries

[24] Fogel, *Railroads*, p. 137.
[25] *ibid.*, p. 139.
[26] *ibid.*, p. 140.
[27] *ibid.*, pp. 145, 146.

between 1859 and 1899 need not be undertaken in this paper.[28] However, the iron and steel industry requires further consideration. It is frequently said that the introduction of the Bessemer process radically reduced the cost of producing steel and ushered that industry into a new era. As measured by value added, the production of basic steel products rose from 4% of the output of the iron industry in 1859 to 23% in 1880.[29] Moreover, the consumption of steel was dominated by rails. Table 4.2 shows that in 1871 some 52% of all steel ingots were consumed in the production of rails. The rail share rose steadily from that date to 1881, when it stood at 87%, after which it declined to 50% in 1890.

The fact that the rail share of steel production fluctuated between 50 and 87% for a period of twenty years appears to suggest that the market for rails was indispensable to the emergence of a modern steel industry in the United States. This opinion also seems to have been nourished by the inverse relationship between the average output of Bessemer mills and the prices of the products of these mills (see Table 4.3), a relationship that suggests economies of scale.

There is, however, another way of looking at the data contained in Table 4.2. Stress on the share of total output consumed by rails in any given year beclouds the extremely rapid rate at which non-rail steel consumption grew and the rapidity with which that type of consumption exceeded the total steel production of a given year. This feature is brought forward in Table 4.4. Table 4.4 shows that the time required for the non-rail consumption of steel to exceed the total production of a given year varied from two to nine years, the average being about six years. Consequently, if the non-rail demand for steel was inelastic over the range of prices involved the observed scale of operations could have been achieved with an average lag of six years, even in the absence of rails.

It is possible to estimate the maximum gain to the nation made possible by rail-induced economies of scale. The computation turns on

---

[28] Albert Fishlow, 'Productivity and technological change in the railroad sector, 1840–1910' (unpublished paper presented to the Conference on Research in Income and Wealth, Chapel Hill, September 1963), Table 6; Robert E. Gallman, 'Commodity Output, 1839–1899', Conference on Research in Income and Wealth, *Trends in the American Economy in the Nineteenth Century*, Vol. 24 of *Studies in Income and Wealth* (Princeton, 1960), p. 43.

[29] *Eighth Census, Manufacturing*, pp. clxxviii, clxxx, clxxiii, clxxxv, clxciv; U.S. Bureau of the Census, *Tenth Census of the United States: 1880, Report on the Manufactures of the United States*, Vol. II (1883), pp. 748, 749, 753, 755, 757, 758, 759, 760. The term 'iron industry' as used here includes forges, bloomeries, blast furnaces, rolling mills and steel mills.

TABLE 4·2 *The production and consumption of steel, 1871–90*
(thousands of net tons)

	(1) Production of crude steel	(2) Steel consumed in rails	(3) Steel consumed in all other production	(4) Col. 2 as a percentage of Col. 1
1871	82	44	38	52
1872	160	108	52	67
1873	223	147	76	66
1874	242	166	76	69
1875	437	332	105	76
1876	597	471	126	79
1877	638	494	144	77
1878	820	640	180	78
1879	1,048	792	256	76
1880	1,397	1,107	290	79
1881	1,779	1,549	230	87
1882	1,945	1,670	275	86
1883	1,874	1,481	393	79
1884	1,737	1,279	458	74
1885	1,917	1,234	683	64
1886	2,870	2,022	848	70
1887	3,740	2,713	1,027	73
1888	3,247	1,781	1,466	55
1889	3,792	1,937	1,855	51
1890	4,790	2,396	2,394	50

Sources and Notes:
Column 1. American Iron and Steel Association, *Annual Report of the Secretary,
1889*, p. 63; *Annual Report, 1890*, p. 48.
Column 2. Total production of steel rails multiplied by 1·143. A.I.S.A. *Annual
Report, 1886*, p. 43; *Annual Report, 1888*, pp. 36, 61; *Annual Report, 1896*, p. 68.
Column 3. Column 1 minus Column 2.

the availability of the open-hearth furnace. The optimum plant size of
the open-hearth mill was about one-tenth that of a Bessemer mill.[30] In
1880 open-hearth mills had an average production of only 3,500 net tons;
in 1890 the average product was 9,000 net tons.[31]

If the absence of rails reduced the scale of operation to such a level that

[30] Peter Temin, *A History of the American Iron and Steel Industry from 1830–
1900* (unpublished doctoral dissertation, Massachusetts Institute of Technology,
1964), p. 206.
[31] *Tenth Census, Manufacturing*, pp. 743, 756; Temin, *A History*, p. 252; U.S.
Bureau of the Census, *Eleventh Census of the United States, Manufacturing*,
Part III, p. 412.

TABLE 4·3 *The average product of Bessemer steel mills and the average price of steel rails*

		(1) Average product of Bessemer mills, in thousands of net tons	(2) Average price of Bessemer steel rails in dollars of 1890, dollars per net ton
1	1870	21	73
2	1880	90	62
3	1890	99	36

Sources and Notes:
Column 1. The 1870 entry refers to a calendar year, while the entries for 1880 and 1890 represent production in census years. In computing average product, furnaces using the Clapp–Griffith and Robert–Bessemer processes were excluded. Thomas Dunlap (ed.), *Wiley's Iron Trade Manual* (New York, 1874), p. 187; A.I.S.A., *Annual Report, 1896*, p. 69; *Eleventh Census, Manufacturing*, Part III, pp. 411–12.
Column 2. Calendar year prices were deflated by the Warren–Pearson wholesale price index. The current dollar prices for the three years were $120, $76 and $36 per net ton. A.I.S.A. *Annual Report, 1896*, p. 84; U.S. Bureau of the Census, *Historical Statistics of the United States, Colonial Times to 1957* (Washington, D.C.; 1960), p. 115.

the cost of Bessemer steel exceeded the cost of open-hearth steel, consumers of Bessemer steel would have made their purchases from open-hearth mills. Hence the maximum gain to society from the economies of scale in Bessemer plants induced by rails was the price differential between Bessemer and open-hearth steel. In 1880 the average differential in the delivered price of Bessemer and open-hearth steel was $10 ·19 per net ton. Non-rail consumption of Bessemer steel was 112,200 net tons. Hence the maximum gain due to economies of scale induced by the railroad in the production of non-rail steel was only $1,144,000 or 0·01% of gross national product. By 1890 the average price differential fell to $4.02 per ton, while the production of non-rail Bessemer steel rose to 1,740,000 net tons. The indicated maximum gain attributable to railroad-induced economies of scale in 1890 is thus $6,995,000 or 0·06% of gross national product.[32]

[32] A.I.S.A., *Annual Report, 1896*, p. 69; *Eleventh Census, Manufacturing*, Part III, p. 417; *Historical Statistics*, p. 139.
    Even the small figures indicated in this computation over-state the gain attributable to railroad induced economies of scale. The computations assume that the superior quality of open-hearth steel was of no value to consumers of the

TABLE 4·4 *Time required for non-rail consumption of domestic steel to exceed total production of steel*

(1) Year to which non-rail consumption applies	(2) Non-rail consumption of steel, thousands of net tons	(3) Nearest year in which total steel production fell short of non-rail consumption	(4) Time lag in years (Col. 1 − Col. 3)
1871	38	1869	2
1872	52	1869	3
1873	76	1869	4
1874	76	1869	5
1875	105	1871	4
1876	126	1871	5
1877	144	1871	6
1878	180	1872	6
1879	256	1873	6
1880	290	1874	6
1881	230	1873	8
1882	275	1874	8
1883	393	1874	9
1884	458	1875	9
1885	683	1877	8
1886	848	1878	8
1887	1,027	1878	9
1888	1,466	1880	8
1889	1,855	1881	8
1890	2,394	1885	5

Sources:
Column 2. Table 4·2.
Column 3. Table 4·2; A.I.S.A., *Annual Report, 1889*, p. 63.

It thus appears that a modern steel industry would have emerged even in the absence of a demand for rails. While the increase in the scale of operations may have lagged behind that actually observed, it does not appear likely that the average lag would have exceeded six years. In any

---

Bessemer product. One would expect that for at least some purchasers of Bessemer steel there was a positive value to the superior features of open-hearth steel, although they obviously believed that the incremental benefit was less than the price differential between the two products. The computations also assume the existence of a completely inelastic demand curve for non-rail Bessemer steel. However, if the demand curve had some degree of elasticity, then to some consumers the incremental value of steel over other alternatives was less than the observed differential in the price of Bessemer and open-hearth steel.

case, the maximum social loss of a slower growth in the scale of operations would have been barely one-twentieth of 1% gross national product. Perhaps the most striking difference in the first quarter century of the development of a modern steel industry in the United States would have been the predominance of open-hearth over Bessemer mills.

THE EFFECT OF RAILROADS ON TECHNOLOGICAL INNOVATIONS

In discussing the effect of railroads on the introduction and diffusion of inventions, a distinction has to be drawn between innovations limited exclusively, or largely, to the operation of railroads and innovations that had a major impact outside of the railroad industry. The former category of devices will be denoted by the term 'restricted', the latter by the term 'transcending'.

Most inventions which arose out of the operation or construction of railroads fall into the category of restricted devices. Such items as air brakes, block signals, car trucks, automatic coupling devices, track switches, pullman cars and equalising bars were mere appurtenances. While they may have been important to the efficient operation of railroads, they had no significant application outside of this industry during the nineteenth century. Nor did the railroads' demand for these items induce the rise of industries or production processes of transcending economic significance. They made no independent contribution to economic growth. Rather they defined the conditions under which railroads operated – conditions that in varying degrees explain how it was that railroads were able to produce a low-cost transport service.

There are, however, certain innovations associated with railroads to which transcending significance has been attached and which therefore require further consideration. The two that will be considered here are: cheap methods of producing steel and the telegraph.

The belief that the railroads' demand for improved rails was responsible for the inventions that led to low-cost steel production rests on shaky foundations. It was not the problem of how to produce better rails that led Henry Bessemer into the series of experiments that resulted in the Bessemer converter. As J. S. Jeans has pointed out, Bessemer's experiments stemmed from a desire to improve the effectiveness of artillery. A major obstacle to such improvement was the inadequacy of cast iron for cannon firing heavy projectiles. Bessemer pursued his research on metallurgy with the aim of 'producing a quality of metal more suitable than any other for the construction of heavy ordnance'.[33] William Kelly, who independently discovered the Bessemer process in the United States, was engaged not in the production of heavy rolled forms but in the production of cast-iron kettles.[34] And the immediate factor that stimulated the Siemens brothers to develop the open-hearth furnace was their desire to find industrial applications for their earlier discovery – the regenerative condenser.[35]

The point is that metallurgical research in the mid-nineteenth century was induced by the rapidly growing demand for iron in a wide variety of production processes. Cheap steel had potential marketability not only for the fabrication of rails but also for ships, boilers, bridges, buildings, ordnance, armour, springs, wire, forgings, castings, chains, cutlery, etc. Metallurgical innovators could have been, and were, lured to search for improved products and processes by the profit that was to be earned from sales in all markets for iron and not just in the railroad market.

It is, of course, true that during the initial decades following the discovery of the Bessemer process most of the steel that poured from converters was destined for the fabrication of rails. From 1867 to 1883 about 80% of all Bessemer steel ingots were so consumed.[36] This fact seems to suggest that railroads played an essential role in making cheap steel available on a large scale.

The problem is, however, more complex than it first appears. The fact that rails used four-fifths of Bessemer steel production – in some years the share approached or exceeded 90% – raises the question of whether the Bessemer process was, during this period, a restricted or a transcending innovation. If Bessemer steel had been used exclusively for railroad purposes one could give an unequivocal answer to the question. Like block signals or air brakes, it would fall into the category of an appurtenance that contributed to economic growth only in and through railroads; Bessemer steel would have increased real national income only because it increased productivity in the railroad industry.

But in fact some Bessemer steel was used for non-rail products. In 1880, 8·9% of all such metal was turned into bars; 5·7% into rods; 0·2% into structural shapes, sheets and boiler or other plate. In total,

---

[33] J. S. Jeans, *Steel: Its History, Manufacture, Properties and Uses* (London, 1880), pp. 44–5.
[34] *The National Cyclopaedia of American Biography*, 46 vols. (New York, 1898–1963), Vol. XIII, p. 196.
[35] Leslie Stephen and Sidney Lee (eds.), *The Dictionary of National Biography*, 22 vols. (Oxford, 1921–2), Vol. XVIII, pp. 241–2.
[36] A.I.S.A. *Annual Report, 1889*, pp. 63, 65; note to column 2 of Table 4.2 above.

169,645 net tons of Bessemer steel were rolled into products other than rails.[37] While some of these shapes were also consumed by railroads, it may be assumed that the bulk was not. Was the amount of Bessemer steel used for non-railroad purposes large enough to warrant the classification of the Bessemer process as a transcending innovation?

While a definitive answer to this question requires more thorough research than was possible for this paper, available data suggest that the tentative answer should be: 'No.' In 1880 Bessemer steel accounted for only a minuscule share of the most important non-rail forms of rolled ferrous metal. Bessemer steel accounted for 9·79% of rolled bar, 0·57% of structural shapes and 0·50% of sheets and plates.[38] At the time when Bessemer steel was most rapidly displacing wrought iron as the basic raw material for rails it was unable to dislodge wrought iron from its dominance as an input in the production of other products of rolling mills. According to Peter Temin, Bessemer steel 'was subject to mysterious breakages and fractures that made people prefer iron' for most non-rail purposes.[39]

In later years the fall in the relative price of steel led to a situation in which most rolling-mill products were made from this material. By 1909 over 89% of rolling-mill output other than rails was made from steel. However, most of this steel came not from converters but from open-hearths. In the production of those forms for which demand was increasing most rapidly – plates, sheets, structural shapes, wire, etc. – open-hearth steel was preferred because of its superior qualities and its competitive price.[40]

Thus superior alternatives to Bessemer steel in non-rail uses were available at comparable prices through the later nineteenth century. Bessemer steel does not appear to have provided the basis for the remarkable growth of productivity in other industries that it did in the railroad sector.[41] Although the rapid expansion of Bessemer production

[37] ibid., Tenth Census, Manufacturing, pp. 743, 758.
[38] Tenth Census, Manufacturing, pp. 754, 755, 758.
[39] Temin, A History, p. 315.
[40] Temin, A History, pp. 207–12, 315, 325–34, 395–6. It should be stressed that only a negligible proportion of open-hearth steel was used for the production of rails. In 1880 the figure was 10%, by 1890 it had fallen to less than 1%.
[41] According to Albert Fishlow ('Productivity and Technological Change') the substitution of steel rails for iron rails, the increased power of locomotives and the increased capacity of freight cars account for 50% of the increase in total factor productivity between 1870 and 1910. He further indicates that steel rails were a necessary condition for the utilisation of heavy engines. They may also have been a necessary condition for the larger capacity of freight cars.

between 1867 and 1890 is attributable to the market for rails, the Bessemer process appears to have been a restricted rather than a transcending innovation.

Unlike the case of Bessemer steel, there was little connection between the railroads and the early growth of the telegraph industry in the United States. The first telegraph line was established in 1844. Just eight years later the nation was laced with lines totalling 17,000 miles.[42] By 1852 the telegraph network connected all of the major eastern and southern cities. St. Louis, Milwaukee, Chicago, Detroit and Toledo had telegraphic connection with the Atlantic coast well before the completion of the railroad link. In the United States, said the Superintendent of the Census, 'the telegraphic system is carried to greater extent than in any other part of the world, and the numerous lines now in full operation form a net-work over the length and breadth of the land. They are not confined to the populous regions of the Atlantic coast, but extend far into the interior, climb the sides of the highest mountains, and cross the almost boundless prairies.'[43]

The demand that induced the remarkably rapid rate of construction emanated not from railroads but from other businesses. Bankers, stock-brokers, commodity brokers and newspapers were the largest purchasers of telegraphic service.[44] The railroads did not try systematically to employ the new device until the basic wire network had been completed. The Erie railroad, which began to use the telegraph for the dispatching of trains in 1851, was the first to do so. Despite its successful experience, most other railroads did not immediately become convinced of the advantages of the system. As late as 1854, a reporter for the *London Quarterly Review* could write that 'the telegraph is rarely seen in America running beside the railway'.[45]

What, then, is the basis for the view that railroads played a funda-mental role in the growth and diffusion of the telegraph? It appears to rest primarily on the operating efficiencies achieved as a result of the alliance between the two systems. Once the alliance was formed, tele-graph companies could utilise railroad men 'to watch the line, straighten poles, re-set them when down, mend wires and report to the telegraph company'.[46] Consequently, by making use of railroad track-walkers and

---

[42] U.S. Bureau of the Census, *Report of the Superintendent of the Census for December 1, 1852* (1853), pp. 111–13.
[43] *ibid.*, p. 106.
[44] Robert Luther Thompson, *Wiring a Continent* (Princeton, 1947), pp. 47, 242.
[45] *ibid.*, pp. 203–10.
[46] *ibid.*, p. 213.

other railroad maintenance men, telegraph companies were able to reduce maintenance costs below what they would have been. Such savings were, no doubt, reflected in lower rates that probably stimulated the growth of the telegraph service. Given the existence of railroads, the telegraph was no doubt aided by the alliance. However, it by no means follows that the observed rate of growth of the telegraph industry was higher than it would have been in the absence of railroads. It must be remembered that by speeding up the distribution of mail, railroads provided consumers with a better substitute for the telegraph than would otherwise have been available. Consequently, whether railroads made the volume of telegraphic business larger or smaller than it would have been in their absence is at this point a moot question.

THE SOCIAL SAVING OF RAILROADS[47]

It is possible to set an upper limit to the increase in national income attributable to the reduction in transport costs made possible by railroads. The main conceptual device used in this computation is the 'social saving'. The social saving in any given year is defined as the difference between the actual cost of shipping goods in that year and the alternative cost of shipping exactly the same goods between exactly the same points without railroads. This cost differential is in fact larger than the 'true' social saving. Forcing the pattern of shipments in a non-rail situation to conform to the pattern that actually existed is equivalent to the imposition of a restraint on society's freedom to adjust to an alternative technological situation. If society had had to ship by water and wagon without the railroad it could have altered the geographical locus of production in a manner that would have economised on transport services. Further, the sets of primary and secondary markets through which commodities were distributed were surely influenced by conditions peculiar to rail transport; in the absence of railroads some different cities would have entered these sets, and the relative importance of those remaining would have changed. Adjustments of this sort would have reduced the loss of national income occasioned by the absence of the railroad.

For analytical convenience the computation of the social saving is divided into several parts. We begin with the estimation of the social saving on the inter-regional distribution of agricultural commodities. In

[47] Unless otherwise stated, Fogel, *Railroads,* Chapters II and III, is the source for all of the computations presented in this section.

1890 most agricultural goods destined for inter-regional shipment were first concentrated in the eleven great primary markets of the Midwest. These farm surpluses were then trans-shipped to some ninety secondary markets located in the East and South. After arriving in the secondary markets the commodities were distributed to retailers in the immediately surrounding territory or exported.

Of the various forms of transport in use in 1890, the most relevant alternative to railroads was waterways. All of the eleven primary markets were on navigable waterways. Lakes, canals, rivers and coastal waters directly linked the primary markets with secondary markets receiving 90% of the inter-regional shipments. Consequently, it is possible to compute a first approximation of the inter-regional social saving by finding the difference between payments actually made by shippers of agricultural products and the payments they would have made to water carriers if shippers had sent the same commodities between the same points without railroads.

The agricultural tonnage shipped inter-regionally in 1890 was approximately equal to the local deficits of the trading regions of the East and South plus net exports. The local net deficits of a trading area are computed by subtracting from the consumption requirements of the area its production and its changes in inventories. The average rail and water distances of an inter-regional shipment are estimated from a randomly drawn sample of the routes (pairs of cities) that represent the population of connections (i.e., all possible pairings) between primary and secondary (deficit) markets. The water and rail rates per ton-mile for the various commodities are based on representative rates that prevailed in 1890 over distances and routes approximating to the average condition. The application of observed water rates to a tonnage greatly in excess of that actually carried by waterways is justified by evidence which indicates that water transport was a constant- or declining-cost industry.

Using these estimates of tonnages shipped, rates and distances, it appears that the actual cost of the inter-regional agricultural transport in 1890 was $87,500,000, while the cost of transporting the same goods by water would have been only $49,200,000. In other words, the first approximation of the inter-regional social saving is negative by about $38 million. This odd result is the consequence of the fact that direct payments to railroads included virtually all of the cost of inter-regional transport, while direct payments to water carriers did not. In calculating the cost of shipping without the railroad one must account for six additional items of cost not included in payments to water carriers. These items are cargo losses in transit, trans-shipment costs, wagon haulage costs from water points to secondary markets not on waterways, capital costs not reflected in water rates, the cost resulting from the time lost when using a slow medium of transport, and the cost of being unable to use water routes for five months out of the year.

The first four of the neglected costs can be estimated directly from available commercial data. Insurance rates measure the average cargo loss per dollar of goods shipped by water. Trans-shipment rates were published. Data on the capital invested in the construction and improvement of waterways were also published. The quantity of goods required by secondary markets not on waterways is indicated in the calculation of the net deficits of trading areas. And estimates of the cost of wagon transport are available.

It is more difficult to determine the cost of the time lost in shipping by a slow medium of transport and the cost of being unable to use water routes for about five months during each year. Such costs were not recorded in profit and loss statements, or publications of trade associations, or the decennial censuses, or any of the other normal sources of business information. Consequently, they must be determined indirectly through a method that links the desired information to data which are available. The solution to the problem lies in the nexus between time and inventories. If entrepreneurs could replace goods the instant they were sold they would, *ceteris paribus*, carry zero inventories. Inventories are necessary to bridge the gap of time required to deliver a commodity from its supply source to a given point. If on the average inter-regional shipments of agricultural commodities required a month more by water than by rail, and if water routes were closed for five months out of each year it would have been possible to compensate for the slowness of water transport and the limited season of navigation by increasing inventories in secondary markets by an amount equal to one-half of the annual receipts of these markets. Hence the cost of the interruptions and time lost in water transport is the 1890 cost of carrying such an inventory. The inventory cost comprises two elements: the foregone opportunity of investing the capital represented in the additional inventory (which is measured by the interest rate) and storage charges (which were published).

When account is taken of the neglected costs the negative first approximation is transformed into a positive social saving of $73 million (see Table 4·5). Since the actual 1890 cost of shipping the specified commodities was approximately $88 million, the absence of the railroad would have almost doubled the cost of shipping agricultural commodities inter-regionally. It is therefore quite easy to see why the great bulk of agricultural commodities were actually sent to the East by rail, with water transport used only over a few favourable routes.

TABLE 4·5 *The social saving in the inter-regional distribution of agricultural commodities* (in millions of dollars)

First approximation	−38
Neglected cargo losses	6
Trans-shipping	16
Supplementary wagon haulage	23
Neglected capital costs	18
Additional inventory costs	48
Total	73

While the inter-regional social saving is large compared to the actual transport cost, it is quite small compared to annual output of the economy – just six-tenths of 1% of gross national product. Hence the computed social saving indicates that the availability of railroads for the inter-regional distribution of agricultural products represented only a relatively small addition to the production potential of the economy.

The estimation of the social saving is more complex in intra-regional trade (movements from farms to primary markets) than in long-haul trade. Inter-regional transport represented a movement between a relatively small number of points – eleven great collection centres in the Midwest and ninety secondary markets in the East and South. But intra-regional transport required the connection of an enormous number of locations. Considering each farm as a shipping point, there were not eleven but 4,565,000 interior shipping locations in 1890; the number of primary markets receiving farm commodities was well over a hundred.[48] These points were not all connected by the railroad network, let alone by navigable waterways. The movement of commodities from farms to primary markets was never accomplished exclusively by water or by rail.

[48] In the intra-regional case the term 'primary markets' refers not merely to the eleven great midwestern collection centres but also to cities that served as collection centres for intra-regionally traded commodities. Thus, while New York City was a secondary market for the corn, wheat, beef and pork of the North Central states, it was a primary market for the dairy products, fruits and other commodities produced by local farmers.

Rather it involved a mixture of wagon and water or wagon and train services.

A first approximation of the intra-regional social saving (a) can be computed on the basis of the relationship shown in the equation:

$$a - x\left[w(D_{fb}-D_{fr})+(BD_{bp}-RD_{rp})\right]$$

where x = the tonnage of agricultural produce shipped out of counties by rail;

   w = the average wagon rate per ton-mile;

   B = the average water rate per ton-mile;

   R = the average rail rate per ton-mile;

   D_{fb} = the average distance from a farm to a water shipping point;

   D_{fr} = the average distance from a farm to a rail shipping point;

   D_{bp} = the average distance from a water shipping point to a primary market;

   D_{rp} = the average distance from a rail shipping point to a primary market.

The first term within the square bracket $w(D_{fb}-D_{fr})$ is the social saving per ton attributable to the reduction in wagon transport; the second term $(BD_{bp}-RD_{rp})$ is the social saving per ton on payments to water and rail carriers. One of the surprising results is that only the first term is positive. In the absence of railroads, wagon transport costs would have increased by $8.92 for each ton of agricultural produce that was shipped intra-regionally by rail. However, payments to water carriers would have been $0·76 per ton less than the payments to railroads. In other words, the entire first approximation of the a estimate of the social saving – which amounts to $300 million – is attributable not to the fact that railroad charges were less than boat charges but to the fact that railroads reduced the amount of expensive wagon haulage that had to be combined with one of the low-cost forms of transport.

To the $300 million obtained as the first approximation it is necessary to add certain indirect costs. In the long-haul case the first approximation of the social saving omitted six charges of considerable importance. However, in the intra-regional case three of these items are covered by the first approximation. Wagon haulage costs are included in the equation. Trans-shipment costs would have been no greater in the non-rail cases than in the rail case. In both situations bulk would have been broken when the wagons reached the rail or water shipping points, and no further trans-shipments would have been required between these points and the primary markets. Since all government expenditures on rivers and canals financed out of taxes rather than tolls were assigned to inter-regional agricultural shipments, their inclusion in the intra-regional case would represent double counting.

Three indirect costs do have to be added to the first approximation. These are cargo losses, the cost of using a slow medium of transport, and the cost of the limited season of navigation. As is shown by Table 4·6,

TABLE 4·6 *The preliminary intra-regional social saving* (in millions of dollars)

First approximation	300·2
Cargo losses	1·3
Cost of slow transportation	1·7
Cost of the limited season of navigation	34·0
Total	337·2

these neglected items amount to only $37 million, which, when added to the first approximation, yields a preliminary *a* estimate of $337 million or 2·8% of gross national product.

The preliminary estimate of the agricultural social saving is based on the severe assumption that in the absence of railroads all other aspects of technology would have been unaltered. However, it seems quite likely that in the absence of railroads much of the capital and ingenuity that went into the perfection and spread of the railroad would have been turned towards the development of other cheap forms of land transport. In these circumstances it is possible that the internal-combustion engine would have been developed years sooner than it actually was, thus per-mitting a reduction in transport costs through the use of motor trucks.

While most of such possibilities of a speed-up in the introduction and spread of alternative forms of transport have not been sufficiently explored to permit meaningful quantification at the present time, there are two changes about which one can make fairly definite statements. These are the extension of the existing system of internal waterways and the improvement of common roads. Neither of these developments required new knowledge. They merely involved an extension of existing technology.

As has already been pointed out, in the absence of railroads it would have been technologically and commercially feasible to build canals in the North and South Central states. A 5,000-miles system of such canals would have brought all but 7% of agricultural land within 40 'airline' miles of a navigable waterway. In so doing these waterways would have reduced the combined inter- and intra-regional social saving from $410 million to $287 million. Similarly, improvement of roads could have cut the cost of wagon transport by 39%, thus still further reducing the total agricultural social saving to $214 million.

It is possible to estimate roughly the social saving on non-agricultural commodities by extrapolating the social saving per ton-mile on agricultural commodities to non-agricultural commodities.[49] To do so, two adjustments must be made. First, the figure of $214 million presented as the agricultural social saving already includes substantial elements of the social saving on non-agricultural items. Although all of the capital costs of the improvement of waterways were charged to agricultural commodities, most of this cost should be distributed among non-agricultural items. Similarly, the wagon rates used in the computations assumed zero return hauls, so that these rates cover most of the additional wagon cost that would have been incurred in shipping non-agricultural commodities to farms. It is probable that 35% of the $214 million should be assigned to the social saving induced by railroads in transporting products of mines, forest and factories. In other words, the 'pure' agricultural social saving is about $140 million. Given that 20,000 million ton-miles of railroad service were required for the shipment of agricultural commodities in 1890, the agricultural social saving per ton-mile of railroad service was $0·0070.

Second, available evidence suggests that the social saving per ton-mile was less on non-agricultural products than on agricultural ones. Products of mines dominated the non-agricultural commodities carried by railroads. Coal alone represented 35% of the non-agricultural tonnage in 1890. Iron and other ores brought the mineral share to over 50%. As has been previously shown, a relatively small extension of the canal system could have brought most mines into direct contact with waterways. Thus, very little supplementary wagon transport would have been

---

[49] This extrapolation involves a series of uncertain assumptions. The hazards involved in such an extrapolation are discussed in Fogel, *Railroads*, pp. 219–24. A reliable estimate on the total social saving can be obtained only by applying to non-agricultural commodities the detailed methods of estimation used in the agricultural case. It seems probable that such a computation will reveal that the social saving on all freight was well below 5% of gross national product (c.f. *ibid.*, p. 223). However, pending such a computation, estimates of the social saving on all freight – including the one given in this paper – should be considered tentative and largely illustrative.

required on these items. Moreover, the cost of increasing inventories to compensate for the slowness of, and interruptions in, water transport would have been quite low. The total value of products of mines was well below the value of the agricultural commodities shipped from farms. As a consequence, the opportunity cost of the increased inventories of minerals would have been well below that found for agriculture. Additional storage charges, if any, would have been trivial. Minerals required neither very expensive storage facilities nor shelters. They were stored on open docks or fields.

These general considerations are supported by estimates compiled by Albert Fishlow which reveal that in 1860 the social saving per ton-mile on non-agricultural commodities was only 46% of that for agricultural goods.[50] This ratio applied to the figure of $0·0070 indicates that in the case of non-agricultural freight the social saving per ton-mile in 1890 was $0·0032. On this basis the social saving made possible by the 59,000 million ton-miles of non-agricultural freight service provided by railroads in 1890 was $189 million. The last figure added to the 'pure' agricultural saving yields a total of $329 million on all commodities. Thus, the availability of railroads for the transport of commodities appears to have increased the production potential of the economy by about 3% of gross national product.

IMPLICATIONS FOR THE SPACE EFFORT[51]

If space activities should make a major contribution to economic growth it seems highly unlikely that it will take the same form as the contribution made by railroads. The central feature of the developmental impact of railroads was not so much that they induced or made possible new economic activities but that by reducing transport costs they facilitated processes and activities which were well under way prior to their advent. The cheap form of inland transport service purveyed by railroads speeded the commercialisation of agriculture, widened the market for

[50] Albert Fishlow, *Railroads and the Transformation of the Ante Bellum Economy* (Princeton, Harvard University Press, 1966), Chapter II; Fishlow, *Economic Contribution*, Table A.5. Fishlow estimates that the social saving on passenger traffic in 1890 was $300 million (see Fishlow, *Railroads*, Chapter II).

[51] It is worth repeating the caveat stated at the beginning of this essay. No evaluation of the impact of railroads on American development can be complete without a consideration of the cultural, political, military and social consequences of such an innovation. I have focused on economic aspects of railroads, and my consideration of the implications of the railroad experience for the space effort is limited to the economic effects outlined in the preceding pages.

manufactured goods and promoted regional specialisation. While the scope of these effects and the net benefit accruing to the economy from them was much less than is usually presumed, they were none the less large enough to warrant the investment made in railroads.

The present cost of rocket transport between points on earth is now far more expensive than alternative services. It is conceivable that future improvements may reduce the cost of rocket transport to such a level that the movement of persons between the most distant points on earth will become commercially feasible.[52] But experience thus far offers no basis for assuming that rockets will, in the foreseeable future, provide a superior alternative to boats, trains, trucks, pipelines and planes for the transport of the freight now normally carried by these mediums. Moreover, since the development of supersonic jets will soon reduce the flying time between the most distant points on earth to about six hours, the maximum time saving in earth transport that could be brought about by rockets is only about five hours.

As for access to resources, it does not seem likely that rockets will match the quite limited contribution of railroads to the expansion of the available supply of traditional economic resources. Even if other planets of the solar system have agricultural lands several times more productive than the best prairie soils or ore deposits richer than the Mesabi mines in their heyday, the cost of transporting the products of these planets to earth would, in existing circumstances, be prohibitive. The mining of planetoids or other extra-terrestrial bodies, as has sometimes been proposed, would therefore become practical only if there were a very sharp decrease in the cost of space transport and/or a very sharp rise in the cost of available resources on earth. Considering the substitutability of materials and the rapid rate of innovation in synthetics, the likelihood of a contribution in this area during the foreseeable future seems very small.

With respect to the development of technology, the experience of railroads offers little basis for assuming that the devices required for space transport will lead to innovations that markedly affect productive technique in other spheres of activity. Most of the devices invented to improve railroads had no significant applications outside of this industry. And in the case of Bessemer steel, a product with many applications that was clearly promoted by railroad requirements, the economy independently produced an extremely effective substitute: namely open-hearth steel.

[52] Leston Faneuf, 'Application of space science to earth travel', *Peacetime Uses of Outer Space*, ed. Simon Ramo (New York, 1961), pp. 86–109.

It is also important to keep in mind the fact that the huge investment devoted to railroad construction may have, by diverting resources, retarded technological development in other fields. A case in point is the relatively late realisation of commercially useful motor vehicles. The decisions that led society to invest billions of dollars in railroads between 1830 and 1890 while allocating paltry sums to the perfection of motor vehicles may have delayed the advent of motor transport by several decades.

Given the information generally available in 1830, the preference for railroads over the horseless carriages is quite understandable. Although carriages powered by steam engines were sufficiently perfected to be commercially successful in the absence of railroad competition, they were less efficient than the early railway.[53] The experience gained as the railroad system expanded revealed specific ways in which locomotives, cars and track could be improved. With millions of dollars invested in new railroads annually, and with virtually each new extension of the system embodying some technological advance, the efficiency gap between the railroad and the horseless carriage became increasingly great – perhaps to the point that the latter no longer appeared to be a practical alternative. At any rate, it is interesting to note that the pace of experimentation on horseless carriages and wagons does not appear to have regained the peak attained in the twenties and thirties until half a century later. By then it cost the Minnesota farmers as much to haul a ton of wheat 15 miles by wagon as it did to ship the same quantity 375 miles by rail. And the railroad network was too dense significantly to reduce the cost of wagon haulage by further additions to the system. Thus, motor vehicles were perfected and put into commercial production when the developmental potential of railroads had more or less run its course.

Could the horseless carriage have been made commercially viable sooner than it actually was? The crucial step in the perfection of motor vehicles appears to have been the substitution of the internal-combustion engine for the steam engine as the power source in horseless carriages. However, 'not only the fundamental internal-combustion engine theory, but even that of the diesel engine' was published as early as 1824.[54] Consequently, one cannot at this point foreclose the possibility that in

[53] D. C. Field, 'Mechanical road-vehicles', in *A History of Technology*, eds. Charles Singer and others (New York and London, Oxford University Press, 1958), Vol. V, pp. 420–6.
[54] Orville Charles Cromer, 'Internal combustion engines', *Encyclopaedia Britannica* (Chicago, 1961), Vol. 12, p. 494; Field, 'Mechanical road-vehicles', pp. 426–34.

the absence of railroads more capital and talent would have been devoted to the perfection of the horseless carriage, and that as a result the engineering knowledge and technical skills required to produce effective motor vehicles would have emerged decades sooner than it actually did. In weighing the benefits of technological innovations such as telemetry, compact power sources, reinforced plastics and new metal alloys that have been induced or accelerated by the space effort, one must take into account alternative devices that could have been developed if the resources devoted to the space effort were applied to other activities.

The preceding discussion does not necessarily imply that the space effort will fail to contribute to the expansion of the nation's production potential. There is a very important asymmetry between the railroads and rockets. While railroads increased the area of economically accessible territory, they did not affect the physical accessibility. All parts of the earth's surface were penetrable before the invention of railroads. Indeed, the various territories of the world were explored by man before they were traversed by rails. However, it is impossible to explore the solar system without rocket-ships. The development of space-craft, unlike the railroad, thus offers man access to knowledge that cannot be obtained in any other way. The knowledge gained from space exploration may have enormous consequences for the biological and physical sciences. The advances in these sciences made possible by space exploration may in turn lead to a technological and commercial revolution far more portentous than that which followed from the scientific breakthroughs of the seventeenth, eighteenth and nineteenth centuries. In this respect the space effort has a chance of affecting economic life far more radically than did railroads. Examination of the railroad experience cannot aid in predicting the value of the scientific knowledge that may be gained from space exploration.

5.1 Some implications of recent work in historical demography

JOHN T. KRAUSE

Current population theory depends heavily on the hypothesis that a demographic revolution occurred in West European countries roughly between 1750 and 1880.[1] According to this hypothesis, European death rates averaged at least 35 per 1,000 prior to 1750; hence, even very high birth rates did not enable populations to recover rapidly from the effects of catastrophes, which are supposed to have been frequent and intense. Only after the advances, mainly hygienic, which began about 1750 did the death rate commence a long-term decline. Because fertility remained high, West European populations grew more rapidly than they had ever done. Eventually, urbanization and industrialization sapped the forces which maintained high birth rates, and low fertility became the major cause of low Western rates of growth. Since currently under-developed populations have high vital rates, it has been suggested that demographic principles are transcultural and that Western demographic patterns will be repeated.

A growing body of evidence suggests that this theory is incorrect. Some writers argue that increased fertility caused the rapid demographic

John T. Krause (1959) *Comparative Studies in Society and History*, I, No. 2, (The Hague), pp. 164–88.
[1] A. Landry, *La révolution démographique* (Paris, Librairie du Recueil Sirey, 1934); M. Buer, *Health, Wealth and Population in the Early Days of the Industrial Revolution* (London, G. Routledge and Sons Ltd, 1926); R. B. Vance, 'The demographic gap: dilemma of modernization programs' in *Approaches to Problems of High Fertility in Agrarian Societies* (New York, Milbank Memorial Fund, 1952), pp. 9–17; F. Notestein and I. Taeuber, 'The changing fertility of the Japanese', *Population Studies*, I (1947), pp. 2–28. The English evidence has provided the most commonly cited model for these developments; for a fuller bibliography see H. J. Habakkuk, 'English population in the eighteenth century', *Economic History Review*, 2nd ser., VI (1953), pp. 117–33.

growth of England, Ireland, and French Canada. Studies of France, although frequently undermining the traditional argument on the height of eighteenth-century mortality, have generally brought forward new arguments to support the accepted view; but their new arguments have been sharply criticized. Then, generalizations on the relationship between nutrition and mortality in the currently under-developed countries when applied to the pre-industrial West suggest that Western mortality levels have been exaggerated. As knowledge of the factors which affect fertility increases, it seems that the effectiveness of Western controls over birth have been underestimated. While all the above points will be discussed in this article, the historical data on Scandinavia, England, Ireland, French Canada, and France will be subjected to closest scrutiny.

I

Of primary importance are studies of eighteenth century Scandinavia.[2] Crude birth and death rates are available from the early 1720s for Sweden and Finland, and from 1735 for Norway, Denmark, and Iceland. Annual data on marriages are also available for the different countries beginning at various times during the century. Then, starting in 1750 for Sweden and in 1751 for Finland, age distributions make possible the calculation of some refined rates, especially in the case of Sweden. Not until 1800 were reliable age distributions made in the other Scandinavian states, except for the isolated instance of Iceland whose census of 1703 provides evidence on age, sex, and civil status.

Not only are the data plentiful, by comparison with other areas, but in the case of Sweden after 1750 the abundant material enables one to test the data for internal consistency on a scale unknown in other lands of the time. While Swedish statistics for 1750–1800 undoubtedly are somewhat deficient, they are probably more accurate than those of England or France in the mid-nineteenth century, or those of the early twentieth-century U.S.A.

[2] The best introduction to these data is H. Gille, 'The demographic history of northern European countries in the eighteenth century', *Population Studies*, III (1949), pp. 3–65. G. Sundbärg, *Bevölkerungsstatistik Schwedens 1750–1900* (Stockholm, P. A. Norstedt & Söner, 1907); E. Heckscher, 'Swedish population trends before the Industrial Revolution', *Economic History Review*, 2nd ser., II (1950), pp. 266–77; G. Utterström, 'Some population problems in pre-industrial Sweden', *Scandinavian Economic History Review*, II (1954), pp. 103–65. B. Boëthius, 'New light on eighteenth century Sweden', *Scandinavian Economic History Review*, I (1953), pp. 143–77.

Increasing the importance of the Swedish statistics, a comparison of the crude rates indicates that, except for Finland whose birth-rate was above the Scandinavian average, Swedish demographic traits appear to have been very similar to those of the other Scandinavian countries. According to E. Heckscher, eighteenth-century Sweden's backward economy made her typical of Western and Central Europe in earlier centuries, thus further increasing their value.[3]

That the populations of the United States and New France doubled every 25 or 30 years is evidence of extremely high fertility. While it has been estimated that there were 952 children aged 0–4 per 1,000 women aged 15–45 in the U.S. of 1800, a fertility rate higher than any in the world today, marital fertility rates cannot be calculated.[4]

For Canada, whose economic conditions were similar to those of the U.S., there is a large body of data. Unfortunately, some important materials have not been studied, and the two most important studies disagree.[5] G. Sabagh, who relied on the baptisms and the censuses of 1666, 1667, and 1681, argued that the age-specific marital fertility rates were similar to those of Western Europe between 1850 and 1900. On the other hand, J. Henripin, whose major source was a genealogy, found that the age-specific marital fertility rates were 20 to 25 per cent higher than the West European levels of the late nineteenth century.

While this paper cannot fully explore the Canadian data, a brief analysis may resolve the conflict. Both Henripin and Sabagh use the censuses of 1666, 1667, and 1681 which give detailed data on age (for single years from 0–9, then by five year age-groups until age 19, and by 10 year age-groups for those aged 20 and above), sex, and marital status. Thanks to Sabagh, the women of child-bearing age have been divided into five year age-groups. Then, there are eight less detailed censuses between 1692 and 1734 which make possible the calculation of sex-ratios, the percentage of the population under age 15, and the percentage of women aged 15 and over who were married or widowed.[6] In addition,

[3] E. Heckscher, 'The place of Sweden in modern economic history', *Economic History Review*, IV (1932), pp. 1–22.

[4] W. S. Thompson and P. K. Whelpton, *Population Trends in the United States* (New York, McGraw-Hill, 1933), p. 263.

[5] G. Sabagh, 'The fertility of the French Canadian women during the seventeenth century', *American Journal of Sociology*, XLVII (1942), pp. 680–9. J. Henripin, *La population canadienne au début du XVIIIe siècle*, cahier no. 23 of Travaux et Documents de l'Institut National d'Études Démographiques (Paris, Presses Universitaires de France, 1954).

[6] The basic materials on censuses and vital statistics are to be found in the *Census of Canada 1871*, Vols. IV and V. B. Sulte, *Historie des Canadiens Français*,

other censuses give data on sex-ratios and the number of women who were married or widowed. While these censuses were carefully compiled, there is undoubtedly some under-enumeration, especially of infants, and misstatement of age.[7]

The voluminous Canadian statistics, beginning in 1621, include the annual numbers of baptisms, burials, and marriages. The preface to volume IV of the Census of 1870–1 indicates that some registers have been lost and that others are incomplete, but concludes that omissions were slight for the period as a whole. The gaps are probably most important for the seventeenth century. For example, out of about 2,060 baptisms in 1677–81 there were 2,022 children alive in 1681, an amazing survival ratio of 0·982. Some under-enumeration of the 0–4 age group is likely and immigration was negligible by the late 1670s, hence a significant omission of births is probable, about 20 per cent if one assumes a survival ratio of 0·800. Death rates of nine per 1,000 for 1671–80 and 18 for 1681–90 provide further evidence of deficient registration; age distribution cannot explain these low figures because of the large size of the 0–4 age-group and because the high fertility must have affected infant and maternal mortality rates significantly. Apparently, registration improved after the 1680s. In testing the completeness of baptismal registration in the early eighteenth century, Henripin found that only 1.5 per cent of the baptisms were omitted; but, as he notes, his test probably understates omission, and a few registers are missing for the period.

The extent of omissions in the number of baptisms in the seventeenth century invalidates Sabagh's estimates and increases the plausibility of Henripin's. However, even the latter's may be too low. He tested his estimated age-specific marital fertility rates, which were based on early eighteenth-century data, by applying them to the appropriate age-groups of married women in 1666, 1667, and 1681. He then compared

----

8 vols. (Montréal, Wilson et Cie, 1882–4), IV, pp. 52–78, and V, pp. 53–88, gives the nominal lists of 1666, 1667, and 1681. The calculation of the percentage of women over age 14 who were married depends on the assumptions that all married women were over that age, a highly probable assumption, and that the general summaries include the widows among the married women. This is shown by the censuses prior to 1706 whose results have been given in some detail.
[7] That the early Canadian censuses were probably far more accurate than those for most pre-industrial populations is indicated by the evidence given by A. J. Pelletier, 'Canadian censuses of the seventeenth century', *Papers and Proceedings . . . of the Canadian Political Science Association*, II (1930), pp. 20–34. His comments are relevant to the eighteenth-century censuses as well. The census of 1734 is said to have been the most accurate of the early censuses.

the number of estimated births with the observed number of baptisms in the given year. Estimated and observed totals matched closely for 1666 and 1667; however, the difference in 1681 was fairly marked: 522 estimated and 486 observed. Henripin suggested some plausible reasons which may partially account for the difference, but omissions were more than enough to make up the difference. The same factor would also affect the observed totals of 1666 and 1667 so that Henripin's estimated age-specific marital fertility rates seem too low.

Further, using his estimated age-specific marital fertility rates and his estimated percentages of married women in the various female age-groups, Henripin calculated a gross reproduction rate. Then, assuming that the French life table which was constructed by Duvillard (to be discussed shortly) was applicable to New France, he found a net repro-duction rate of 1·93, thus indicating that the population almost doubled every 30 years. That the female population did in fact double every 30

TABLE 5·1 *Percentage of women aged 15 and over who had never been married at census dates*

1681	1692*	1695*	1698*	1706	1719	1720	1721	1734	1851
21	31	32	32	32	43	43	47	37	38

* includes a small number of Indians.
Source: *Census of Canada 1870–1*, IV, pp. 11–57 and V.

years seems to confirm his estimates. The assumption about mortality may be relatively accurate; the numbers of survivors aged 0–4 in 1719 and in 1734 from the baptisms of the preceding 15 years are in the neighborhood of expectations based on that table. However, his esti-mated percentages of women who were married are probably too high. His genealogical data provide no information on the extent of nuptiality and so, using the censuses of 1666, 1667, 1681 and 1871, he estimated the percentages of married women in each age group about 1720 by interpolation. The assumption, that the fall from the seventeenth-century heights to the 1871 levels was gradual, is probably incorrect. While the census data after 1681 do not give the numbers of married women in each age group, they indicate that the decline was rapid after 1681. For 1706–34 about 40 per cent of the women over the age of 15 had never been married, or almost double the figure for 1681 and above that of 1851. Hence, if the net reproduction rate was about 1·93, as seems probable, he has underestimated marital fertility.

Hence, this brief examination of the Canadian data has shown that

Henripin's estimated age-specific marital fertility rates are more accurate than Sabagh's. But, Henripin, whose rates are quite high, apparently also erred on the side of understatement. However, the exact amount by which his rates should be corrected is unknown; hence, in the ensuing analysis, Henripin's rates will be used.

Generalizations on eighteenth-century French demography have usually been based on local data, in part life tables, which were compiled by various eighteenth-century demographers.[8] In general, the studies indicate that mortality during the last decades of the old regime was at least 33 per 1,000, and it has been frequently stated that rates had been higher in earlier periods.

Undoubtedly, the recent work has invalidated this evidence. For example, J. Bourgeois-Pichat points out that the eighteenth-century life tables are based on deaths alone.[9] For such tables to measure life expectation accurately, birth and death rates must be constant and equal over a long period. If the population was growing, as was the French after 1750, then such tables understate life expectation, and exaggerate mortality.

But even properly constructed tables would have overstated mortality in terms of modern definitions. As P. Goubert notes, still-births were often included among the deaths;[10] thus, implied comparisons between eighteenth-century and modern rates are misleading. Assuming that correct infant mortality rates were 200 per 1,000 live births and that the still-birth rate was 40 per 1,000 live births, the inclusion of the still-births among both baptisms and burials results in an infant death rate of 231 per 1,000. If they were included only among the burials, then the rate is 240 per 1,000, an exaggeration of 20 per cent. Increasing the importance of Goubert's observation, ergotism was occasionally important in rye-consuming regions during wet seasons and many epidemics cause spontaneous abortions and still-births; further complicating the comparison of eighteenth-century rates with those of later periods is the possibility of infanticide, which will be discussed later.[11]

[8] E. Levasseur, *La population française*, 3 vols. (Paris, Arthur Rousseau, 1889–92), I, pp. 251–6, and II, pp. 293–306.
[9] J. Bourgeois-Pichat, 'Evolution de la population française depuis le XVIIIe siècle', *Population*, VI (1951), pp. 635–62, 642.
[10] P. Goubert, 'Une richesse historique en cours d'exploitation. Les registres paroissiaux', *Annales: économies, sociétés, civilisations*, IX (1954), pp. 83–93, 86. Moheau, *Recherches et considérations sur la population de la France* (Paris, Librairie Paul Geuthner, 1912), p. 171, gives *mort-nés* as a major cause of death. Unfortunately, the exact meaning of the term '*mort-né*' is unknown.
[11] H. Chaumartin, *Le mal des ardents et le feu de Saint-Antoine* (Paris, 1946); H. and F. Hotelling, 'Causes of birth rate fluctuations', *Journal of the American*

Goubert has also shown that the eighteenth-century demographers erred in their local studies by including the deaths of *nourrissons* whose baptisms had been registered elsewhere, thus further falsifying infant death rates. Here again, there is a complicating factor – the foundlings, whose numbers increased sharply in the eighteenth century.[12] The children were usually sent to nurse in the countryside where indifferent care led to high death rates. Auvergne, which figures heavily in the studies of Moheau and Messance, was a favorite dumping ground for Parisian foundlings.

Of course, these qualifications to the accuracy of the traditional data apply to both life tables and crude vital rates. And in the case of the latter, another factor makes for exaggeration: incomplete census. Unless strong evidence to the contrary exists, all early censuses must be presumed to be understatements. This is especially true of eighteenth-century France where taxation bore so heavily on the lower classes and where militia service was so dreaded (some children were castrated so that they would escape it).[13] For example, those who took a census of French Flanders assumed that about 20 per cent of the populace escaped enumeration.

Although some work thus shows that the commonly cited data overstate mortality, most recent studies nonetheless reaffirm the conclusion that high death rates were the major obstacle to French demographic growth. Based on a relatively few parish registers, these studies emphasize the sharp rise in the number of deaths in 1693–4 and 1709 when burials greatly exceeded baptisms. By contrast, baptisms annually exceeded burials in the France of the 1770s, except in 1779, even

Statistical Association, XXVI (1931), pp. 25–49. Montesquieu, *Lettres persanes*, letter no. CXX and by the same author, *Esprit des lois*, Book XXVI, chapter III; J. P. Brissot de Warville and E. B. Bernardi, *Les moyens d'adoucir la rigueur des loix pénales en France* (Chalons-sur-Marne, Chez Seneuze, 1781), pp. 45, 107–9, Table 7.
[12] S. T. McCloy, *Government Assistance in Eighteenth-Century France* (Durham, Duke University Press, 1946), pp. 238–59, contains important data on both *nourrissons* and foundlings. R. Mols, *Introduction à la démographie historique des villes d'Europe du XIVe au XVIIIe siècle*, 3 vols. (Louvain, Editions J. Duculot, 1954–6), II, pp. 303–5.
[13] United Nations, *Population Census Methods* (New York, 1949), p. 13; M. Marion, *Dictionnaire des institutions de la France aux XVIIe et XVIIIe siècles* (Paris, Auguste Picard, 1923), pp. 377–9; S. T. McCloy, *The Humanitarian Movement in Eighteenth-Century France* (University of Kentucky Press, 1957), p. 212. A. des Cilleuls, 'La population française avant 1789', *Revue générale d'administration*, 1885, p. 424, n. 5.

although several serious grain shortages occurred.[14] Hence, conclude
these scholars, *crises frumentaires*, such as those of 1693–4 and 1709,
which had prevented any rapid or sustained demographic growth before
1750 no longer did so after that date.[15]

R. Baehrel proves that fluctuations in the number of deaths are affected by most of the factors which make the crude death rate such a poor
measure of mortality and that fluctuations in themselves give little data
on levels of mortality.[16] Also, it might be noted that still-births, exposure, and infanticide were probably most common during time of
hardship and thus exaggerate crisis mortality correspondingly. Therefore, the parish register studies do not prove that French mortality
had averaged more than 30 per 1,000 during the old regime.

Bourgeois-Pichat uses an intricate argument to show that mortality
was a constant 35 per 1,000 between 1700 and 1770.[17] He starts with the
life table which was constructed by E. Duvillard, a table which is based
on 2,290,672 living and 101,542 deaths. Unfortunately, Duvillard

---

[14] C. E. Labrouse, *La crise de l'économie française à la fin de l'ancien régime et
au début de la révolution* (Paris, Presses Universitaires de France, 1944), I,
pp. xxviii and 184–9; J. Meuvret, 'Les crises de subsistences et la démographie
de l'ancien régime', *Population* I (1946), pp. 643–50; J. Meuvret, 'Les mouv-
ments des prix de 1661 à 1715 et leur répercussions', *Journal de la société de
statistique de Paris*, LXXXV (1944), pp. 109–18. Goubert, *op. cit.*, and same
author, 'En Beauvaisis. Problèmes démographiques du XVIIe siècle', *Annales:
économies, sociétés, civilisations*, VII (1952), pp. 453–68. One of the arguments
is of special interest. Using data for the 1690's from the *généralités* of Rouen,
Clermont-Ferrand, Carcassonne, and the city of Roubaix, one author implies
that the crisis of 1693–4 brought about an excess of deaths over births for
France. On the other hand, France for the years 1770, 1771, 1772 and 1773, as
well as 1770–84, showed an excess of baptisms over burials, even though there
were several periods of acute shortage of grain. Yet, had the author chosen
different areas for comparison, the results would have been quite different. The
généralités of Dauphiné, Montauban and Provence, not to mention other areas,
had an excess of baptisms over burials in the 1690's. In 1778–87, on the other
hand, the *généralités* of Bretagne, Tours, Orleans, La Rochelle and Roussillon
had an excess of burials over baptisms. I should mention that Goubert does not
suggest the use of the average age of death in his latest work, 'Des registres
paroissiaux à l'histoire (indications pratiques et orientations de recherches)',
Bulletin d'histoire moderne et contemporaine (Comité des Travaux historiques et
scientifiques), 1956, pp. 5–19. His use of the average age of death was criticized
by L. Henry, 'Une richesse démographique en friche: les registres paroissiaux',
Population, VIII (1953), pp. 281–90; by R. Baehrel, 'Statistique et démographie
historique: la mortalité sous l'ancien régime. Remarques inquiètes', *Annales:
économies, sociétés, civilisations*, XII (1957), pp. 85–99, and by the same author,
'Histoire et démographie', same journal, XII (1957), pp. 629–38.
[15] I do not discuss the use of the national data for 1770–84 to estimate vital
rates. Without an adequate estimate of total population, such rates are invalid.
[16] Baehrel, *op. cit.*   [17] Bourgeois-Pichat, *op. cit.*

mentioned neither the localities nor the period covered, writing only that the data referred to the period before 1789. Bourgeois-Pichat assumed that the age-specific death rates of the life table were constant for the period 1700–70. Accepting Vauban's estimate of 19 million French in 1700 and estimates of 25 or 26 million in 1789, he concludes that the annual rate of increase was a constant four per 1,000. Hence, the population was stable (the age-specific birth and death rates were constant), and he was able to calculate the age distribution for 1770. His results agree with those obtained by P. Vincent for 1775 on the basis of other data.[18] Bourgeois-Pichat therefore concludes that the consistency of the results guarantees the validity of the assumptions which make up his argument.

Unfortunately, a large body of evidence contradicts his findings. Leaving aside the validity of the estimates for 1700 and 1789, students of the period generally agree that the population declined during the last part of the reign of Louis XIV.[19] That the population was virtually stationary between 1720 and mid-century is shown by the hearth counts and by d'Avenel's economic data.[20] Expilly's material on the baptisms and burials of over 16,000 parishes in a 12 year period, mainly 1752–63, gives a vital index (baptisms divided by burials) of 1·266, or far above the 1·079 of 1778–87. A vital index of 1·266 implies an annual rate of increase of about seven per 1,000 or higher than Bourgeois-Pichat's constant four per 1,000. Expilly's data, as E. Esmonin points out, have never been used in modern analysis; yet, with the exception of the national data for 1770–87, Expilly's is the largest sample available, dwarfing those of Messance, Moheau, and Duvillard.[21] It has the further

[18] P. Vincent, 'French demography in the eighteenth century', *Population Studies*, I (1947), pp. 44–71, 50.

[19] J. J. Spengler, *France Faces Depopulation* (Durham, Duke University Press, 1938), pp. 17–18, summarizes the findings.

[20] G. d'Avenel, *Histoire économique de la propriété, des salaires, des denrées*, 7 vols., 2nd ed. (Paris, Imprimerie nationale, 1913), III, pp. 229 and 424–44. Hearth counts place the population at 20,905,413 in 1720, 17,017,737 in 1745, and 18,017,000 in 1755. The 1720 figure has long been taken as referring to 1762, see E. Esmonin, 'L'abbé Expilly et ses travaux de statistique', *Revue d'histoire moderne et contemporaine*, IV (1957), pp. 241–80, 274; Fr. de Dainville, 'Un dénombrement inédit au XVIIIe siècle: l'enquête du Controleur générale Orry – 1745', *Population*, VII (1952), pp. 49–68; J. Conan, review of Dainville's article, *Revue d'histoire économique et sociale*, XXXII (1954), pp. 328–9. While the hearth coefficients may not have been the same for each hearth count, it is unlikely that the difference between 1720 and 1745–55 would disappear completely.

[21] The data are given in the appendices to vols. III and IV of J. J. Expilly, *Dictionnaire géographique, historique et politique des Gaules et de la France*,

advantages of widespread, known geographical and temporal coverage.

Hence, Bourgeois-Pichat's key assumption of a constant annual rate of increase of four per 1,000 is invalid. To say that the average was four per 1,000 is not enough, the rate must be constant to produce a stable population. In any case, the assumption of constant age-specific death rates is highly questionable, as shown by the Swedish evidence. Without a stable population, his estimated age distribution for 1770 is invalid. Even had he been able to derive validly an age distribution which resembled Vincent's, which was mainly based on the Burgundian census of 1786, the similarity would not be convincing.[22] Whether the 1700 Burgundian parishes in 1786 had an age distribution similar to that of the more than 40,000 French parishes of 1770 is unknown; regional variations are important today and were probably more important then. Duvillard's life table thus remains unconfirmed.

The validity of Bourgeois-Pichat's conclusions is thus doubtful as is that of other attempts to show that eighteenth-century French mortality was over 30 per 1,000. While the eighteenth-century demographers overestimated death rates, the amount by which they did so is unknown, and in any case, the typicality of their data is unknown. Therefore, eighteenth-century French data will be used only in an incidental way in the following analysis.

England has furnished the classic model of the fall of mortality, a model which is based on crude birth and death rates going back to 1700 and on explanations of the fall. However, both bases have been sharply criticized in recent writings.[23] While trends of vital rates for the period

---

6 vols. (Paris, Desaint and Saillant, 1762–70). Oddly enough, most copies of Vol. IV do not contain this appendix, as Esmonin, *op. cit.*, points out. Not having access to a Vol. IV which contained data on 8,000 parishes I am indebted to Prof. Esmonin who graciously furnished me with the missing data.

[22] Vincent, *op. cit.*, p. 51. It should also be noted that Duvillard's data undoubtedly contain still-births, foundlings, etc.

[23] K. H. Connell, 'Some unsettled problems in English and Irish population history', *Irish Historical Studies*, VII (1951), pp. 225–34; Habakkuk, *op. cit.*; J. Krause, 'Changes in English fertility and mortality, 1781–1850', *Economic History Review*, 2nd ser., XI (1958). T. McKeown and R. G. Brown, 'Medical evidence related to English population changes in the eighteenth century', *Population Studies*, IX (1955), pp. 119–41, support the traditional position. However, they deny that medical science was an important factor; their stress is on environmental improvements, an argument which I examined. The few statistics cited by McKeown and Brown are mainly for London. In addition to Habakkuk's objection to the use of London data (*op. cit.*, pp. 125–7), I might note that the statistics refer to burials in London, not to deaths of Londoners. As the city increased in size during the century, burial space became increasingly expensive and many cheap burial grounds opened outside the city. More and more burials,

1700–80 cannot be validly estimated now, fertility was probably the major demographic variable between 1781 and 1850. Previous investigators did not devote enough attention to the changing adequacy of registration of baptisms and burials. Likewise, the factors which have been used to explain the falling mortality have been rejected by most recent writers. Indeed, an examination of the probable factors which affected mortality suggests that death rates may have risen between the 1780s and 1810s. Likely causes of changes in fertility after 1780 are: industrialization with its child labor before 1833; the Speenhamland system of poor relief, which existed between 1795 and 1834; enclosure, which increased demand for labor after 1780, and others which were less important.

While marriage undoubtedly became earlier and more prevalent between 1781 and 1821, it is not possible to compute marital fertility ratios, nor is exact measurement of change possible. Even birth rates, measured on a per 1,000 basis, are risky before the 1840s; hence, the fertility ratio for England and Wales in 1821 is the only one which will be used in the subsequent discussion. While much work remains to be done on England, there is now little reason to believe that secular changes in the mortality were of great importance prior to the late nineteenth century.

The Irish evidence is in many respects poorer than the English. No statistical data exist on movements of the vital rates between 1780 and 1830, after which date evidence indicates that marriage became increasingly delayed and less prevalent. Fortunately, the census of 1841 provides data on age distribution and civil status, from which some conclusions can be extracted for later discussion of fertility and marital fertility. Connell concludes that these census results are relatively accurate and there seems to be little reason to disagree with his judgment, although some omission of children and some misstatement of age is highly probable.

While the statistical evidence leaves much to be desired, Connell's argument that the birth rate was the major variable seems to be solid, at least as solid as can be expected in the absence of statistics.[24] He shows

---

especially of the lower classes, occurred outside the limits of the Bills of Mortality; hence, a large part of the seeming decline of London's mortality during the eighteenth century is explained on the basis of the deteriorating registration of deaths.

[24] K. H. Connell, *The Population of Ireland, 1750–1845* (Oxford, Clarendon Press, 1950). Not even M. Buer argued that mortality was the major factor in Irish population growth. In a note which had no specific reference to her text she took much the same position in regard to Ireland as that taken by Connell,

that the increased cultivation of the potato, the switch from pasture to arable, the opening of new land for cultivation, and the increase of rack-renting produced parcellization of holdings. The rapid increase in the number of holdings made possible the formation of new families so that age of marriage fell and marriage became more prevalent. Such developments could not be continued indefinitely and so after 1830, or perhaps somewhat earlier, the decline in the rate of founding new families set in. On the other hand, no important data suggest that mortality declined significantly after 1780.

II

TABLE 5·2 *Average annual rates of increase (per 1,000)*

Canada, 1698–1765	27	Iceland, 1735–1800	1
Finland, 1735–1800	12	Ireland, 1781–1841	12
Sweden, 1735–1800	5	India, 1871–1941	6
Denmark, 1735–1800	3		

Sources: Census of Canada 1870–1, IV, pp. 40 and 65. Gille, *op. cit.*, p. 38. Connell, *op. cit.*, p. 25. Davis, *The Population of India and Pakistan* (Princeton, Princeton University Press, 1952), p. 27.

Evidently, the rate of growth varied considerably among pre-industrial Western societies. The Canadian rate is about as high as the highest in the world today and the U.S. rate was probably comparable. On the other hand, Iceland's is remarkably low. Whether the birth rate or the death rate explain the variations in the rate of increase is the next problem.

There are few available statistics on mortality, except for the Scandinavian countries, in which the crude death rate averaged about 28 per 1,000 during the period 1735–1800, except in Iceland where the rate was nearly 32.[25] The evidence indicates that the lowest rates of the century occurred between 1721 and 1735. While age-specific death rates are available only for Sweden, they seem to have been broadly similar in all the Northern countries, except Iceland. That the Icelandic crude death rate was only about 13 per cent higher than those of the other countries

although she did not present the wealth of supporting detail and the discriminating appreciation of the problems which he has. That many of her generalizations on Ireland contradict her position on England is obvious, see Buer, *op. cit.*, pp. 263–5.

[25] Gille, *op. cit.* The table of death rates, p. 65, contains two errors for Iceland. In 1784 and 1785 the death rates were 113·8 and 132·9 per 1,000 respectively, instead of 11·4 and 14·4 per 1,000.

is important because the average annual death rate in 1784 and 1785 was 122 per 1,000 and between 1735 and 1800 it had been over 50 per 1,000 in three other years. Because low death rates followed catastrophes, the average was not greatly different from the other countries. The Swedish data also contain a warning to those who generalize from local catastrophes to conclusions about national death rates over a long period. While the Swedish crude death rate was about 28 per 1,000 between 1735 and 1800, the death rate in the province of Värmland in 1742 was about 112 per 1,000.[26] Probably, some villages in Värmland had even higher death rates.

Other data are much more scanty and less reliable. The Canadian death rate between 1700 and 1770 was about 33 per 1,000. While this rate is about 18 per cent higher than the Scandinavian, one should not assume that hygienic or medical factors were responsible for the difference. Causes of the high Canadian crude death rates were: the large percentage of children aged 0–4 with their high death rates, the probable effect of the high fertility in raising child and maternal mortality rates (see below), and the warfare of 1740–8 and 1754–63. The death rate for England and Wales in 1811–20 was about 26–8 per 1,000, a rate which may have been somewhat lower in the 1780s. Connell's discussion suggests that the Irish death rate was not higher than 25–30 per 1,000 between 1780 and 1841. West European crude mortality thus seems far removed from the Indian average of over 40 per 1,000 between 1871 and 1940.[27]

Whether or not West European mortality in earlier periods was generally high by comparison with the rates cited above is unknown. However, some studies of the underdeveloped countries and of European economic history may shed some light on the problem. Recent investigators have stressed the importance of *chronic* shortage of food as a major cause of high mortality in the under-developed countries today.[28]

[26] Utterström, *op. cit.*, pp. 128–9.
[27] W. S. Thompson, 'La population des Etats-Unis d'Amérique', *Population*, III (1948), pp. 115–26; Krause, *Changes in English Fertility and Mortality*; Connell, *The Population of Ireland*, pp. 184–237; Henripin, *op. cit.*, p. 103.
[28] M. Cépède and M. Lengellé, *Economie alimentaire du globe* (Paris, Librairie de Medicis, 1953), esp. pp. 279–85. W. S. Thompson, *Population Problems*, 4th ed. (New York, McGraw-Hill, 1953), pp. 48–9. Both works agree that death rates which are consistently over 30 per 1,000 indicate a chronically short food supply. The generalization is not necessarily true for urban areas, but would appear to be so for most rural areas. I shall give few references on the remainder of this discussion of mortality because the points will be covered in greater detail in a forthcoming book.

Not only do most contemporary populations have insufficient calories, but a lack of animal proteins and protective foods is at least equally serious.[29] A large variety of evidence suggests that West European diets were generally far more adequate, both quantitatively and qualitatively, than are those of contemporary under-developed peoples.[30] Data compiled by E. Heckscher show that the diet of sixteenth-century Swedish agricultural servants was sufficient in calories and contained large amounts of animal proteins. While Swedish dietary levels were lower in the next two centuries, they remained well above those of the modern Indian. The Irish diet was probably adequate even by modern standards. Other data on food consumption are extremely sketchy, but it appears that medieval France and England were similar to sixteenth-century Sweden in that food was plentiful, if monotonous by our standards. No doubt there were famines, just as there were in the eighteenth century, but there is evidence to show that famine has been greatly exaggerated as a factor in demographic history.[31] This statement does not mean that there were no periods of high mortality. When contending armies ravaged the countryside, starvation and epidemics were often common, as is true to a lesser extent of the twentieth century.

An indirect approach to the problem is also possible. Students of economic growth now seem to agree that *per capita* income was greater in European countries during the early stages of industrialization than

---

[29] For an eloquent discussion of food shortage in the world, see J. de Castro, *The Geography of Hunger* (Boston, Little Brown & Co, 1952).
[30] E. F. Heckscher, *An Economic History of Sweden* (Cambridge, Mass., Harvard University Press, 1954), pp. 68–70. More detailed data are found in his *Sveriges Eknomiska Historia fràn Gustav Vasa*, 2 vols. (Stockholm, Albert Bonniers Förlag, 1936–49), II, appendix, pp. 16–19. Also see the comments made by Boëthius, *op. cit.*, pp. 155–8; Connell, *The Population of Ireland*, pp. 151–6; Krause, *Changes in English Fertility and Mortality;* C. Creighton, *A History of Epidemics in Britain*, 2 vols. (Cambridge University Press, 1891), I, p. 67; P. Boissonnade, *Life and Work in Medieval Europe* (New York, A. A. Knopf, 1927), p. 261. There is little doubt that diets in the U.S. and Canada were sufficient. Even for West European areas for which we possess little information, the chances are that dietary levels were well above those of currently under-developed peoples because the major cereal was wheat or rye and livestock and fishing played prominent roles in the economy. Most contemporary under-developed populations subsist on rice, maize, or starchy roots which tend to cause beri-beri, pellegra, or multiple deficiency diseases.
[31] A. M. Carr-Saunders, *The Population Problem* (Oxford, The Clarendon Press, 1922), p. 249; K. Davis, *The Population of India and Pakistan* (Princeton, Princeton University Press, 1949), p. 41; R. Pernoud, *Lumière du moyen âge* (Paris, B. Grasset, 1946), pp. 221–35, esp. 223.

in the under-developed countries today.[32] Yet, it is interesting to note that the second half of the eighteenth century, instead of being a period of rising levels of living as is often claimed, was one of sharply declining real wages at least in England, France, Spain, and Sweden;[33] but, even after the decline, the living levels were probably far above those of the modern Indian. Moreover, sketchy evidence suggests that relatively high real wages have been characteristic of European society at least as far back as the thirteenth century.[34] Hence, there is reason to believe that European living levels were rarely as low as those of the currently underdeveloped countries.

Where malnutrition reigns today, malaria is (or was until the recent D.D.T. campaigns) endemic and epidemic on a scale which West Europeans probably never knew.[35] The annual number of malaria cases in India has been estimated at 100,000,000. While the disease normally has a low case mortality, it causes more deaths, more sickness, and greater loss of working power than any other disease in India. And, by lowering bodily resistance, it increases the death rate from other diseases. Relatively adequate nutrition and absence of malaria are not the only factors which explain the probable low level of West European mortality, but they are in all likelihood the most important.

Thus far, I have not mentioned infant mortality, for which rates of at least 300 per 1,000 live births have often been cited as evidence of generally poor health conditions in the eighteenth century. But these rates are not as solidly based or as informative as they seem. First, accurate calculation of the infant mortality rate is difficult. Even early twentieth-century rates of the U.S. cannot be relied upon because of the

[32] S. Kuznets, 'Population, Income and Capital', in L. Dupriez (ed.), *Economic Progress* (Louvain, Institut de Recherches Economiques et Sociales, 1955), pp. 27–46.
[33] Krause, *Changes in English Fertility and Mortality*; C. E. Labrousse, *Esquisse du mouvement des prix et des revenus en France au XVIIIe siècle*, 2 vols. (Paris, Librairie Dalloz, 1933), II, pp. 362 and 492; E. J. Hamilton, *War and Prices in Spain, 1651–1800* (Cambridge, Mass., Harvard University Press, 1947), pp. 204–16; Boëthius, *op. cit.*, p. 154.
[34] P. Razous, 'L'évolution de l'agriculture française métropolitaine a travers l'histoire', *Journal de la société de statistique de Paris*, LXXXV (1944), pp. 56–85, 80. G. F. Steffen, *Studien zur Geschichte der Englischen Lohnarbeiter*, 3 vols. (Stuttgart, Hobbing and Büchle, 1905), I, p. 112. A considerable amount of statistical and non-statistical data can be cited in support of the general outline presented in these works.
[35] Davis, *op. cit.*, pp. 53–4; E. J. Pampana and P. F. Russell, 'Malaria: A World Problem', *Chronicle of the World Health Organization*, IX (1955), esp. pp. 33–94, 33–9; M. Sorre, *Les fondements biologiques de la géographie humaine*, 2 vols. (Paris, A. Colin, 1942–3), I, pp. 354–66.

deficient registration of both births and deaths. Rates for most earlier societies are even more insecure. As mentioned earlier, still-births were often included among the burials in France, as was also true for most Catholic populations, and England. While the inclusion of still-births could inflate infant mortality rates greatly, there are other factors which raise infant death rates, but which have nothing to do with health. Illegitimacy and exposure of infants became increasingly common in the course of the eighteenth century, especially in the cities where the phenomena reached amazingly high proportions – in the Paris of 1772 the number of foundlings was equal to about 40 per cent of the baptisms.[36] While the illegitimate infant mortality rate was undoubtedly far higher than the legitimate, the death rates of foundlings were incredibly high, often surpassing 500 per 1,000. Infanticide, too, is a possibility. G. Sundbärg once described the high infant mortality of rural, south Germany in the late nineteenth century as a major demographic mystery. But S. Peller, who has studied the region, believes that infanticide is the explanation; some evidence indicates that the phenomenon was also important in the eighteenth century.[37]

Second, caution must be observed in the comparison of even accurate rates. The usually cited rates refer to cities, and urban infant death rates were, like mortality in general, much higher than rural during the nineteenth century. Europe was predominantly rural so that the urban rates are misleading indicators of national rates. Further, high fertility was very possibly a cause of high infant mortality; hence, all comparisons of infant mortality rates should be accompanied by fertility rates of the populations concerned.[38] If these lines of argument are valid, a

[36] Mols, *op. cit.*, II, pp. 299–305, and III, pp. 149–50; McCloy, *Government Assistance in Eighteenth-Century France*, pp. 238–59. It has been estimated that prior to 1767 2,690 children out of 2,800 admitted annually to London workhouses did not live to be a year old. Death rates for the period after 1767 are not known.

[37] The statement is based on conversation with Dr S. Peller. Supporting his view is the fact that infant mortality rates in Bavaria, Würtemburg and Saxony seem out of proportion to the mortality of ages 1–4 and older. Brissot de Warville and Bernardi, *loc. cit.*; M. Rubin, 'Population and birth rate, illustrated from historical statistics', *Journal of the Royal Statistical Society*, LXIII (1900), pp. 596–625, 616–17. Also note the quotation from the royal speech to the Estates in 1756, Utterström, *op. cit.*, p. 146. L. Schöne, *Histoire de la population française* (Paris, Arthur Rousseau, 1893), p. 138, gives some evidence on infanticide in the seventeenth century.

[38] McKeown and Brown, *op. cit.*, p. 129; L. Henry, 'La mortalité infantile dans les familles nombreuses', *Population*, III (1948), pp. 631–47; Gille, *op. cit.*, p. 50. Gille expressed himself more definitely in conversation than he did in the article. Also, the French Canadians of the late nineteenth century had lower

number of consequences follow. The usually cited infant death rates greatly exaggerate pre-industrial European infant mortality, especially among infants born to families which wanted to keep them alive. Also, the decline of infant mortality during the nineteenth and early twentieth centuries was probably due in large part to changed social customs, particularly the decline of fertility, illegitimacy, exposure, neglect, and infanticide. Medicine has been important in the twentieth century, but its significance for earlier centuries has been exaggerated. Finally, I believe that these considerations lessen the utility of the infant death rate as a measure of general health conditions in historical demography; it should be used only with the greatest caution. In general, the evidence on mortality thus indicates that the death rate was not the primary determinant of the rate of growth – the Canadian population had the highest rate of growth and the highest crude mortality among the pre-industrial Western populations which are considered here.

While it has often been stated that postponement of marriage and the practice of celibacy was more common in the pre-industrial West European countries than in the under-developed countries today, the data in the tables stress the difference strongly.[39] Even Canada of 1681 with its large percentage of women in the marriageable age groups and a considerable excess of males over females was not able to equal the precocity of Indian marriage. As noted earlier, there are questions about the interpretation of the Canadian census of 1734, but in any case the number of celibate *canadiennes* seems very high in view of the numerous factors which tended to promote early marriage: royal pressure, economic conditions, and religious injunction.[40] Clearly, the problem needs

---

age-specific death rates for ages over 14 than did the rest of Canadians, but under the age of 14 the reverse was the case. The most obvious explanation is that the high fertility of the French Canadians caused high infant and child mortality. Another instance of this type is provided by the Hutterites, see J. W. Easton and A. J. Mayer, 'The social biology of very high fertility among the Hutterites. The demography of a unique population', *Human Biology*, XXV (1953), pp. 206–64, 237–9.

[39] F. Lorimer and others, *Culture and Human Fertility* (Paris, Unesco, 1954), pp. 164–217; Carr-Saunders, *op. cit.*, p. 264. That the marriage habits of fourteenth century Englishmen were probably not greatly different from the eighteenth century Scandinavians is suggested by J. T. Krause, 'The medieval household: large or small?', *Economic History Review*, 2nd ser., IX (1957), pp. 420–32, 431. That many tenants were unmarried in the ninth century may be inferred from the Polyptyque of the Abbot Irminon, see Schöne, *op. cit.*, p. 73.

[40] Sulte, *op. cit.*, II, p. 97; G. Langlois, *Histoire de la population canadienne-française* (Montréal, Albert Lévesque, 1934), pp. 205–6; H. Miner, 'Changes

TABLE 5·3 *Percentage of women aged 15 and over who were married, widowed or single*

Country		Marr.	Wid.	Single	Country		Marr.	Wid.	Single
India	1931	70·6	25·8	3·6	Sweden	1750	50·3	15·1	34·6
Turkey	1935	65·9	21·9	12·2	Canada	1734	62·5		37·5
Canada	1681	75·9	3·0	21·1	Ireland	1841	46·7	12·4	40·9
Finland	1751	55·6	13·7	30·7	Iceland	1703	28·3	8·5	63·2

Sources: Gille, *op. cit.*, p. 25. *Census of Canada*, 1870–1, IV, p. 57. *Census of Ireland*, 1841, pp. 438–9. *Demographic Yearbook*, 1949–50.

TABLE 5·4 *Married women as a percentage of the women in each age-group*

Country	15–9	20–4	25–9	30–4	35–9	40–4	45–9
India 1931	83·9	90·0	87·3	82·6	70·0	62·2	46·6
Turkey 1935	23·2	80·8	90·8	90·8	87·5	76·6	65·2
Canada 1681	30·7	76·9	91·7	94·8	89·8	93·4	89·6
Ireland 1841	16·8		67·3		72·4		
Sweden 1750	4·4	27·0	55·5	71·3	78·9	78·6	74·6
Iceland 1703	0·1	4·8	20·1	39·3	47·3	52·4	48·5

Sources: Sabagh, *op. cit.*, p. 689; *Census of Ireland*, 1841, pp. 483–9; Gille, *op. cit.*, p. 27. *Demographic Yearbook*, 1949–50.

more study, and abundant materials make possible such research. However, the Canadian is possibly not as unique a case as it seems. Finland had large tracts of vacant land as a result of the disasters of the Great Northern War. Yet, while the Finnish crude marriage rates were regularly higher than the Swedish, the percentage of women over age 14 who were single was not greatly different in the two countries. Even the Swedish figures may exaggerate the picture for earlier periods because in 1747 the laws against parcellization of farms had been relaxed; this development may have permitted a short period of relatively early marriages (the age of marriage rose appreciably between 1750 and 1800).[41]

The Irish and Icelandic populations are ones in which marriage had become less frequent. Connell shows that marriage had become increasingly delayed and less prevalent between 1831 and 1841. Although the

in rural French Canadian culture', *American Journal of Sociology*, XLIV (1938), pp. 365–78.
[41] B. J. Hovde, *The Scandinavian Countries, 1720–1865*, 2 vols. (Boston, Chapman and Grimes, 1943), I, pp. 286–8.

data indicate that marriage was slightly earlier in Ireland than in Sweden, there is no reason to believe that Irish marriage levels had been similar to those of the under-developed countries today. The low Icelandic figures can be attributed to the hard years of the 1690s and early 1700s. The sea around Iceland froze over in 1695 and 1696 and inland bodies of water which had not been known to freeze were solid in those years. Apparently, unfavorable conditions continued for a number of years, and perhaps worsened, because the population declined about a third between 1703 and 1708.[42] Such a decline is hardly surprising in view of the low marriage levels.

Further evidence that marriage was closely tied to ability to provide for a family is given by the very scanty evidence on class-differentials in nuptiality. The Danish census of 1787 shows that there was a direct relationship between height of social class and frequency of marriage, a finding which is corroborated by some Italian data.[43] Occasionally, legislation restricted the rights of the lower classes to marry. In the case of the English industrial workers, the laborer reached his maximum earning power early in life and prior to 1833 the child was an economic asset, not a liability. An apparent exception to the generalization is furnished by the Speenhamland areas of England, where the level of living declined sharply after 1780 and yet the age of marriage probably fell. But, it must be remembered that the unmarried laborer had difficulty in obtaining work and that the larger the family, the higher the payments to the head of the family.

As might be expected, there were considerable differences in fertility. Crude birth rates in 1735–1800 were: Sweden, 33·6; Finland, 40·7; Iceland, 33·1; and French Canada, 58·8 (for 1700–70). Evidently, nuptiality does not explain these differences. In the past, broader and more detailed comparisons have been limited by the absence of satisfactory birth data. However, in addition to the ratio of children aged 0–4 per 1,000 women of child-bearing age, which is being used increasingly in the analysis of under-developed populations, two similar rates are possible. First, the ratio of children aged 0–4 per 1,000 married women aged 15–49 makes possible an approximate measure of marital fertility. Second, to compensate for variations in the age distribution of wives, I multiplied each five year age-group (or ten year age-group in the case of Ireland) by the percentage of women who are fecund in the age group,

[42] K. Gjerset, *History of Iceland* (New York, Macmillan Company, 1925), pp. 320–2.
[43] Rubin, *op. cit.*, pp. 596–606; Mols, *op. cit.*, II, p. 222.

as estimated by L. Henry.[44] The resulting ratio of children aged 0–4 per 1,000 fecund married women, hereafter referred to as the age-weighted marital fertility rate, provides a rough measure of age-specific marital fertility and makes possible the use of large bodies of census data, which

TABLE 5·5 *Fertility as measured by census data*

Population	Children 0–4 per 1,000 women aged 15–49	Children 0–4 per 1,000 married women aged 15–49	Age-weighted marital fertility rate
Canada 1681	1,174	1,632	1,942
Sweden 1750	511	997	1,391
Finland 1751	681	—	—
Iceland 1703	245	882	1,366
England 1821	605	—	—
Ireland 1841	595	1,451a	1,746a
India 1931b	629	779	934
Turkey 1935	720	948	1,187

a. The figures are for women aged 15–44. Comparable figures for Sweden are 1,175 and 1,472 and for Canada are 1,661 and 1,980 respectively. b. I have used the census of 1931 rather than that of 1951 because Davis, *op. cit.* has commented on the accuracy of the earlier census and because difficulties of partition may have affected some of the results of the later census.
Sources: Sabagh, *op. cit.*, p. 689. Gille, *op. cit.*, pp. 56–9. Krause, *op. cit. Census of Ireland, 1841*, pp. 438–9. *Demographic Yearbook, 1949–50.*

otherwise are not useful in this connection. With the exception of Canada and Finland, all populations in the table previously had fertility rates which were below those of India and Turkey. However, omitting Iceland, the West European countries, for which data were available, had higher ratios of children aged 0–4 per 1,000 married women aged 15–49 than do India or Turkey. Finally the age-weighted marital ferti-lity rates of the West European populations are higher, often far higher, than those of India or Turkey. The Canadian is more than double the Indian and errors in the data are unlikely to account for much of the difference.

[44] L. Henry, *Fecondité des mariages. Nouvelle méthode de mesure*, cahier no. 16 of the Institut National d'Etudes Démographiques (Paris, Presses Universitaires de France, 1953), p. 99. The ratio of children aged 0–4 per 1,000 women aged 15–49 is discussed by R. R. Kuczynski, *The Measurement of Population Growth* (London, Sidgwick and Jackson, 1935), pp. 96–9. My suggested rates, in addition to the qualifications noted by Kuczynski, do not take illegitimacy nor the reproductive activity of recently widowed women into account. However, these factors are not important enough to explain the differences which will be discussed shortly.

While the rates in both tables are likely to be too low, the height of the Hutterite and Canadian fertility rates is surprising. Especially surprising because many Hutterite women over the age of 35 possibly have had hysterectomies or other sterilizing operations,[45] and as mentioned earlier, the Canadian rates for the early eighteenth century are probably

TABLE 5·6 *Annual age specific marital fertility rates (per 1,000 women) for selected populations*

Population	15–9	20–4	25–9	30–4	40–4	45–9	Total fertility ratio
Hutterites, 20th century	574	554	510	450	219	38	13·7
Canada, about 1720	492	510	496	484	231	30	13·3
Sweden 1775–1800	522	467	382	323	121	29	10·3
Bengali areas (rural) 1945–6	118	323	288	282	100	33	6·8

Sources: J. W. Eaton and A. J. Mayer, *op. cit.*, p. 230. Henripin, *op. cit.*, p. 73. Gille, *op. cit.*, p. 31. Lorimer, *op. cit.*, pp. 25–7. Lorimer gives similar data for other under-developed societies which are broadly similar to the Indian.

too low. Among the modern Hutterites and the French Canadians in 1681 almost all women over the age of 20 were married; hence, there is no ground for the belief that only the most fertile women were married. That the high Hutterite and French Canadian rates were caused by some unknown genetic factor seems improbable (see below).

But the contrast between the West European populations and the modern Indian, which is broadly typical of many under-developed countries today is very striking. Clearly, J. de Castro's argument that there is an inverse relationship between consumption of animal proteins and fecundity is invalid.[46] The West European populations which are included in both tables had higher intakes of animal protein and more balanced diets than those of most underdeveloped countries of today. However, de Castro's suggestion that nutrition affects fecundity is important.

Experiments on animals show that well-balanced diets result in earlier sexual maturation, increased chances of pregnancy and of giving birth to healthy offspring, and a longer period of reproductive activity than do inadequate diets. While data on human beings can rarely be obtained

[45] Eaton and Mayer, *op. cit.*, pp. 254–5.
[46] J. de Castro, *op. cit.*, pp. 70–2, and particularly 162–3. Some have assumed that de Castro's argument is a correlation between protein consumption and fertility, but his main point is that large amounts of proteins reduce the ability to have children.

under experimental conditions, abundant evidence indicates that well-balanced diets promote high human fecundity.[47]

One of de Castro's arguments should be examined in more detail. He rightfully argues that a shortage of animal proteins is a major cause of malfunctioning of the liver, perhaps the most common nutritional disorder in the world today, and that a defective liver fails to inactivate estrogens, which are important female sex hormones. He concludes that malnourished women, having an excess of estrogens, are more fecund than the well-fed women of advanced countries. While the consequences of an excess of estrogens are not well understood, de Castro's thesis is probably invalid. It has been argued that dysfunctional uterine bleeding, which is so common among malnourished women (thus rendering them at least temporarily sterile), is a long-term result of an excess of estrogens.[48] On the other hand, Gilman and Gilman reject this explanation on the ground that malnutrition should cause a sharp drop in the production of estrogen. On the basis of their own clinical studies, they point out that liver disease is frequently associated with amenorrhea and a small uterus, both symptoms of estrogen deficiency and low fertility.[49] Then, de Castro does not discuss the effect of an excess of estrogens on the male. In the U.S. it has been estimated that 40 per cent of all barrenness in marriage is caused by male infertility. There is evidence which shows that the upsetting of the balance between estrogen and testosterone results in disturbed spermatogenesis and finally in the destruction of reproductive tissue.[50]

Some indirect evidence which suggests that nutritional diseases lower Indian fertility is given by K. K. Mathen, who points out that the ratio of children aged 0–4 per 100 women aged 15–44 was generally low in the

[47] The references are so numerous that I shall cite only a few of those which I found to be most pertinent. C. Mazer and S. L. Israel, *Diagnosis and Treatment of Menstrual Disorders and Sterility*, 3rd ed. (New York, P. B. Hoeber, 1951), *passim*; M. G. Wohl and R. S. Goodhart (eds.), *Modern Nutrition in Health and Disease* (Philadelphia, Lea and Febeger, 1955), *passim*, and in some ways most important, J. Gilman and T. Gilman, *Perspectives in Human Nutrition* (New York, Grune and Stratton, 1951), *passim*. On nutritional diseases in India, see Davis, *op. cit.*, pp. 58–61. De Castro cited the experiments conducted by Slonaker on rats as evidence of the deleterious effects of animal proteins on fecundity. But these experiments were carried out in the 1930s before many amino acids were known. It is now clear that the feeding of incomplete proteins often results in great damage. A well balanced diet is necessary, see Wohl and Goodhart, *op. cit.*, pp. 113 and 136. I am indebted to Dean T. S. Sutton for advice on the animal experiments.

[48] Mazer and Israel, *op. cit.*, pp. 323–4.

[49] Gilman and Gilman, *op. cit.*, pp. 424 and 434.

[50] *ibid.*, pp. 426 and 496; Mazer and Israel, *op. cit.*, p. 462.

rice-consuming areas, where the possibility of malnutrition was greatest; for example, the ratio was only 55 in South India, whereas in the wheat-eating North-west it was 76.[51] His data do not take nuptiality into account, but the age-weighted marital fertility rate of the Punjab was nearly 40 per cent higher than that of Madras in 1931.

Disease also reduces the fertility of many under-developed populations today. In modern American fertility clinics patients are given a complete physical examination because even local infections sometimes impair fecundity.[52] While no satisfactory morbidity statistics exist for the populations with which this paper is concerned, the severe malnutrition of the under-developed countries indicates that morbidity is probably higher in those populations than it was in the early European. And there are some diseases, such as malaria, yellow fever, yaws, syphilis, and gonorrhea, which are especially significant in sterility and which are now far more widespread than they ever appear to have been in Europe. As has been mentioned above, prior to the recent anti-mosquito campaign, India had about 100,000,000 cases of malaria annually, which probably increased both permanent and temporary sterility to a significant extent.[53] Also, quinine, which was important in the treatment of malaria in India, impairs fertility temporarily. While malnutrition and infectious disease by no means exhaust the list of factors which probably lower the marital fertility of the under-developed countries, they are probably the most important factors.[54]

[51] K. K. Mathen, 'Rice diet and population trends', *Indian Journal of Medical Research*, XLIV (1956), pp. 491–9, 498.
[52] Lane-Roberts, *op. cit.*, pp. 146–51; Mazer and Israel, *op. cit.*, pp. 140 and 411; J. Macloed, 'Effect of chickenpox and pneumonia on semen quality', *Fertility and Sterility*, II (1951), pp. 523–33.
[53] Mazer and Israel, *op. cit.*, pp. 462–3; Lane-Roberts, *op. cit.*, pp. 146–51; Pampana and Russell, *op. cit.*, pp. 35–6; *Census of India*, 1951, Vol. I, Part 1.A, p. 132.
[54] C. V. Kiser, 'Fertility trends and differentials among non-whites in the United States', *Millbank Memorial Fund Quarterly*, XXXVI (1958), pp. 149–97, 190–6, ascribes a large part of the amazing increase of non-white fertility since 1940 to improved health conditions, particularly the reduction of venereal disease (which is so widespread in many under-developed countries). Among the factors which would also affect fertility are length of nursing period, the non-marriage of widows, and taboos on sexual activity at various periods. There is little information on the length of the lactation period in the different regions of India. One can get widely varying estimates: World Health Organization, 'Infant nutrition in the sub-tropics and tropics', *Chronicle*, IX (1955), pp. 217–28, and H. Peters, S. Israel and S. Purshottam, 'Lactation period in Indian women: duration of amenorrhea and vaginal and cervical cytology', *Fertility and Sterility* (1958), pp. 134–44. One would think that a short period is probable because of the effect of malnutrition on ability to lactate. If Davis is correct in

It will be noted that the Irish age-weighted marital fertility rate is not far below that of French Canada in 1681. Rural Ireland had a rate of 1811 (based on ages 15–44), which is even closer to the Canadian total and is almost twice the Indian. It is probable that the omission of Irish children was greater than that of the Canadian, thus further closing the gap. While other evidence indicates that Irish marital fertility was extremely high, the height is quite impressive because several factors possibly decreased fecundity. Food shortages were relatively frequent in the 1830s, health conditions were deteriorating, and probably an increased number of Irish husbands went to England in search of work. That Irish marital fertility rates nonetheless remained extremely high is evidence that the Hutterite and Canadian marital fertility rates were not the result of peculiar genetic traits.

Before considering the Swedish age-specific fertility rates, a brief examination of recent comments on birth control is necessary. A number of writers, among them Gille and Goubert, have suggested that birth control was important among some pre-industrial European populations.[55] Gille shows that the number of births per 1,000 existing marriages was consistently higher in eighteenth-century Finland than in the other Scandinavian countries and that a close association is found between economic fluctuations and annual variations in the birth rate. Considering that Canadian marital fertility was probably much higher than the Finnish, Gille's conclusion that birth control was important in eighteenth-century Scandinavia seems sound. Goubert, basing himself on the sharp decline of conceptions during periods of hard times, suggests that primitive methods of birth control were used at least as early as the 1630s. If it were true that birth control was used in combination with postponement of marriage to control fertility, then one could easily understand the seeming fact that West European living levels have long been higher than those prevailing in the under-developed countries today.

The lowness of Swedish age-specific marital fertility rates, by comparison with the Canadian, confirms Gille's contention (Norwegian and Danish marital fertility appears to have been very similar to the Swedish). It is unlikely that differences in dietary and health levels account for the dissimilarity between Scandinavian and Canadian marital fertility. The decline between age-groups 20–4 (or 25–9 for that matter) and

---

believing that the taboo on the remarriage of Hindu widows reduces fertility then there is another reason to believe that improved health will raise fertility.
[55] Gille, *op. cit.*, pp. 31 and 39; Goubert, *Une richesse historique*, pp. 90–2.

35–9 is far more marked than for other populations in the table and is similar to that shown by many populations which practise birth control. Then, there is evidence to show that abortion was widespread, that prolonged nursing of infants was sometimes practised to reduce fecundity, and that Danish women occasionally resorted to 'prostitutes' devices' to prevent conception.[56] The Scandinavian example is important because a money economy, a capitalistic spirit, and urbanization, so often cited as causes of birth control, were conspicuously unimportant. Rather, it seems that peasants desiring to maintain a given level of living acted to restrain reproduction. Without such a reduction of fertility, the rate of natural increase would have been two or three times as great as it was. If a peasant society, such as that of Scandinavia, practised birth control on a significant scale, there is certainly no *a priori* ground for believing that it could not have been done at earlier periods.

There is other evidence on birth control. R. Mols presents ratios of baptisms to marriages, a crude measure of marital fertility, for a large number of European cities at different periods between 1500 and 1800.[57] Taking all the rates together, the median is slightly under 3·9, a ratio which is virtually the same as the Swedish. More important data are furnished by nine Prussian territories for different periods of the late seventeenth and the first half of the eighteenth century.[58] The median for these 'territory-time' units is about 3·84 baptisms per marriage; interestingly enough, the ratios tend to rise between the 1690s and the 1750s. Slightly more than 80 per cent of the units had four baptisms or less per marriage. Going back much further, medieval French and Italian sermons frequently denounced the parishioners for having small families.[59]

---

[56] Rubin, *op. cit.*, p. 617; Hovde, *op. cit.*, II, p. 759. Although not mentioned by Hovde one would suspect that *coitus interruptus* was used. Apparently, it was the major means of controlling fertility in nineteenth-century France, and is still important in some countries. On abortion in France, see Montesquieu, *Lettres persanes*, letter no. CXX.

[57] Mols, *op. cit.*, III, pp. 216–23.

[58] R. Price, *Observations on Reversionary Payments*, 4th ed., 2 vols. (London, T. Cadell, 1783, II), pp. 313–16. Price took the data from P. Süssmilch, *Die Göttliche Ordnung in den Veränderungen des menschlichen Geschlechts . . .*, 3rd ed., (Berlin, 1765).

[59] J. Michelet, *Satanism and Witchcraft* (New York, The Citadel Press, 1939), pp. 112 and 161, not only mentions the French medieval sermons, but he points out that a considerable number of sixteenth-century peasants knew that cold douches prevent conception. For the information on the Italian sermons I am indebted to Prof. R. Lopez (personal communication). Much is sometimes made of the silence of historical sources as evidence that birth control was not prac-

The lowness of the Icelandic levels of nuptiality obviously resulted in very low fertility rates and in a low ratio of children aged 0–4 per 1,000 women aged 15–49; however, the age-weighted marital fertility rate is similar to the Swedish. If the annual age-specific marital fertility rates of Sweden in 1775–1800 are applied to the Icelandic data of 1703, one finds a birth rate of about 16 per 1,000. Such rates may have existed prior to 1703. The lowness of the birth rate apparently played a major role in the decline of the Icelandic population at this time. Yet, it is striking that even in time of great hardship, the Icelandic age-weighted marital fertility rate was still significantly higher than that of the contemporary Indian and was as high as the Swedish.

III

The most obvious feature of the foregoing analysis is the great variation in fertility. The French Canadians and the Hutterites maintained higher birth rates over far longer periods than has been thought possible. On the other hand, Scandinavian birth rates (except the Finnish), averaged 30–3 per 1,000, or lower than the 40 per 1,000 usually postulated for pre-industrial west European populations. The Icelandic birth rate was probably about 16 per 1,000 around 1703 and certainly played an important role in the decline of the population. A range in 'normal' birth rates of 30 to 60 per 1,000 is far wider than demographers have considered possible for pre-industrial populations of the West.

To some extent, differences in fertility were caused by variations in nuptiality. The difference in Western societies is striking, for example, that between Iceland in 1703 and Canada of 1681. Yet, nuptiality does not account for all the observed differences, marital fertility also varied considerably. Because nutrition and health probably played relatively slight roles in reducing fecundity and because there is evidence on abortion and the prevention of conception, it is likely that some pre-industrial West Europeans practised family limitation. Had they not

tised. While a variety of factors might explain such silence, one should remember that the subject of birth control is still taboo in many quarters and that some important writers have implied that it is inconsequential in the advanced countries of the twentieth century. J. Brownlee, 'The history of the birth and death-rates in England and Wales taken as a whole from 1570 to the present time', *Public Health*, XXIX (1916), pp. 211–22, and 228–38 was considered by many to be the authoritative work on English historical demography, but one of the main points of the article was to show that long-term variations in racial physiology can explain changes in the birth rate. Also, de Castro does not seem to ascribe much importance to contraception. Others could also be cited.

done so, rates of increase would have greatly exceeded economic growth.

There is thus ground for the tentative hypothesis that the birth rate was the major determinant of population growth in pre-industrial Western societies. That population growth was slight between the middle ages and 1800 may be explained by restrictions placed on marriage and on marital fertility, restrictions which were tightened during time of crisis. On the other hand, when conditions for rapid economic expansion became favorable (to over-simplify somewhat), the restrictions became less effective, as in French Canada, Ireland after 1780, England of the early industrial revolution, and probably the U.S. Successful operation of these restraints on fertility generally prevented the arable land–man ratio from deteriorating to the point found in most under-developed countries today. I do not mean to imply that other variables were not operative, but I think that the demographic traits of Western society were favorable to the maintenance of relatively high levels of living, which in turn made for lower death rates than are found in most of the under-developed countries today.

If this tentative hypothesis is correct, several important consequences follow. First, contrary to the point which is sometimes made, mortality did not necessarily prevent the growth of high densities of population in European society prior to 1800. In so far as *grandes mortalités* occurred, we should expect that fluctuations of total population, fertility, and mortality would have been marked. Hence, use of the S curve or stable population analysis is likely to be invalid, unless there is good reason to believe that conditions had been relatively constant for the period which is being discussed. Second, if birth rates had customarily been in the low thirties, the age distribution would have contained a higher percentage of persons in the economically active age-groups than is suggested by the usual estimates. Also, if the argument on mortality is correct, it would probably follow that the European labor force was more active and more efficient than those of the contemporary under-developed societies.

Third, the accepted explanation of the spread of birth control after the 1870s, a response to urbanization and industrialization, may have to be modified. Some writers have noted that the Catholic French of the early 1800s, although engaged primarily in agriculture and the traditional handicraft production, apparently restricted family size. However, this phenomenon either has been dismissed as a recent occurrence, possibly stimulated by the Napoleonic Code, or left unexplained. While the position of early nineteenth-century France is anomalous in the traditional description of Europe's demographic past, it poses no such problem for the hypothesis suggested in this paper. If West Europeans had long been accustomed to the practise of family limitation, both by postponement or avoidance of marriage and by limiting marital fertility, the problem is to explain the partial breakdown of those practices in some countries at some times. Looked at from this position, the rapid decline in Western fertility after 1880 is a reversion to earlier customs which had fallen into disuse, customs which could then be carried out more efficiently with improved devices.

Fourth, the foregoing points indicate that West Europeans on the eve of industrialization were in a much more favorable position than are most underdeveloped countries today. As a result of the high mortality and of relatively low fecundity, marriage is earlier and more frequent in those countries than it had generally been among pre-industrial West Europeans. Hence, there is the possibility that improved nutrition and health will increase birth rates fantastically.[60] While nutritional improvements may not come rapidly, there is always the possibility of a breakthrough by means of chlorella, leaf protein,[61] or other means. And, in the immediate future the reduction, and possibly eradication, of malaria and some other diseases in many regions should raise the fecundity of the inhabitants. Without a tradition of restricting births by means of delayed marriage and of birth control, it may be extremely difficult to cope with the problems created by rising fertility – the problems are arduous enough now. As Shri R. A. Gopalaswami points out, reduction of improvident maternity will be difficult and costly,[62] and it may well be that modernization programs will have to stress postponement of marriage, celibacy, and birth control much more heavily than they have done in the past.

However, the tentative hypothesis that fertility was the primary determinant of demographic growth in the pre-industrial and early industrial West is far from having been proved, and it may be incorrect. Many gaps exist in our knowledge of even nineteenth-century demographic phenomena. The exaggerated emphasis on medicine and hygiene has made research on fertility seem unnecessary. As a result, we know far too little

[60] There are several recent instances in which improved health has been cited as a partial explanation of increased fertility: Lorimer, *op. cit.*, pp. 137–9; United Nations, *The Population of Central America (including Mexico)*, 1950–80 (New York, 1954), p. 9; Kiser, *op. cit.*, pp. 190–6.
[61] N. W. Pirie, 'World hunger as a biochemical problem', *Journal of the Royal Society of Arts*, CVI (1958), pp. 511–28.
[62] *Census of India*, 1951, I, Part 1.A, pp. 216–28.

about variations in age of marriage, degree of celibacy, size of completed family, and birth control. As Henripin and Henry have demonstrated, age-specific marital fertility rates and other refined measures can occasionally be obtained from parish registers and genealogies. And the many early censuses, which have thus far yielded little precise information, may be analyzed by means of the age-weighted marital fertility rate and methods which have been devised by the Population Division of the U.N. If rates and methods were the only knowledge required, perhaps the analysis could be carried out quickly. Unfortunately, questions of typicality and causes necessitate comprehensive knowledge of the population which is being studied. While the problems are thus difficult, their solution may help clarify important problems of the twentieth century.

5.2 Implications of the demographic history of developed countries for present-day under-developed nations

RICHARD A. EASTERLIN

In a recent issue, John T. Krause has raised the specter that improved nutrition and health in the under-developed countries 'will increase birth rates fantastically'.[1] Coupled with the present and prospective declines in mortality in these countries this would pose a formidable prospect indeed for solution of 'the population problem', and the argument therefore calls for careful evaluation. The available historical evidence provides one basis for such appraisal, and the purpose of the present note is to point to one case in which the evidence conflicts with Krause's hypothesis.

Krause's argument itself rests on the use of historical data. His analysis cannot be fully summarized here, but the principal burden of the argument – and the part with which the present note is concerned – involves a comparison of the pre-industrial situation of more developed Western areas with the current situation in under-developed nations. This is perhaps a rather generous description of the procedure, since a number of the examples, such as the twentieth-century Hutterites, Iceland, mid-nineteenth-century Ireland, and the French Canadians, are rather suspect from the point of view of 'typicality'. Indeed, if, after eliminating such problematical evidence, one traces the argument through from table to table in Krause's paper (that is, from Tables 5·3 through 5·6, which comprise the heart of his analysis), one concludes that it rests virtually on a comparison of pre-industrial Sweden with present-day India.

Richard A. Easterlin (1960) *Comparative Studies in Society and History*, II, (The Hague), pp. 374–8.
[1] John T. Krause, 'Some implications of recent research in demographic history', p. 182, (present volume).

The essential steps in the argument are as follows:

1 In present-day under-developed countries there are proportionately more persons married than in the pre-industrial stage of the more developed nations. Moreover, of particular importance for fertility, the age at marriage is much lower.

2 At a given age, the fertility of marriage in present-day under-developed countries is considerably less than in the pre-industrial stage of more developed nations. This is presumably due to poor health and nutrition rather than the operation of conscious controls over fertility, which, it is argued, were already in operation in the pre-industrial stage of the developed nations.

3 Hence the improvement of health and nutrition in the under-developed areas is likely to precipitate a rise in marital fertility, and given the greater extent and earlier age at marriage, birth rates may increase fantastically.

Since a central feature of the analysis is the distinctive marriage pattern in present-day under-developed countries, one is naturally led, in attempting to evaluate the argument, to search for examples of more developed countries where pre-industrial marriage patterns were closer to those of current under-developed nations. One area where such cases can be found is Eastern and Southeastern Europe.

Tables 5·7 and 5·8 present the relevant figures for Bulgaria, a nation for which data were readily accessible, for comparison with Krause's figures for Sweden and India. It will be noted that in Bulgaria in 1934, 71 per cent of the women over 15 years of age were married, a figure identical with that for India, and much higher than that of Sweden in 1750. With regard to age at marriage, the percentage of women married at an early age in Bulgaria was considerably higher than in Sweden. It is true, though, that the percentage married in Bulgaria was less than in India for the important age groups 15–19 and 20–24, though not, it should be noted, for the later age groups. However, examination of the data for the countries covered in the United Nations *Demographic Yearbook*, the source for the figures, shows India to be at one extreme of a frequency distribution of countries by percentage of women married at given ages, rather than representative of the underdeveloped countries. For example, for the age group 15–19, there are only two other areas, Korea and Mozambique, for which the proportion of women married exceeds even 40 per cent. By comparison with the more typical pattern for the under-developed nations covered in the Yearbook, the Bulgarian

TABLE 5·7 *Married women as a percentage of women in specified age group*

	15 and over	15–19	20–24	25–29	30–34	35–39	40–44	45–49
Sweden, 1750	50	4	27	56	71	79	79	75
Bulgaria, 1934	71	17	65	88	92	93	90	84
India, 1931	71	84	90	87	83	70	62	47

Sources: Sweden and India – Krause, *op. cit.*, p. 172 (figures have been rounded). Bulgaria – United Nations, *Demographic Yearbook, 1954*, p. 51 (Southern Dobruja is excluded).

TABLE 5·8 *Average annual age specific marital fertility rates per 1,000 women*

	15–19	20–24	25–29	30–34	40–44	45–49
Sweden, 1775–1800	522	467	382	323	121	29
Bulgaria, 1906–10 (est. range)	24–141	302–465	356–405	303–329	129–143	58–69
Bengali areas (rural), 1945–46	118	323	288	282	100	38

Sources: Sweden and India – Krause, *op. cit.*, p. 175. Bulgaria – for each age group the estimate was made by dividing the 1906–10 figure for births per 1,000 women by the estimated percentage of the group married. The latter was not known for 1906–10 and had to be estimated. On the assumption that in 1906–10 the percentage of women married in each age group was higher than in 1934, two calculations were made, one on the basis of the actual 1934 age specific figures for percentage of women married, the other, assuming the percentage married was 100 per cent in each age group. The results yield a range within which the 1906–10 marital fertility rates would fall if the assumption is correct that the percentage of women married in each age group was higher in 1906–10 than in 1934. If one reasoned that the 1906 figures for percentage of women married were perhaps not much different than in 1934, the true 1906–10 marital fertility rates would lie near the upper limit of the range. But account should be taken of the fact that the present calculation assigns illegitimate as well as legitimate births to married women, and this tends to bias upwards the estimated marital fertility rates. The basic data are from L'Institut National d'Etudes Démographiques. *Le Mouvement Naturel de la Population dans le Monde de 1906 a 1936* (1954), p. 82 and United Nations, *Demographic Yearbook 1954*, p. 51.

figures for percentages of women married at these early ages are not out of line at all. Finally, while exact figures for age-specific marital fertility in Bulgaria at a pre-industrial date are not available, the rough approximations that can be made of the pre-World War I situation, suggest levels at the early ages falling somewhere between those given for India and pre-industrial Sweden (Table 5·8).

On the whole, then, the evidence suggests a pattern for Bulgaria approximating more closely that for India than does the pre-industrial situation of Sweden. Much of what has been said to characterize the situation of present-day under-developed nations might have been said of Bulgaria prior to World War I – more frequent and earlier age at marriage coupled with lower fertility of marriage, presumably due to poor health and nutrition. What then, was the course of fertility in Bulgaria from World War I on, a period during which Bulgaria may be considered to have entered, however haltingly, into the process of modern development? Did the birth rate rise fantastically?

Table 5·9 tells the story. The birth rate did not rise, but fell. In 1906–10, the crude birth rate was 42·1, one of the highest in Europe and quite comparable to the levels in underdeveloped areas today. By 1935–9 it had dropped to 24·2, and by 1955–6 to 19·8. Moreover, the decline was exceedingly sharp in comparison with the experience of some of the older developed nations. Thus the United Nations figures show a decline from around 39·6 in the early twenties to 24·2 in the late thirties, an average drop in the rate of about a point per year.

TABLE 5·9 *Annual average crude birth rate per 1,000, Bulgaria, 1906–10 to 1955–56*

Period	Birth rate	Period	Birth rate
1906–10	42·1	1920–24	39·6
1911–15	38·8	1925–29	34·2
1916–20	26·5	1930–34	30·3
1921–25	39·0	1935–39	24·2
		1940–44	22·1
		1945–49	24·6
		1950–54	21·6
		1955–56	19·8

Sources: 1906–10 through 1921–25 – L'Institut National d'Etudes Démographiques, *op. cit.*, p. 72. 1920–24 through 1955–56, United Nations, *Demographic Yearbook, 1954*, pp. 258–259, and *Demographic Yearbook, 1958*, p. 213. Before 1941, Southern Dobruja is excluded.

This one example does not of course constitute conclusive refutation of Krause's hypothesis. There is need for bringing more countries into the comparison and for more intensive examination of the underlying factors in the various situations. It is worth noting, however, that the patterns for other countries in this area, such as Russia and Yugoslavia, would probably prove to be much like that of Bulgaria. Indeed, in searching for insights into prospective demographic trends in under-developed areas, one wonders at the relative neglect of countries such as these, where precipitous declines in fertility are known to have occurred. Certainly they would seem to call for thorough study along with the experience of older developed nations.

5.3 On the possibility of increasing fertility in the under-developed nations

JOHN T. KRAUSE

In the last issue Richard A. Easterlin criticized some arguments which I have advanced. Because I think that his main point is at least partially irrelevant, I shall briefly summarize my argument. I suggested that demographic growth in the pre-industrial West was determined primarily by levels of fertility, levels which depended in large part on economic factors, and that mortality has been the major variable in the demographic growth of most less developed countries today mainly because they do not control fertility in the interest of the maintenance of a given standard of living. From this basic difference, I drew a number of consequences. Among them, but by no means the most important, was the one to which Easterlin devoted most attention. It was my statement: 'Hence, there is the possibility that improved nutrition and health will increase birth rates fantastically.'[1] Easterlin omitted the first six words of the sentence from his quotation.

After implying, without evidence, that many of my historical statistics were atypical, Easterlin devoted himself mainly to an examination of Bulgarian statistics. Using the census of 1934, he pointed out that female marriage was about as early and as frequent as that found in most under-developed countries today. Also, his estimated Bulgarian age-specific marital fertility rates for 1906-10 were broadly similar to the modern Indian. Without evidence he presumed that the low Bulgarian marital fertility rates were the result of poor health and malnutrition, as may be the case in India. Having satisfied himself that Bulgaria was quite similar

John T. Krause (1960) *Comparative Studies in Society and History*, II, (The Hague), pp. 485-7.
[1] J. T. Krause, 'Some implications of recent work in historical demography', p. 182, (present volume).

to most under-developed countries today, he asked: 'What then, was the course of fertility in Bulgaria from World War I on, a period during which Bulgaria may be considered to have entered, however haltingly, into the process of modern development?'[2] Not surprisingly, he found that birth rates fell sharply between 1920–24 and 1935–39 and concluded that he had provided a partial refutation of my 'hypothesis'.

Even if his argument were valid, it would of course not be a refutation of the statement which I made. I did not write that *all* newly developing populations would have rising fertility, and I have cited some instances of rising fertility.[3] Then, as a refutation of my suggestion that economic growth might bring increased birth rates, Easterlin cited Bulgaria whose birth rates fell at a time when per capita real incomes were probably *falling*.[4] If anything, his figures may show that Bulgarian birth rates were much affected by economic factors. And his assertion that the low marital fertility rates resulted from the same causes as the Indian seems most improbable.[5] Some Bulgarian statistics which Easterlin did not cite may shed further light on the matter.

It will be noted that birth and marriage rates went up. Further, there is no evidence that Bulgarian death rates were at levels which were found in most modern less developed countries before the advent of modern methods of public health, methods which could hardly have affected Bulgarian death rates of the late nineteenth and early twentieth centuries.

[2] R. A. Easterlin, 'Implications of the demographic history of developed countries for present-day under-developed nations', p. 188 (present volume).

[3] Krause, p. 182. Also, the rise in the birth rates in the formerly malarial regions of Ceylon from 39 to 50 per 1,000 is impressive, if not fantastic. Ceylon, Department of Census and Statistics, *Fertility Trends in Ceylon*, Monograph no. 3 (Government Press, 1954). I am indebted to Dr Sarkar for this last reference.

When I wrote my article, I had not yet seen L. Henry's 'Charactéristiques démographiques des pays sous-développés: Natalité, Nuptialité, Fécondité', in *Le 'Tiers Monde', Sous-développement et développement*, ed. G. Balandier (Paris, Presses Universitaires de France, 1958), pp. 138–49. Henry also finds some cause for alarm, although his emphasis is somewhat different from mine. I would agree that in some countries various customs limit fertility and that modernization may break down these customs. Another work on customs and fertility is A. M. Carr-Saunders, *The Population Problem* (Oxford, Clarendon Press, 1922).

[4] H. Prost, *La Bulgarie de 1912 à 1930* (Paris, Editions Pierre Roger, 1932), especially p. 219. Colin Clark, *The Conditions of Economic Progress*, 2nd ed. (London, Macmillan, 1951), pp. 160–1.

[5] Bulgaria was probably more like Turkey than India and Turkish marital fertility seems to have been about 25 per cent higher than the Indian, see Table 5·5 of my article.

It may well be that Easterlin has discovered another population type, one which is somewhat similar to my pre-industrial Western, but differs in that it was geared to a different standard of living and in that marital fertility was controlled more than marriage. However, it is also possible that the break-up of the large estates and the sharing of the *zadruga* lands

TABLE 5·10 *Bulgarian crude marriage, birth, and death rates (per 1,000)*

Period	Marriage rate	Birth rate	Death rate
1888–90	8·4	36·3	19·2
1891–95	8·2	37·6	27·8
1896–1900	8·3	41·0	23·9
1901–05	10·0	40·7	22·5
1906–10	9·3	42·1	23·8

Sources: Bulgarie, Direction Générale de la Statistique, *Mouvement de la population dans le Royaume de Bulgarie en 1912* (Sofia, 1923), p. VII.

after the end of Turkish misrule in combination with partible inheritance led to earlier and more frequent marriage.[6] The Slavic countries clearly need *detailed* investigation by people who know the languages and who are familiar with the cultures.

In regard to his dismissal of many of my historical statistics on the ground that they 'are rather suspect from the point of view of "typicality"' (his quotation marks around the word 'typicality'),[7] I can only say that it is difficult to reply to a remark of this kind. It is true that they are suspect in the light or darkness of the traditional hypothesis of demographic transition, but I am criticizing that hypothesis. On the other hand, I fully agree with Easterlin that India is an extreme instance, but I think that extreme instances are sometimes of great analytical value, especially when they have data for long periods of time. I do not think that the world's second largest population is as irrelevant as Easterlin seems to imply. Finally, I used statistics from only a relatively few countries because I knew something about materials with which to interpret the statistics – disembodied demography can be misleading.

[6] This supposition, and it is no more than that, is based on W. E. Moore, *Economic Demography of Eastern and Southern Europe* (Geneva, League of Nations, 1945), pp. 250–2.
[7] Easterlin, p. 185.

6 A demographic and genetic study of a group of Oxfordshire villages

C. F. KÜCHEMANN, A. J. BOYCE
AND G. A. HARRISON

In recent years ever more attention has been given to the demographic structure of small human communities since it is becoming increasingly apparent that evolutionary forces must be studied in an ecological context. This awareness has led to a number of studies of primitive human communities in different parts of the world in which it is surmised that the evolutionary forces operating are similar to those that have occurred throughout the major phase of human evolution.[1]

These studies of primitive communities have revealed many important parameters of human population dynamics but they are inevitably limited to conditions prevailing at the present day. One of the great advantages in studying evolution in human populations, however, is that for many communities there is a recorded history which can be used for reconstructing the demographic and genetic structure of these communities over a period of several hundred years. Several workers have made use of such material,[2] and increasing attention is being given by histori-

C. F. Küchemann, A. J. Boyce and G. A. Harrison (1967), *Human Biology*, **39** (Detroit), pp. 251–76.
Acknowledgements: We gratefully acknowledge the invaluable help given to us in this study by the Rev. E. H. W. Crusha, Rector of Charlton-on-Otmoor. We also wish to express our gratitude to the Medical Research Council and to the Wenner-Gren Foundation for Anthropological Research, who financed the project.
[1] For example, D. F. Roberts, 'A demographic study of a Dinka village', *Human Biology*, **28** (1956), pp. 323–49; J. V. Neel, F. M. Salzano, P. C. Junqueira, F. Keiter and D. Maybury-Lewis, 'Studies on the Xavante Indians of the Brazilian Mato Grosso', *American Journal of Human Genetics*, **16** (1964), pp. 52–140.
[2] For example, J. W. Eaton and A. J. Mayer, 'The social biology of very high fertility among the Hutterites. The demography of a unique population', *Human Biology*, **25** (1953), pp. 206–64; J. Sutter and Tran-Ngoc-Toan, 'The

cal demographers to the investigation of demographic parameters using historical records.[3] Most of these studies, however, have tended to concentrate either on demographic parameters or on genetic ones and little attention has been given to the inter-relationship between the two types of parameter. The present study is concerned with these inter-relationships and consists of an attempted reconstruction of the genetic and demographic structure over several hundred years of an Oxfordshire country parish.

MATERIALS AND METHODS

The community studied, the parish of Charlton-on-Otmoor, consists of the village of Charlton-on-Otmoor itself and two hamlets, Fencott and Murcott and at the present day has an area of 4155 acres (16·8 sq. km). Charlton lies seven miles (11 km) to the north-east of Oxford (see Fig. 6·1) and with Fencott and Murcott is part of a complex of seven villages surrounding the area of Otmoor. This is a plain four square miles (10·4 sq. km) in extent, lying roughly 200 ft (60 m) above sea level. The seven villages have had rights of common on the moor since Anglo-Saxon times and have always formed a community to some extent economically independent of and isolated from neighbouring areas.

The first source of data consists of the parish registers which provide a record of baptisms, marriages and burials in Charlton, Fencott and Murcott from 1578 to the present day. The information from the three registers was linked together as far as possible in order to ascertain the life history of each individual, and individuals were linked together into families to reveal the relationships of each individual to present and past relatives. When linking marriages to baptisms or defining families uncertainty occasionally arose. Ambiguous cases were normally excluded from further analysis except where one possible interpretation seemed very much more likely than the alternatives. The parish records are of

problem of the structure of isolates and their evolution among human populations', *Cold Spring Harbor Symp. Quant. Biology*, **22** (1957), pp. 379–83; L. L. Cavalli-Sforza, 'Some data on the genetics of human populations', *Proc. 10th International Congress of Genetics*, **I** (1959), pp. 389–407; L. Beckman, 'Breeding patterns of a north Swedish parish', *Hereditas*, **47** (1961), pp. 72–80; N. and A. Freire-Maia, 'The structure of consanguineous marriages and its genetic implications', *Annals of Human Genetics, London*, **25** (1961), pp. 14–39; B. Bonné, 'The Samaritans: A demographic study', *Human Biology*, **35** (1963), pp. 61–89.
[3] D. V. Glass and D. E. C. Eversley (eds.), *Population in History: Essays in Historical Demography* (London, Arnold, 1965).

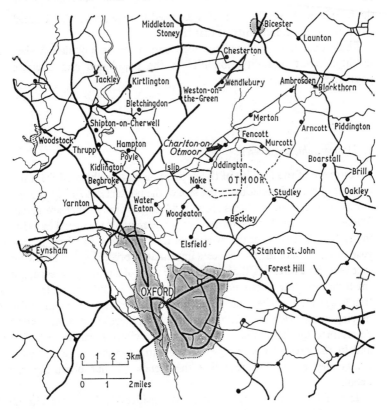

FIG. 6·1 Map of the Charlton-on-Otmoor Area.

the Anglican Church and from the beginning of the nineteenth century there have been a number of Nonconformists in the parish. However, the majority of these have been Methodists who have usually used the Anglican church for baptisms, marriage and burial. The parish register material is not necessarily complete and one of the principal difficulties in this investigation is the lack of knowledge of the reliability of the data in any particular period and also of the variations in reliability. However, some check on the reliability can be obtained from the second source of data which consists of the census records obtained at ten-year intervals since 1801. These provide information about the numbers of people living in the community during the last 160 years. In addition, the enumerators' returns for the 1861 census, which was one of the first to ask for complete details of the ages, relationships and birthplaces of the members of each household, were used to reconstruct the detailed structure of the community at that time.

These data were analysed for such parameters as population size, fertility, infant mortality, mobility of the population and effective population size.

RESULTS

1. Demographic parameters

An estimate of the fertility of the population can be obtained from the number of births in relation to the size of the population. In Fig. 6·2 the annual numbers of baptisms from 1578 to the present day are given. These are presented in the form of a 25-year moving average. The value for each year consists of the average of the number of baptisms in that year and in each of the twelve years immediately preceding and following that year. By expressing the results in the form of a moving average, the small year-to-year fluctuations are smoothed out and the underlying trends are more easily seen. The choice of interval in calculating the moving average is necessarily arbitrary. It is, however, to some extent determined by the numbers of observations within a particular period and in the present case a 25-year grouping appears to be the most satisfactory method of revealing the trends without obscuring the detail.

It would appear that there have been considerable fluctuations in the number of births over this period with relatively large numbers of baptisms being recorded in the early seventeenth and eighteenth centuries and especially in the 1830s. Since this last period there has been a gradual decline in the number of baptisms. The number of births, of course, not only determines the population size but is itself determined by the total number of individuals in the population. Until 1801 there is no way of accurately establishing the size of the population but from 1801 onwards the ten-year census returns give accurate information about the changing size of the population. These changes are shown in Fig. 6·3, and this clearly indicates that within the period from 1801 to the present day the population size reached a maximum in the years 1830–1860. There has been a consistent decline in population size from 1860 to 1930. Furthermore, there is evidence that the population achieved its overall maximum in the years 1830–1860, since seventeenth- and eighteenth-century records, such as Hearth Tax returns, suggest a maximum population size

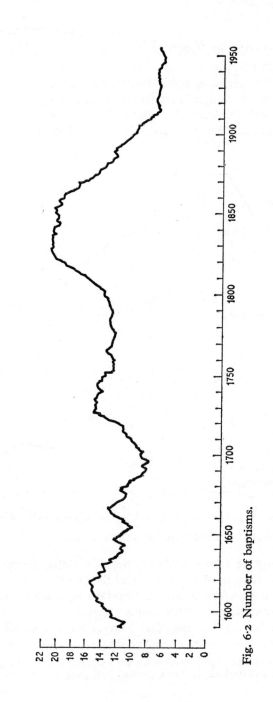

Fig. 6·2 Number of baptisms.

during that period of 450 individuals.[4] It therefore seems reasonable to conclude that the parish has never contained more than 700 individuals.

Within the period in which a direct comparison is possible it is evident that the changes in number of births and population size are closely related. The inter-relation between the two parameters is shown in Fig. 6·4 in the form of the crude birth rate (estimated by the number

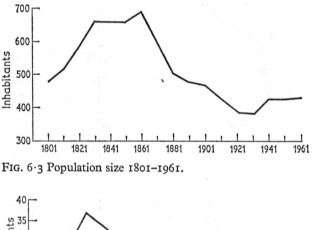

FIG. 6·3 Population size 1801–1961.

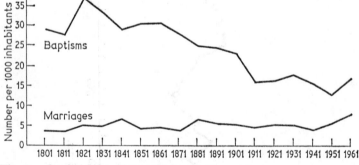

Fig. 6·4 Crude birth and marriage rates 1801–1961.

of baptisms per 1000 individuals). Notwithstanding the relationship between the number of births and population size, the number of births has decreased more rapidly than the size of the population from the early part of the nineteenth century, that is to say, there has been a gradual decline in the crude birth rate. This, however, is not associated with any decline in the marriage rate which shows no such clear-cut trend.

[4] M. D. Lobel (ed.), *A History of the County of Oxford* (The Victoria History of the Counties of England; Oxford University Press, 1959).

Another factor which determines fertility is age at marriage. This is not recorded in the marriage register until the early nineteenth century and to determine the ages of people marrying in Charlton prior to this it is necessary to have a record of their births. In the sixteenth and seventeenth centuries, however, the number of marriage records which can be linked with baptismal records is very small. For this reason, ages at marriage have been studied only from 1700 and have been based entirely on linked records. About 40% of the marriages can be linked to baptismal records (154 marriages). Ages at marriage are shown in Fig. 6·5a. The value for each year is the average age at first marriage for all the marriages which occurred in that year and in the twelve years before and twelve years after the year in question. It is clear that the age at marriage of the males is consistently greater than that of the females except at two periods: 1835–50 and 1910–30. It is also clear that there have been considerable variations in age at marriage over the period. An examination of the age at marriage of the females shows that there was a gradual rise in the early part of the eighteenth century followed by a fall and then a rise again during the nineteenth century. There was a very marked rise in the early twentieth century followed by a decline from 1930 onwards.

The average size of the completed families of Charlton-born women who had at least one child is shown in Fig. 6·5b. In constructing this figure, only the families of first marriages were considered and families in which either parent died during the reproductive period were excluded. Fig. 6·5b shows that for Charlton-born women there was a decline in family size from the early eighteenth century to 1765 followed by a subsequent rise and fall. There has been a continuing decline from 1840 to the present day. What is of special interest is the close relationship between the age at marriage of the female (Fig. 6·5a) and family size in the early part of the period, from 1700 to 1820. An increase in age at marriage of the female corresponds to a decline in total family size and the subsequent fall in age at marriage corresponds to a rise in total family size. By contrast, in the latter part of the period studied, in the nineteenth and twentieth centuries, there is no apparent relationship between age at marriage and family size.

Fig. 6·5b is based on 154 families in which the mother was both born and married in the parish. However, the 3,713 baptisms recorded in the parish during the period studied can be organized into 1,316 families and these provide a more reliable estimate of the change in average size of the family. Fig. 6·6 shows, in the form of a 25-year moving average,

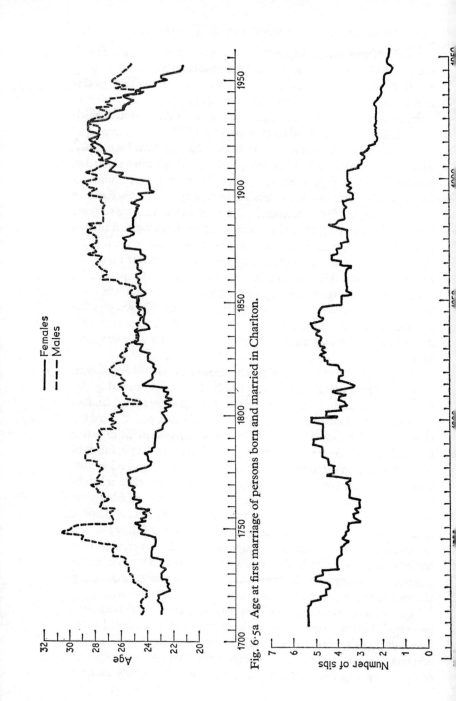

Fig. 6·5a Age at first marriage of persons born and married in Charlton.

the change in family size. The lower graph is based on all 1316 families and the upper on the 727 families with more than one child. It is clear that the exclusion of singleton families produces little change in the pattern of variation. The estimate of family size at any particular time, on the other hand, is markedly affected.

The proportion of singleton families in those families which were most probably completed (because of the known death, after the reproductive period, of the mother) is considerably less than in the total sample of families (14% compared with 45%) although the relative proportions of families of other sizes are similar. This suggests that many of the singleton families were incomplete families and that a more reliable picture of the actual size of families is obtained if singleton families are excluded. Further evidence to support the exclusion of singletons is provided by the fact that in the completed families the average size of the family is very similar to the average size in the total sample when singleton families are excluded (4·6 compared with 4·3). A residence in the parish of only a few days is sufficient for the establishment in the records of a singleton family whereas at least nine months residence is necessary for the establishment of families of two or more children.

The graph of change in family size (Fig. 6·6) shows that there was an increase in family size in the early seventeenth century followed by a fall and subsequent rise in the early eighteenth century. This rise is followed by a fall and a gradual rise to a maximum at the end of the eighteenth century. Since then the average size of the family has gradually fallen. What is of particular interest is the general similarity in shape between the graph of number of baptisms (Fig. 6·2) and that of average family size (Fig. 6·6). (The displacement of approximately ten years in the concordance between the two graphs is due to the fact that in the graph of family size each sibship is tied to the date of birth of the first child.) There is a positive association between family size and number of baptisms, particularly in the seventeenth and eighteenth centuries, and this suggests that the two peaks in baptisms in this early period were partly due to increases in fertility.

Not only does the mean family size vary from time to time but there are indications that the variation in family size also changes with time. These variations, expressed as the square of the coefficients of variation in family size, which allows for differences in mean family size, are plotted in the form of a 25-year moving average in Fig. 6·7. Crow (1958)[5] has pointed out that this parameter is an important measure of the potential intensity of selection due to differential fertility. It is clear that

[5] J. F. Crow, 'Some possibilities for measuring selection intensities in man', *Human Biology*, 30 (1958), pp. 1–13.

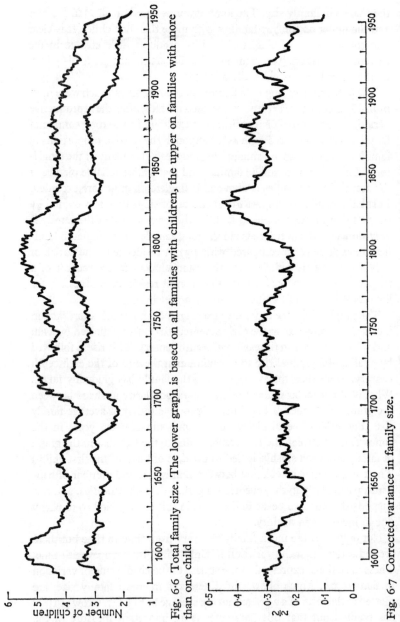

Fig. 6·6 Total family size. The lower graph is based on all families with children, the upper on families with more than one child.

Fig. 6·7 Corrected variance in family size.

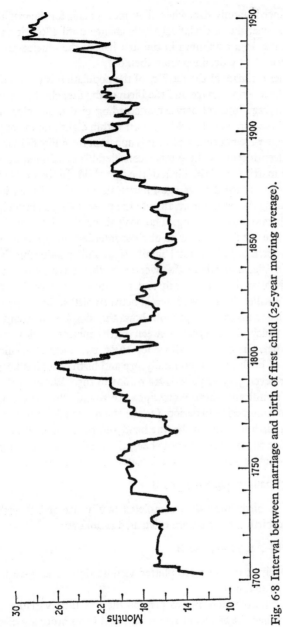

Fig. 6·8 Interval between marriage and birth of first child (25-year moving average).

the variance in family size, when allowance is made for the magnitude of the mean size, showed relatively little change until 1800, it then rose considerably to a maximum in the first half of the nineteenth century and intermittently declined from then on.

Another estimate of the fertility of the population is provided by the interval between marriage and the birth of the first child (Fig. 6·8) and by the average interval between succeeding births. In calculating the first of these parameters children born within eight months of the date of marriage were not considered. It is apparent from Fig. 6·8 that during the eighteenth century there was a considerable increase in the interval between marriage and the birth of the first child. In the first half of the nineteenth century the average interval decreased and then increased again during the period from 1870 to the present day, a period in which the birth rate was declining. The analysis of birth interval is complicated by the fact that there is an obvious interdependence between birth interval, birth order and total family size. This relationship is clearly shown in Fig. 6·9a where the average birth interval, over the whole period, is plotted against family size and shows, as might be expected, that the smaller the average interval between births, the larger the final family size tends to be. Fig. 6·9b shows that despite this trend there is one in which the interval between births increases with increasing birth order. In order to allow for these two factors the linear regression of birth interval on family size and birth order has been calculated for seven 50-year periods from 1601 to 1950. Within each of these periods significant linear regressions are found and these show little variation from period to period. On the assumption that the relationship between birth interval on the one hand and birth order and completed family size on the other has not changed with time, a further regression for the whole period has been calculated and found to be:

$$I = 42\cdot248 - 2\cdot449\ S + 1\cdot556\ B$$

where I is birth interval, S completed family size and B birth order. Adjusted birth intervals were calculated as follows:

$$I' = I + 2\cdot449\ S - 1\cdot556\ B$$

and the adjusted values are plotted against time as a 25-year moving average in Fig. 6·10.

With the exception of two periods there is little variation in birth interval when the effects of family size and birth order are eliminated. The gradual rise from 1840 to 1925 could be due either to deliberate spacing of children by birth control methods or to incompletely effective contraceptive devices. The peculiarly large values from 1630–1690 are difficult to explain but the changes in average birth interval at this period show a close inverse relationship with the changes in family size. Both

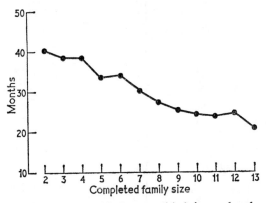

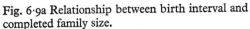

Fig. 6·9a Relationship between birth interval and completed family size.

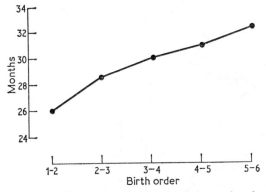

Fig. 6·9b Relationship between birth interval and birth order.

parameters, however, are interdependent and if this were a period of incomplete registration just such an inter-relation would be expected. It is of interest to note that this period coincides with the Civil War and the interregnum following it when only civil registration was legal.

Another potential measure of the fertility of the population is the

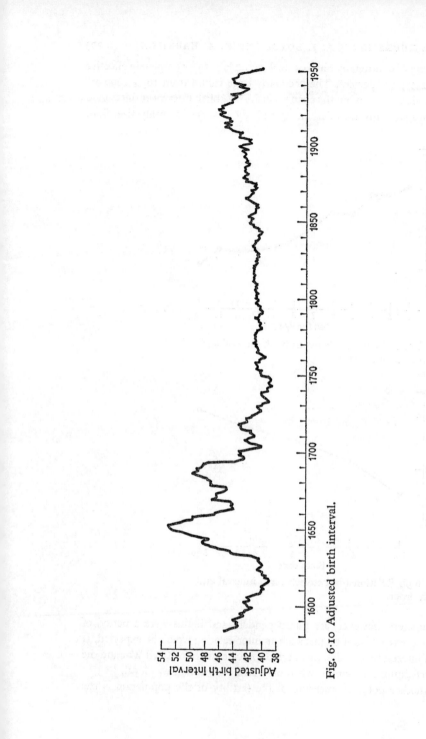

Fig. 6·10 Adjusted birth interval.

number of childless marriages. Over the whole period there are 440 marriages for which no subsequent baptisms are recorded. However, in only 71 of these cases does one or other of the marriage partners occur in the burial register and in only 25 cases is the death of both partners recorded. It seems likely, therefore, that the majority of these apparently childless marriages are only cases of the marriage being contracted in the parish with the family subsequently taking up residence elsewhere and the data are inadequate for analysing changing patterns of complete infertility.

The other primary factor which determines population size is mortality but estimating mortality rates from parish records in a community subject to considerable emigration is unfortunately impossible since the chances of a record occurring of the death of a person whose birth is also recorded increase progressively with increasing age. However, it seems unlikely that this factor affects estimates of mortality of infants and in Fig. 6·11 the number of children who die within the first twelve months of life for every 1,000 children born alive has been plotted in the form of a 25-year moving average. There are considerable fluctuations in the rate of infant mortality with comparatively high rates observed in the early parts of the seventeenth and eighteenth centuries and in the middle of the nineteenth century. It is clear that the great improvement in infant survival has come about quite recently in this rural area and a very great drop in mortality has taken place only since the end of the nineteenth century. In the early part of the period, from 1600 to 1730, there is a very close correspondence between the pattern of infant mortality and the change in sibship size. This correspondence is also apparent in the period from 1850 to the present day.

2. Genetic parameters

Of the many forces that determine the genetic structure of a community the distance over which marriage partners are obtained is probably one of the most important because marriage distance determines the magnitude of the gene pool. For this reason, the marriage distances of people living in the parish were examined. Table 6·1 gives the numbers of marriages, in different 50-year periods, in which one partner or both partners were resident in the parish at the time of the marriage. These figures show that over the whole period a large number of marriages were contracted in which one partner came from outside the parish (it may also be noted that over the whole period there were 20 marriages in

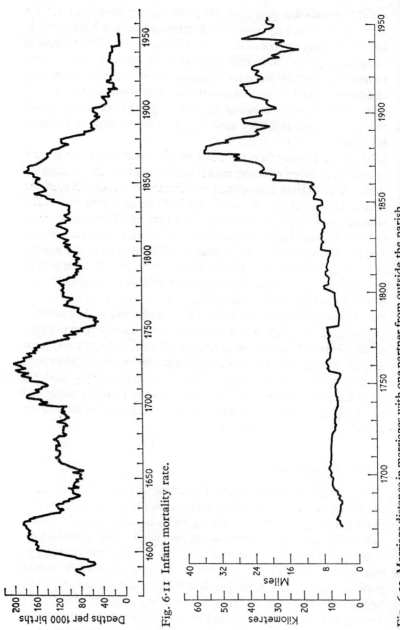

Fig. 6·11 Infant mortality rate.

Fig. 6·12 Marriage distance in marriages with one partner from outside the parish.

which both partners were from outside the parish; these have not been included in the table). It is clear that in the latter part of the period there is a marked increase in the proportion of marriages in which one or the other partner came from outside the parish. The table also shows that at every period the number of marriages in which the male came from outside is greater than the number in which the female came from outside and this reflects the custom of having the marriage ceremony in the parish of the bride. It is likely, however, that in these circumstances of inter-parochial marriage the wife subsequently took up residence in her husband's parish and this accounts for the fact that throughout the period many people were living in Charlton whose marriage was contracted outside the village.

TABLE 6·1 *Marriages within and between Parishes.*

Period	Both partners within parish	Husband from another parish	Wife from another parish	Percentage of marriages with 1 partner from another parish
1651–1700*	24	7	8	38·5
1701–1750	87	28	14	32·6
1751–1800	86	43	4	35·3
1801–1850	100	34	10	30·6
1851–1900	72	50	15	47·4
1901–1950	32	50	5	63·2
1951–1965	18	28	4	64·0
Total	419	240	60	41·7

* Before 1651 the place of residence of the marriage partners does not appear in the marriage register.

Although the percentage of outside partners is high, the distance over which these were obtained is quite small during the major part of the period studied. This is evident from Fig. 6·12 which shows the average marriage distance (in the form of a 25-year moving average) in those marriages in which one partner came from outside the parish. Until the middle of the nineteenth century the average marriage distance remained remarkably constant, in the region of 6 to 8 miles (10–13 km). After 1860, however, there is a dramatic increase in the average marriage distance followed by considerable fluctuations. The largest fluctuations in the latter part of this period are due mainly to occasional marriages contracted over very large distances.

The total amount of immigration into the parish can be more fully analysed by examining the census returns. The most informative of the censuses available from this point of view are those of 1851 and 1861 in which the birthplaces and relationships are given for members of each household in the parish. An analysis has been made of the composition of the village of Charlton itself using the enumerators' returns for the 1861 census. At that time there were 375 individuals living in the village. The estimated size of the breeding population, however, was lower and consisted of 140 individuals. Membership of the breeding population was based on residence in the village at the time of the census and the possession of children who had not themselves had children. The effective size of this breeding population[6] which takes into account the average size and variance in size of families was 96. Of the 140 individuals in the breeding population, 100 were born outside the village. The comparative contribution of the immigrants to the next generation compared with the contribution of the non-immigrants was in the ratio 2·03 : 2·30 (where one parent was local and the other an immigrant, their contribution was distributed between the immigrant and non-immigrant groups). This ratio of contributions indicates an effective immigration rate of 62·67% and thus a coefficient of breeding isolation of 60·16.[7]

Of the 71% who were born outside the village, 65% came from within a radius of six miles (9·6 km) and Fig. 6·13 shows the contributions to the breeding population of Charlton in 1861 made by villages lying within this radius. The figure also shows the size of the villages at that time. Nearness to Charlton is obviously the most important factor determining the contributions of the different villages although size and distance are not the sole determinants of the size of contributions. There are, for instance, in the west and south-west several villages which in spite of their size and nearness to Charlton have contributed nothing to the breeding population of Charlton in 1861. It is of some interest in this connection to see that these particular villages are separated from Charlton by the river Cherwell (see Fig. 6·13) and although this in 1861 could hardly have acted as a strong physical barrier to movement, it nevertheless appears to have acted as a cultural break between the populations.

Finally, the inter-relationship between the contribution of a village

[6] S. Wright, 'Size of population and breeding structure in relation to evolution', *Science*, **87** (1938), pp. 430–1; J. F. Crow, 'Breeding structure of populations, II Effective population number', in *Statistics and Mathematics in Biology*, ed. O. Kempthorne and T. Bancroft, J. Gowen and J. Lush (Iowa State College Press, 1954).
[7] G. W. Lasker and B. A. Kaplan, 'The coefficient of breeding isolation: population size, migration rates and the possibilities for random genetic drift in human communities in northern Peru', *Human Biology*, **36** (1964), pp. 327–38.

(after allowance has been made for its size) and its distance from Charlton can be seen in Fig. 6·14. This shows that the contribution a village makes, in proportion to its size, is not linearly proportional to its distance from Charlton but rather that the nearer villages are contributing

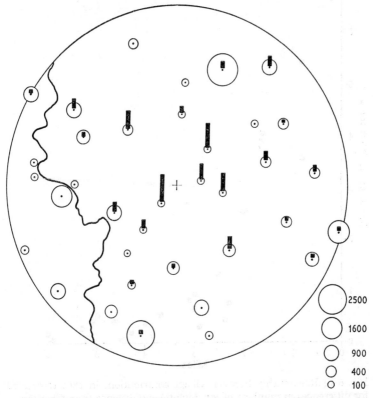

Fig. 6·13 Contributions (Solid Bars) of Surrounding Villages to the Breeding Populations of Charlton in 1861. The area of the circle centred on each village is proportional to the number of inhabitants in that village in 1861. The line on the left of the diagram represents the course of the river Cherwell.

more than one would expect from their distance alone. The form of the relationship has been examined in terms of a model of neighbourhood knowledge[8] and this suggests that the contribution of a village, when

[8] A. J. Boyce, C. F. Küchemann and G. A. Harrison, 'Neighbourhood knowledge and the distribution of marriage distances', *Ann. Human. Genet. London,* **30** (1967), pp. 335–8.

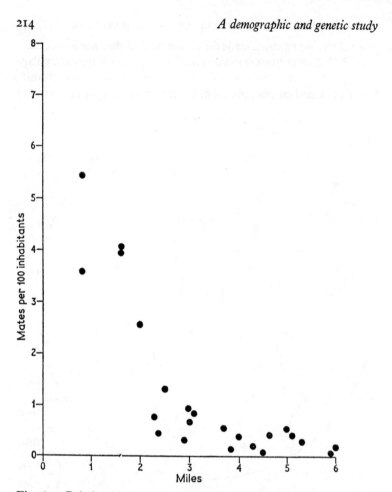

Fig. 6·14 Relationship between village contributions in 1861 (corrected for differences in numbers of inhabitants) and distance from Charlton.

allowance is made for its size, is inversely proportional to approximately the square of its distance from Charlton.

DISCUSSION

It is evident from these results that a considerable amount of information concerning the demographic and genetic structure of a human community can be obtained from parish register and census material, particularly when there is an opportunity of linking up the different types of record so that individual life histories and relationships can be established. Nevertheless, it is important to keep in mind the possibility of bias entering into the analyses as a result of deficiencies in the raw data. This is particularly likely when the analysis is concerned with a fairly open community such as has obviously been in existence in Charlton over the historical period studied. There are problems, for instance, connected with the relationship between place of marriage and place of residence and the more general problems raised by emigration and immigration. The immigration factor is perhaps the most confusing since, from the genetic point of view, the people lost by emigration do not necessarily change the genetic structure of the community. Immigrants, on the other hand, whether or not they differ in gene frequencies from the local inhabitants, will have effects upon the genetic structure of the community. However, emigration can affect estimates of mortality, as has already been mentioned. Incompleteness in the data may also affect the estimates of fertility, especially estimates of family size and birth interval. There is no reason to suppose, however, that the component of error from this source has changed in any systematic manner with time and it seems reasonable to feel confident that the population trends revealed by this study have in fact occurred. Confidence in the validity of the findings is enforced by the concordance between the results derived from different sources of data. For instance, the broad fluctuations in the number of births over the nineteenth and twentieth centuries are very similar to the changes in population based on the extremely reliable census records. Similarly, the judgements about the mobility of the population determined from marriage records are consistent with the analysis based on the 1861 census returns.

Among the most interesting findings of the study are the relationships which have emerged between the different demographic parameters. In considering these relationships it would appear that the whole period can be divided into three segments. The first of these is from the beginning of the seventeenth century until the middle of the eighteenth. In this period there is a close association between the changes in the number of baptisms, family size, average birth interval and infant mortality. There is also a suggestion, though the data are based on a small number of observations, of an inverse association between the age at marriage of women and the size of the family they produce.

The association between number of baptisms on the one hand and family size and birth interval on the other indicates that the changes in the number of baptisms in the seventeenth and early eighteenth centuries were due, at least in part, to changes in fertility although changes in the amount of migration may also have contributed to the changes in the number of baptisms. The inverse association between sibship size and age at marriage of the women suggests that age at marriage was one of the factors regulating fertility at this time.

The association between the infant mortality rate and the average size of the family suggests that the changes in fertility were a direct response to changes in infant mortality or *vice versa*. It is not possible to decide, however, whether the high infant mortality rates arose from the high fertility or, conversely, whether the high fertility represents the result of compensation for high infant mortality.

The second segment consists of the period from 1760 to 1860. The association between the various demographic parameters is less marked than in the earlier period but there are a number of interesting features. During this time the population reached its maximum size and a contributory factor might very well have been the increase in the average size of the family which shortly preceded the marked increase in population. Because this increase in family size was not concurrent with an increase in infant mortality, as in the earlier segment, its effect must have been to increase population size and thereby increase the number of baptisms. No doubt, however, changing patterns of life expectancy and migration rates were also involved in causing the rise in population size.

It is known that important historical events were taking place in Charlton during this period. The Inclosure Acts of the late eighteenth and early nineteenth centuries, which resulted in the inclosure of the whole of Otmoor by 1830, had adverse economic and social effects as is indicated by the fact that they led to the Otmoor Riots of 1831.[9] There are also indications that there was a dramatic rise in the cost of basic foodstuffs such as corn which was not accompanied by comparable rises in wages.[10] It seems reasonable, therefore, to conclude that the late eighteenth and early nineteenth centuries were periods of particular hardship in Charlton. It is also interesting that in the latter part of the period when the population was at its maximum size there was a noticeable increase in the infant mortality rate.

The third segment consists of the period from 1860 to the present day and is characterized by a continuous decline in the size of the population. During this period there is also a decline in the birth rate, in family

---

[9] M. G. Hobson and K. L. H. Price, *Otmoor and its Seven Towns* (Oxford, 1961).
[10] M. D. Lobel (ed.), *op. cit.*

size and an increase in the interval between marriage and the birth of the first child and in the interval between succeeding births. It seems probable, therefore, that the decline in the population size was due to a decline in fertility although increasing migration to urban areas almost certainly played a part. It may be surmised, although no direct evidence is available, that in this period conscious methods of family limitation were increasingly employed and this itself was probably at least partly due to the very marked decline in infant mortality.

It is evident that, in addition to the information about demographic parameters, information concerning the genetic structure of a community may also be obtained from parish registers and census records. In general, it can be said that the genetic structure of a community is determined by its particular composition of genes and the ways in which these genes are combined in genotypes. Evolutionary forces such as selection, mutation, drift and gene flow determine the former while the latter are determined by the mating pattern. In the present study no information has yet been collected on the gene frequencies in known marker systems although it is hoped to establish these as part of future work. Some insight, however, into the role that selection, drift and isolation may have played can be obtained from the present data.

Although the nature of the selective forces operating on the population over the period studied is not known, it has been shown that there have been changes in the variance in family size and this is a prerequisite for selective changes. If it could be assumed that family size is entirely heritable at any one time or that the total variability always had a fixed proportion of heritability, then it could be concluded that selection has been operating differentially on fertility at different times.

In the results it has been shown that there is a period of very high variation in family size in the early part of the nineteenth century and this period corresponds to one when socio-economic conditions were poor. This correspondence suggests that selection for fertility may be particularly great under such circumstances. This high variability in family size does not correspond to a high infant mortality rate and therefore is unlikely to be due to differential compensatory reproduction dependent upon variation between families in infant mortality rate. Instead, it seems likely that the increased variation is a direct consequence of differential fertility under adverse conditions. It has been pointed out, however, by Wrigley (personal communication) that exactly the same result would be found if there were the beginnings of differential family limitation according to social status.

Perhaps one of the most surprising findings of this study is that considerable mobility has characterized this community not only in recent times but also throughout the period studied. The degree of 'endogamy', that is the percentage of marriages in which both partners reside in the same parish, has varied between 36 and 67% with a mean over the whole period of 58%. Cavalli-Sforza[11] found a similar picture of high mobility in parishes in northern Italy with a range of 34 to 77% and a mean of 55% in the period 1800–1950. There is clear evidence of an ever widening pattern of movement around Charlton since the middle of the nineteenth century and it is of interest to note that the railway arrived at Islip, two miles (3·2 km) from Charlton, in 1850. This mobility has profound implications, for, as already indicated, the effective size of the community has at no time been very large and from this information it might be concluded that conditions have frequently been suitable for chance changes in gene frequency to play an important part in determining the genetic structure of the community. However, the immigration rates have been so extremely high throughout the whole of the period that they must have offset any tendency for the population and neighbouring ones to drift in gene frequencies in time or space. Lasker and Kaplan[12] point out that genetic drift is unlikely to be important in populations where the coefficient of breeding isolation is greater than 5; in Charlton, at least in 1861, the coefficient of breeding isolation was 60 and therefore the high immigration rates, rather than the mating pattern within the community, must have been the principal factors determining the genetic structure. If a direct estimate is made through pedigree analysis of the percentage of genes at any locus present in Charlton in 1861 which are still present in the 1965 population, the percentage is found to be of the order of 3%. Although this is certainly a minimal estimate, even a fourfold error would not affect the conclusion that there has been considerable gene flow into and out of the population. What has not yet been fully established, however, is the relationship between the parish of Charlton and the surrounding parishes and it could well be that once this has been established a much more circumscribed genetic unit will become apparent. In other words, although Charlton and its two hamlets do not form a closed gene pool, they may well turn out to be segments of a fairly localised gene pool. This is a point on which further work is planned.

[11] Cavalli-Sforza, *op. cit.*
[12] Lasker and Kaplan, *op. cit.*

SUMMARY AND ABSTRACT

A study has been made of the demographic and genetic structure of the Oxfordshire parish of Charlton-on-Otmoor from 1578 to the present day. Data obtained from parish registers and census returns have been analysed for such parameters as population size, birth rate, age at marriage, family size, birth interval, infant mortality, marriage distance and effective population size.

There is clear evidence of the differing contributions of fertility, mortality and migration in determining the structure of the parish.

7.1 Notes on the historical study of social mobility

STEPHAN THERNSTROM

In recent years sociological work in the field of stratification and social mobility has become, in at least one sense of the term, impressively cosmopolitan. National sample surveys which include data on intergenerational occupational mobility have been carried out in every major Western nation and in a good many non-Western societies as well, and those have inspired some ambitious comparative analyses of social mobility. This development, as S. M. Miller puts it, has had the virtue of making 'the study of mobility one of the few fields of sociology which has overcome national parochialisms'.[1] True as this is, however, it must be said that there are forms of parochialism other than national. Much contemporary research into social mobility suffers from one of these – a parochialism of time rather than of place, as it were, the parochialism of presentism. My purpose here is to suggest what is lost as a result of that parochialism, and to argue that a sense of the past, an ability to see his subject in historical depth, is not a luxury but a necessity for the student of social mobility.

I

Let me begin with a simple, obvious, uncontroversial point – so obvious indeed, that I would blush to make it but for the fact that so few students

Stephan Thernstrom (1967) *Comparative Studies in Society and History*, X (The Hague), pp. 162–72.
An earlier version of this paper was delivered at the 1964 annual meeting of the American Sociological Association. I am very much indebted to Charles Tilly for critical suggestions.
[1] S. M. Miller, 'Comparative social mobility: A trend report and bibliography', *Current Sociology*, 9 (1960), p. 2.

of social mobility seem to have taken it to heart. This is simply that some of the most interesting questions we might ask about the nature of a class structure today cannot be answered without reliable information about the nature of that class structure yesterday—and the day before yesterday, and even the century before yesterday! And that nowhere has the research necessary to supply such knowledge about class and mobility been carried out in sufficient historical depth. Despite the recent avalanche of empirical research on social mobility, appallingly little is known about the process of social mobility in the past and about long-term mobility trends in any society – certainly not in our own.

Consider the familiar controversy over the blocked-mobility hypothesis advanced by the Lynds, Warner and others some decades ago.[2] The question of whether or not American society is on the verge of succumbing to arteriosclerosis has been repeatedly discussed ever since. Clearly this is a question of considerable interest – to the general public as well as to the scholarly world, if the success of such books as *The Status Seekers* be any index. And yet the issue remains largely unresolved, despite some recent studies demonstrating that there has been no diminution in mobility rates in the past two decades.[3] Valuable though this work is, its time perspective is so foreshortened as to be irrelevant to the issue of long-term changes in the openness of the American social order. Rogoff's Indianapolis study reaches farther back into the past, but even that begins no earlier than 1910, while the explicit or implicit point of comparison chosen by proponents of the blocked-mobility theory was *nineteenth-century* America, and there is the further limitation that Rogoff did not study intra-generational mobility at all.[4] Systematic studies of social mobility in nineteenth-century America are still woefully absent. True, the social origins of members of the national business elite of the era have been examined in some detail, and Aronson has recently explored the social composition of the higher civil service in the

[2] W. Lloyd Warner and J. O. Low, *The Social System of the Modern Factory* (New Haven, 1947); Robert S. and Helen M. Lynd, *Middletown: A Study in American Culture* (New York, 1929) and *Middletown in Transition: A Study in Cultural Conflict* (New York, 1937); Elbridge Sibley, 'Some demographic clues to stratification', *American Sociological Review*, 7 (1942), pp. 322–30; D. H. Anderson and P. E. Davidson, *Occupational Mobility in an American Community* (Stanford, 1937); J. O. Hertzler, 'Some tendencies towards a closed class system in the United States', *Social Forces*, 30 (1952), pp. 313–23.

[3] E. F. Jackson and H. J. Crockett, 'Occupational mobility in the United States: A point estimate and trend comparison', *American Sociological Review*, 29 (1964), pp. 5–15; O. D. Duncan, 'The trend of occupational mobility in the United States', *American Sociological Review*, 30 (1965), pp. 491–8.

[4] Natalie Rogoff, *Recent Trends in Occupational Mobility* (Glencoe, Ill., 1953).

first four decades of the Republic, but little, regrettably, can be learned about the range of mobility opportunities at the lower and middle levels from surveys of those who rose to the very top.[5]

The debate about mobility trends in the United States has been conducted without any solid grasp of the nature of the American class structure in the past, or indeed any knowledge that much the same argument about the level of opportunities has been going on in this country for approximately a century! Thus this typical contribution to the debate:

> The man at the bottom of the ladder leading up to the social heavens may yet dream that there is a ladder let down to him; but the angels are not seen very often ascending and descending; one after another, it would seem, some unseen yet hostile powers are breaking out the middle rungs of the ladder.[6]

These are not the words of Lloyd Warner or the Lynds observing Newbury port or Muncie in the Great Depression, but the gloomy verdict of an obscure Boston minister in 1885. Similar complaints about declining opportunities were voiced by artisans threatened by economic change in the Jacksonian era.[7]

That the blocked-mobility hypothesis advanced by modern social scientists is not a blinding new discovery but a restatement of an age-old American complaint does not necessarily discredit the notion, but it should make us wonder a little. If the middle rungs of the social ladder were being wrenched out in the 1880s or in the age of Jackson, how many could have been left for the later destruction described by Warner and the Lynds? If, on the other hand, Reverend Smyth and Jacksonian labor leaders were mistaken in their diagnosis, victims of an innate American tendency to judge the imperfections of the present against a fictitious vanished Golden Age of perfect opportunity in the past, might not the

[5] Sidney Aronson, *Status and Kinship in the Higher Civil Service* (Cambridge, 1964). The business-elite literature is conveniently summarized and analyzed in S. M. Lipset and R. Bendix, *Social Mobility in Industrial Society* (Berkeley, 1959), Chap. IV.

[6] Newman Smyth, *Social Problems: Sermons to Workingmen* (Boston, 1885), pp. 12–13.

[7] Norman Ware, *The Industrial Worker, 1840–1860* (Boston, 1934; paperback ed., Chicago, 1964), *passim*. For similar fears in the latter half of the nineteenth century see the documents in Leon Litwack, *The American Labor Movement* (Englewood Cliffs, N.J., 1962), pp. 3–14. Both Ware and Litwack were insufficiently critical of the testimony they cite, and assumed that if contemporary witnesses *thought* that opportunities were declining, they must have been in fact, an assumption questioned below.

same predispositions shape the perceptions of later American social scientists as well? The ironic coincidence that the idyllic past conjured up by Lloyd Warner in *The Social System of the Modern Factory* was just the period in which Reverend Smyth was lamenting the death of the American Dream strongly suggests that this was indeed the case. Popular mythology about the character of the social order is well worth careful study in its own right, to be sure, but some writers have reflected it instead of reflecting upon it.[8]

A large-scale, systematic quantitative study of social-mobility patterns in nineteenth-century America will be required to allow us to gauge whether any of these dire prophecies of constricting mobility opportunities had any foundation in fact, and, more important, to assess the influence of a host of different variables singled out by those who have speculated about long-term mobility trends in the United States. Was it the mechanization of industry and the consequent destruction of older craft hierarchies which produced the changes Reverend Smyth deplored, and if so, had these processes advanced as far and in the same form in Boston in the 1880s as in Muncie and Newburyport four to five decades later? What of the closing of the frontier, the blocking of mass immigration to our shores, or the narrowing of class differences in fertility? The first of these, difficult though it is to date precisely, was taking place at just about the time at which Reverend Smyth wrote, while the other two had yet to occur at all. Since the *timing* of these and other historical developments which might have influenced the shape of the class structure varied greatly, historical inquiry affords us the opportunity to assign priority to certain variables and to dismiss others.

It is a truism, of course, that the comparative method serves this end. What is not a truism, however, at least not one which conspicuously influences the actual course of social research today, is that additional depth of knowledge about one society can be as fruitful for comparative purposes as additional cross-cultural breadth.[9] Perhaps more fruitful, for it does not rest upon the questionable premise that all societies pass

[8] For further development of this point, see Stephan Thernstrom, ' "Yankee City" revisited: The perils of historical naïveté', *American Sociological Review*, 30 (1965), pp. 234–42.
[9] For a good example from the field of demography, see Aaron Antonovsky, 'Social class, life expectancy, and overall mortality', *Milbank Memorial Fund Quarterly*, 45 (1967), 38–9. For further discussion of the advantages of longitudinal studies over static cross-sectional ones, see Nathan Goldfarb, *An Introduction to Longitudinal Statistical Analysis* (Glencoe, Ill., 1960), and Norman B. Ryder, 'The cohort as a concept in the study of social change', *American Sociological Review*, 30 (1965), pp. 843–61.

through similar stages of development and that in the absence of sufficient historical knowledge about social patterns in the early years of
industrialization in the West we may apply models derived from the
study of the class structure of under-developed countries today. Such
models may or may not be relevant; their possible relevance can only be
demonstrated on the basis of thorough acquaintance with the historical
record. The two research strategies are complementary, of course, but
what requires emphasis is that the one is a poor substitute for the
other.

II

The blocked-mobility hypothesis provides a convenient illustration of
another point which underlines the importance of understanding social
mobility in historical context. The question of how the Industrial Revolution and a host of subsequent economic and technological changes have
affected the social position of the ordinary workingman has generated an
enormous historical and sociological literature, much of it marred by the
failure to grasp that in a mobile society a decline in the status of a
particular occupation is often accompanied by a corresponding shift in
the social stratum from which the occupation draws its labor force. Thus
writers like the Hammonds, Norman Ware, the Lynds, and Warner
misunderstood the implications of their discovery that the position of
the semi-skilled operative in a modern textile mill or shoe factory was in
many ways inferior to that of the artisan who produced similar products
prior to industrialization. They saw industrial change as the engine of
'status degradation' for a large sector of the working class. But this
assumed a simplistic model of an occupational structure in which all
skilled crafts were being wiped out and in which there were no opportunities for upward social mobility, so that the artisans and their children
had no alternative but to suffer status degradation and accept a semi-
skilled factory job.

This model, however, is of doubtful validity. Convincing evidence
that it was the skilled craftsmen of old or their children who made up the
new semi-skilled factory labor force has never been produced by
adherents of the cataclysmic view of industrialization. Resent research
suggests that status degradation was a rare phenomenon, that the skilled
have commonly been able to preserve their position and that their sons
have been likely to find other skilled niches or quite often to enter a
white-collar position of some kind. The new factory labor force, it

appears, has characteristically been recruited by a process overlooked by earlier observers, a process with very different implications for the social structure. By and large it was not declassé artisans but unskilled new-comers – immigrants and migrants from rural areas – who moved into the factories, men for whom factory employment generally meant improved status. An essential aspect of the complex of changes we refer to as urbanization and industrialization has been a cycle of migration and social mobility which has filled the least attractive and least well-rewarded industrial positions with successive waves of newcomers, who appraise their situation with standards formed not in the proud world of the independent artisan but in a subsistence agrarian economy.

We cannot speak too dogmatically about this matter, given the paucity of evidence currently available, but this generalization does hold for the United States, I think. (More about the rest of the world in a moment.) My investigation of working class social mobility patterns in Newbury-port, Mass. in the 1850–80 period reveals this mobility cycle at work there,[10] and my current work with a sample of 8,000 residents of Boston between 1880 and the present, as yet unpublished, has yielded much the same result. Few skilled workmen in the community suffered downward mobility as a result of technological and other developments at any time in this period. Furthermore, the sons of skilled craftsmen rarely dropped down into the ranks of the unskilled or semi-skilled themselves; close to half of them, indeed, attained middle class status.

The same conclusion is suggested by Rogoff's Indianapolis study. This goes back no earlier than 1910, unfortunately, but it is the most comprehensive inquiry available for the period with which it deals, and it has the further advantage of dealing with a Hoosier city quite similar to nearby Muncie, the site of the Middletown research, thus providing a rough check of the accuracy of the Lynds' assumptions about the status degradation wrought by industrialization. Rogoff's tables reveal that fully 49 per cent of the sons of skilled craftsmen in the Indianapolis sample for 1910 were themselves in skilled callings, and another quarter of them had moved into the rapidly expanding non-manual occupations. Few of them had been downwardly mobile in the way foreseen by pro-ponents of the blocked-mobility hypothesis.[11] We can infer from Rogoff's tables and what the Lynds tell us about the precipitous growth of the Muncie population that the semi-skilled factory labor force in

[10] Stephan Thernstrom, *Poverty and Progress: Social Mobility in a Nineteenth Century City* (Cambridge, 1964).
[11] Rogoff, *op. cit.*, p. 44.

both cities was actually composed predominantly of newcomers of lowly origin.

This mobility cycle, in which newly-created jobs of rather lowly status tend to go to those who previously held even lowlier jobs, is easiest to observe in cities with two distinguishing features. If a city's population increased dramatically during industrialization, and if many of the new-comers were members of highly visible ethnic groups, this relationship between inmigration, industrialization and social mobility should leap to the eye. Doubtless it was not accidental that the two major community studies which advanced the blocked-mobility theory – the Yankee City inquiry and the Middletown volumes – were carried out in American cities which happened to lack one of these traits. In the case of Newbury-port, whose total population was little more in 1930 than it was in 1855, it was natural – though utterly mistaken – to assume that the *composition* of the population had changed very little, and that this was a self-contained, static 'old New England community'. In fact, however, this was a radical misconception. Though its total population levelled off in 1855, the composition of the population underwent a number of funda-mental changes. The stable net figure concealed staggeringly high rates of gross movement. A substantial fraction of the city's inhabitants left Newburyport each decade; others – the Irish, later the French-Canadians, the Italians, and so forth – poured in to take their places, a steady stream of newcomers to occupy the lower rungs of the occupa-tional ladder.[12]

That the total Muncie population grew very rapidly during the years of the Middletown study was not conducive to the illusion that the community was sealed off from the larger society in the manner dear to the heart of the anthropologist. But the fact that the Lynds selected a community without a large foreign-born or Negro population – they sought to exclude racial change as a variable and to isolate the social effects of industrialization – blinded them to this mobility cycle in much the same way. In fact, Kentucky, Tennessee, and rural Indiana served as the functional equivalent of the Old World as a source of migrants with little status to lose; it was much easier to overlook newcomers like these, however, and to assume that the sons of the highly-skilled glass-blowers of old Muncie were necessarily a prime source of the new semi-skilled factory labor force.

The bald assertion that factory employment generally meant improved status for migrants like these does raise a troubling problem sociologists

[12] Thernstrom, *op. cit.*, pp. 84–6, 167–8, 195–6.

are only now beginning to grapple with, the problem of how to evaluate movement from an entire social setting to one utterly different. It seems simple enough to say that a foreman enjoys higher status than a factory laborer, and that the owner of the factory ranks above both of them, but the shift of agricultural workers into urban industrial employment obviously defies easy evaluation. There can be a series of distinct clusters of positions which differ in their relationship to the market, life chances, etc. and yet which are roughly equivalent in power, wealth, or prestige. The concept of 'situs' has been developed to describe such a situation.[13] The movement of workers from the agricultural situs to the industrial one may sometimes entail no vertical mobility in either direction, but only horizontal movement into a slot of equivalent rank. This means that it is necessary to investigate in detail the social milieu from which the migrants came in any particular instance, to specify the distribution of social types – large landlord or small, tenant or farm laborer – within the migrant stream, and to employ these categories in examining the experiences of these men after they enter the industrial world. Such a procedure will make it possible to distinguish cases in which migration brought no improvement or even status loss from what I suggest is the more common pattern of general advance.

The sketchy evidence cited above pertains to the United States in the past century. That a similar process has been at work in other societies as well we know from the work of Lipset and Bendix, Morris D. Morris, and others, but this work constitutes the barest beginning toward a full understanding of the matter.[14] One wonders if some of the societal differences which were invisible through the crudely-ground lenses of Lipset and Bendix's microscope, and which they consequently interpreted as variations in national values unsupported by actual differences in social structure, might not be rooted in differences in the way this

[13] Paul K. Hatt, 'Occupation and social stratification', *American Journal of Sociology*, 55 (1950), p. 539. For an excellent historical illustration, see Charles Tilly's discussion of the dual class structure of the Vendée in the 1790s: *The Vendée* (Cambridge, 1964), pp. 79–80, 98–9.
[14] Lipset and Bendix, *op. cit.*, pp. 203–26; Gideon Sjoberg, 'Rural-urban balance and models of economic development', in Neil Smelser and S. M. Lipset, *Social Structure and Mobility in Economic Development* (Chicago, 1966), pp. 235–61; Gunnar Boalt, 'Social mobility in Stockholm: A pilot investigation', *Transactions of the Second World Congress of Sociology* (London, 1954), II, pp. 67–73; Morris D. Morris, 'The recruitment of an industrial labor force in India, with British and American comparisons', *Comparative Studies in Society and History*, II (1960), pp. 305–28; Ronald and Deborah Freedman, 'Farm-reared elements in the non-farm population', *Rural Sociology*, 21 (1956), pp. 50–61.

process operated in different countries. One suspects, for example, that the pace and volume of immigration and internal migration was spectacularly high in the American case, and that the proportion of the urban labor force with prior exposure to the artisan and yeoman traditions that inspired the militant labor protest of the Industrial Revolution in Britain was distinctively low, and that this has a good deal to do with the continuing popular belief that New World society has been uniquely open.[15] Too little is known at present to press this argument very far, but the whole issue demands study by sociologically-inclined historians and historically-minded sociologists.

III

Something should be said about the problem of finding data from which historical studies of social mobility can be written, and about the historian's approach to such data. It has often been assumed that systematic historical studies of social mobility are rare because of the absence of satisfactory evidence. In a great many instances, at least, this is more a rationalization than a reason. True, there are times and places irrecoverably lost to history. But for most relatively modern societies, and some traditional ones (such as ancient China), vast amounts of usable material are still untapped. Thus, for the United States there is a wonderfully rich and virtually untouched source for mobility research – manuscript schedules of the federal census, which from 1850 on provide a primitive social survey of the entire population of the United States. There are city directories, well used by Sidney Goldstein and his colleagues in the Norristown study, which for many communities extend back a century and a half or more; the problem of reliability with early city directories is severe but not insurmountable, and they offer the special advantage for sample studies that respondents are arranged by alphabetical order.[16] Reaching even farther back into the past are local tax and voting records – even when these lack adequate occupational information they make it possible to stratify a community according to property ownership and political participation. In many Western European countries, of course, historical records with relevant fragments of data have survived even longer.

There are maddening difficulties in employing this data, to be sure.

---

[15] cf. E. P. Thompson, *The Making of the English Working Class* (London, 1963).
[16] Sidney Goldstein, *Patterns of Mobility, 1910–1950: The Norristown Study* (Philadelphia, 1958).

Occupational designations are sometimes appallingly vague by modern standards. Until well into the nineteenth century in England and the United States, a 'manufacturer' could be a manual employee or his employer; it was not until the twentieth century that the French 'ouvrier' received its present definition.[17] Where the available records do not supply further information to make the distinctions which we regard as crucial, analytical possibilities are obviously sorely limited.

Instead of bewildering vagueness, we sometimes encounter puzzling concreteness. Consider the difficulties of devising an occupational classification scheme to employ in analyzing Patrick Colquhoun's enumeration of the London population at the close of the eighteenth century, enumerations which include such intriguing occupations as mudlark, scufflehunter, bludgeonman, morocco man, flash coachman, grubber, and bear baiter.[18] Obviously the findings of Inkeles, Rossi, Reiss and others who have investigated the prestige ranking of occupations is of little avail in grappling with the problem. If the example is not very serious, the point is. Whatever the difficulties they create, however, there is the consolation that the curiously antique or exotic labels which often appear in the sources convey a very useful warning. The problem of the mudlark and the scufflehunter suggests two general principles: (1) the need to employ finely calibrated instruments in reconstructing a social structure now vanished; (2) the necessity of paying close attention to the entire social context in which the particular phenomenon under consideration was embedded.

At this level of abstraction, these principles seem singularly harmless platitudes, but they are not, I think, without a cutting edge. If we abide by them in examining some vast problem – changes in the openness of the American social structure since 1700, let us say – I think we would proceed in a manner somewhat different from that in which many contemporary sociologists would proceed. Rather than taking the currently fashionable index of social mobility, the rate of inter-generational movement between manual and non-manual occupations, computing occupational mobility rates at selected intervals, and constructing a simple time series, the historian would insist that a scrupulous examination of the class structure at several strategic points in time and an assessment of the extent of social mobility in terms of categories appropriate to each point in time would be required, and that to arrive at a simple conclusion about trends might be impossible because of the lack of

[17] George Rudé, *The Crowd in History, 1730–1848* (New York, 1964), pp. 196–7.
[18] Thompson, *op. cit.*, p. 55.

comparability of the historically specific categories used. Did the Polish peasants in the mills of Gary in 1910 hold the same relative position in the class system as the indentured servants of Salem in 1710? What was the mobility equivalent in 1910 of the purchase of a farm in the Connecticut River Valley in 1710? Merely to contemplate the multitude of meanings of the occupational designation 'farm owner' through the course of American history is to see some of the inescapable complexities of the problem.

This is not to say that there would be nothing of interest in a crude table which purported to summarize changes in the rate of intergenerational movement between manual and non-manual occupations in America since 1700, any more than that there is nothing of interest in a similar table summarizing crude occupational data for post-World War II Europe and the United States. But this would be but a small first step, and it may not be the wisest step to take first. The concept of social mobility, after all, is an exceptionally rich and complex one, and simple one-dimensional indices which facilitate immediate comparisons of social mobility in radically different social orders may not yield the most rewarding comparisons. The alluring comparability attained by passing disparate sets of data through a sieve so crude that it allows essential features of each set to trickle away is purchased at a very heavy price.

In my own work on working class mobility in nineteenth-century America I quickly found that some of the most important elements of the problem could not be discerned through the lenses of a two-class occupational scheme – or, indeed, any occupational scheme at all. Not only was it useful to distinguish unskilled, semi-skilled, and skilled positions within the broad rubric of manual occupations; it was essential to devote extensive attention to another dimension of social mobility entirely. By far the most important form of upward mobility in the setting I examined was movement between the floating, unstable, propertyless sector of the working class and the settled, respectable, property-owning working class group. Whether these were indeed distinct social classes or different strata of the same class seems to me a verbal rather than a substantive problem. Certainly they were distinct social groups, with different life chances and different styles of life, and movement between them must be regarded as social mobility. To move from the first of these into the second was a less dramatic upward advance than to leap directly into the world of the middle class, but it happened much more often and was in this sense a more important feature of the social scene. Without attention to social mobility of this kind, which requires investigation of patterns of home ownership, savings, and residential continuity among other things, we would know very little about social mobility in this milieu. For other times, other places – seventeenth-century England, let us say – a somewhat different conception of social mobility would be required, as the famous controversy inspired by Tawney's paper on 'The Rise of the Gentry' suggests, and categories appropriate to that specific historical configuration should be utilized.[19] In developing these categories, major boundaries of the stratification system of the particular society – power, wealth, style of life – can be specified, and then inquiry can be made about rates of movement and processes of movement across these boundaries, as well as about shifts in the boundaries themselves which take place in the course of historical development.

Such concern for fidelity to a particular historical context implies a certain chastening of the aspiration to construct a general theory of social mobility through comparative research, but certainly not an abandonment of sociological models and systematic comparative analysis. My aim is not to urge the inviolable uniqueness of each historical moment, but rather to argue that historical data should be employed to edit and refine social theory to make it more sensitive to social reality past and present.

[19] A judicious review of the controversy and selections from the leading contributions is available in Lawrence Stone (ed.), *Social Change and Revolution in England, 1540–1640* (London, 1965). For splendid examples of the sort of historical analysis I have in mind, see Stone's essay on 'Social mobility in England, 1500–1700', *Past and Present*, **33** (1966), 16–55, and his book *The Crisis of the Aristocracy, 1558–1641* (Oxford, 1965).

7.2 The historical study of vertical mobility

STUART BLUMIN

The proposition that nineteenth-century America was a land of un-precedented opportunity for individual advancement – that is, a society with a continuously high rate of upward mobility – has long been one of our most central beliefs about the nature of the American past. Stemming from this fundamental belief have come numerous studies of the concept of success; of the failure of American Marxists, land reformers, workingmen's parties and Utopian communitarians; of the role of government and the church in a 'fluid', success-oriented society, and of the vital question of whether opportunities in contemporary America are not less than they were in the days of the 'self-made man'. 'The American Dream' requires no explanation to indicate that it refers not to salvation, love, fame, or even immortality, but to worldly success, a phenomenon that seems possible only in a society in which actual success is not often an unrealistic goal. Yet, fundamental though it is, the proposition that nineteenth-century American society was highly fluid has all but escaped examination. With the exception of a few attempts to study the social and economic origins of the very small minority of individuals who made it to the very top of society, and of Stephan Thernstrom's pioneering study of the mobility of factory operatives in post-Civil War 'Yankee City',[1] virtually nothing has been published to date to report empirical

Stuart Blumin (1968), *Historical Methods Newsletter*, 1 no. 4 (Pittsburgh), pp. 1–13.
[1] Stephan Thernstrom, *Poverty and Progress: Social Mobility in a Nineteenth Century City* (Cambridge, Mass., 1964). For an excellent analysis of the social origins of wealthy industrialists, see Frances W. Gregory and Irene D. Neu, 'The American industrial elite in the 1870s: Their social origins,' in William Miller (ed.), *Men in Business: Essays in the History of Entrepreneurship* (Cambridge, Mass., 1952), pp. 193–211.

research on the 'openness' of society before the twentieth century.[2] Most likely, the reason for this rather extraordinary gap is a reluctance among historians to recognize that 'openness', 'fluidity', opportunity, and mobility are quantitative concepts that acquire meaning only when expressed in quantitative terms – that is, when they are substantiated by research which seeks to establish the relative frequency of vertical mobility.

The purpose of this article is to assess the possibilities (and the difficulties) of performing this kind of research in a society that is inaccessible to personal interview and that has left us a far from complete record of its transactions. Since this assessment derives from this author's personal experience with a specific set of data, namely, those that pertain to mobility in Philadelphia during the period 1820–1860, it may not be wholly applicable to the study of other areas and other periods. On the other hand, most of the problems that were encountered in Philadelphia are probably characteristic ones, especially those that involve the concepts and methods of the study of mobility.

As the study of vertical mobility has been approached by sociologists almost exclusively through the more tangible method of occupational mobility, it would seem quite natural to approach the historical study of mobility in the same way. For one thing, data exist, in cities at least, in the form of city directories, which would seem to support a study of the occupational history of specific individuals (intra-generational occupational mobility) and possibly of the relationship between the occupations of fathers and their sons (inter-generational occupational mobility).[3] But the calculation of rates of occupational mobility raises a number of very serious questions, some of them concerning the application of this method to the past, and some of them concerning its usefulness in any context.

That there should be any reason to doubt the validity of occupational mobility as a sociological method may seem rather surprising, in light of the nature of its rather extensive bibliography.[4] Yet, the method is based on an inference that has received very little examination, namely, the inference of social mobility from occupational mobility. Since no one would define social status in terms of occupation alone, we cannot accept

[2] See Jackson T. Main, *The Social Structure of Revolutionary America* (Princeton, 1965), for an attempt to deal with this question in the eighteenth century.
[3] See Sidney Goldstein, *Patterns of Mobility, 1910–1950* (Philadelphia, 1958) for an interesting example of how city directories may be used to study mobility.
[4] Raymond W. Mack, Linton Freeman and Seymour Yellin, *Social Mobility: Thirty Years of Research and Theory* (Syracuse, 1957).

the idea that a change in occupation constitutes, by definition, a change in social status. Yet few, if any, who calculate rates of occupational mobility pause to question the validity of inferring the magnitude of social mobility from these rates. 'This practice', write Westoff, Bressler and Sagi, 'has arisen partly as a concession to methodological difficulties and partly from theoretical considerations supported by empirical evidence.'[5] The methodological difficulties (quantifying such concepts as 'status' and 'prestige') are precisely what necessitate an inferential method. Obviously, if it were possible to measure social mobility directly (that is, in terms of its definition), there would be no need to infer it from some other kind of mobility. The 'theoretical consideration' that supports the use of occupational mobility is the apparent importance of occupation as a status indicator. 'From Plato to the present', write Lipset and Zetterberg, 'occupation has been the most common indicator of stratification. Observers of social life – from novelists to pollsters – have found that occupational class is one of the major factors which differentiate people's beliefs, values, norms, customs and occasionally some of their emotional expressions.'[6] Thus, one way of giving substance to the concept of 'openness' in a society is to define social status in a meaningful way and to assume that occupational mobility is a valid indicator of movement from status to status.

There are several reasons why this procedure may not satisfy our objective. One reason, as the above discussion implies, is that the inference of social mobility from occupational mobility may well be invalid. Evidence gathered in support of the inference is generally based on the static relationship between occupation and other indices or dimensions of social class, rather than on the dynamic relationship between occupational mobility and other dimensions of mobility. Using interview data from the recent Norristown study,[7] Robert R. Wharton finds that respondents, asked to list the characteristics that they would use to place individuals in classes representing their own class perspectives, mentioned occupation more frequently than any other characteristic. An average of four characteristics was listed by each person, with 76·3% of the sample mentioning occupation. Wealth was mentioned by 73·1%, but no other single characteristic was mentioned by more than

[5] Charles F. Westoff, Marvin Bressler and Philip C. Sagi, 'The concept of social mobility: An empirical inquiry,' *American Sociological Review*, 25 (1960), p. 378.
[6] Seymour M. Lipset and Hans L. Zetterberg, 'A theory of social mobility,' *Transactions of the Third World Congress of Sociology*, II (1956), pp. 155–6.
[7] Sidney Goldstein, *The Norristown Study* (Philadelphia, 1961).

one-third of the sample.[8] The ranking of occupations, therefore, would appear to be a fairly reliable index to the subjective class perceptions of the residents of Norristown.

On the other hand, Westoff, Bressler and Sagi, using the factor analytic method, find that neither inter-generational nor intra-generational occupational mobility is strongly correlated with twenty other hypothesized indices of social mobility.[9] 'One important and direct implication of this finding is that one cannot safely infer knowledge of one dimension of mobility from knowledge of another.'[10] Thus, occupational mobility, even though it may be the most important dimension of the 'complex multidimensional concept'[11] of social mobility is not necessarily a valid indicator of social mobility.

A second difficulty arises when we attempt to apply concepts and methods developed from research on twentieth-century society to data from an earlier historical period. Modern studies of social mobility rank occupations according to presumed prestige values, either by grouping them into categories such as 'professional', 'white-collar' and 'skilled manual', or by using an empirically derived rank order such as the NORC prestige scale.[12] But how useful are these categories or hierarchies in describing pre-Civil War conditions? Economic change in the past century has transformed the occupational structure, virtually eliminating the master craftsmen, the journeymen craftsmen and a host of forgotten trades such as oystermen, tidewaiter and shallopman. The dominance of the importer-exporter, and even of the merchant-manufacturer, have yielded to the age of professional management, finance and advertising. What is more important, however, is that we cannot assume that today's attitudes toward manual and non-manual work, toward proprietorship and employment, or even toward education, characterized the attitudes of the early nineteenth century. Clearly, the prestige rankings of occupations would have to be created anew before we could define the vertical dimension of occupational mobility in pre-Civil War America. The difficulty of arriving at such an empirical, prestige rank order needs no elaboration.

---

[8] Robert R. Wharton, 'A study of the subjective class system as described by a random sample of respondents in Norristown, Pennsylvania,' unpublished Ph.D. dissertation, University of Pennsylvania (1961), pp. 161–74.
[9] 'The concept of social mobility,' p. 383.
[10] *ibid.*, p. 384.
[11] *ibid.*, p. 385.
[12] National Opinion Research Centre, 'Jobs and occupations: A popular evaluation,' *Opinion News* (September 1, 1947), pp. 3–13.

On the other hand, social mobility may not be the only way of conceptualizing the 'open society'. When Calvin Colton spoke in 1844 of the American 'self-made man',[13] or when Richard Hofstadter a century later described the same fellow as an 'expectant capitalist',[14] it would seem that the kind of mobility that was being invoked was more specifically economic than social. Economic mobility is a far more tangible concept, is no less interesting, and is probably a somewhat more direct conceptualization of the proposition we stated at the outset. It also has the happy attribute of being easily quantifiable in terms of changes in levels of wealth or income. Thus, if we shift our ultimate goal from that of measuring social mobility to that of measuring the closely related but conceptually distinct phenomenon of economic mobility, we may hit upon, if not a necessarily more valid inference, at least a more readily testable one.

What, then, are the possibilities of locating historical data that are appropriate for this test? And if data on wealth and income are available, can they be used to develop rates of economic mobility directly, without having to worry about occupational mobility? In Philadelphia there are three separate sources of information as to individual levels of wealth, each suffering from some form of incompleteness, and apparently nothing at all that may be used to record individual incomes. (A personal tax was more or less based on income, but it varied too little to be of any value.) From the outset, then, we must be content to define economic status in terms of wealth alone.

Undoubtedly the most satisfying sources of information are the manuscript schedules of the Federal Census, which are available on microfilm. The Eighth Census, 1860, lists each inhabitant with his occupation, and with the value of his real and personal property. This latter term, as spelled out in the instructions to the interviewers, includes intangible as well as tangible goods. Of course, the schedules are not wholly reliable, nor are they fully informative. A good deal of dishonesty and even honest inaccuracy undoubtedly permeate the wealth columns. Of far greater significance is the failure of the occupation column to differentiate, in all but a few cases, between master and journeyman craftsmen – a fact which makes analyzing the relationship between occupation and wealth a good deal more difficult. Nevertheless, the schedules of the Eighth Census, for their inclusiveness of both enumeration and informa-

---

[13] Calvin Colton, *Junius Tracts* (New York, 1844), p. 15.
[14] Richard Hofstadter, *The American Political Tradition*, paperback edition, (New York, 1954) p. 57.

tion, are a blessing. If earlier Censuses had been conducted in the same way, the analysis of mobility in *ante bellum* America would be a far simpler pursuit. Unfortunately, the Seventh Census lists no personal property, and previous surveys are little more than population enumerations. A longitudinal mobility study based on these readily accessible, nation-wide, inclusive documents is, unfortunately, impossible.

Local tax records provide a second source of information that, in many localities, may help overcome this difficulty. In Philadelphia, property tax records extend back to the earliest years of the Republic, although there is probably no single year in which useful records exist for the entire city, and there are many years for which nothing exists at all. These records are too sparse to trace individual fortunes over time, but in localities where they may be more complete, such a procedure may be quite feasible.

The third source, probate records, obviously cannot be used to trace the development of individual careers. They might, in some localities, be used to create rates of inter-generational mobility when used in conjunction with city directories. Again, the problem is incompleteness. The Register of Wills in Philadelphia contains only a few hundred entries for the four decades before the Civil War, and most of them, of course, refer to the wills of atypically wealthy individuals. Of the three sources, the probate records proved least useful in the Philadelphia study.

Thus, it proved virtually impossible to study economic mobility in Philadelphia without reverting to the inferential method of occupational mobility. But now that our skepticism has been aroused, it will be necessary to test the validity of the inference. How reliably can we predict changes in individual levels of wealth from changes in occupation? We have already seen that this relationship – that is, between the dynamic variables of occupational mobility and economic mobility – cannot be measured directly. The available data simply do not permit it. But it is possible to analyze the relationship between the static variables of occupation and wealth. Obviously, there must be a strong relationship if the inference is to be justified.

Before discussing the measurement of the strength of the relationship between occupation and wealth, however, there are two other types of relationships that should probably be treated first. Obviously, there can be no vertical mobility if there is no vertical dimension, so we must establish this dimension by creating the best possible rank ordering of occupations. We have already seen that the usual functional or prestige rankings, derived from contemporary experience, are not appropriate to a study of social mobility in the early nineteenth century. Neither will they serve for a study of economic mobility in that period. Therefore, we must rank our occupations empirically, and to do so we may rely upon the data we have already discussed.

There are problems, of course. The failure of census schedules to differentiate masters from journeymen requires that we create an arbitrary procedure for doing so. Although space does not permit a detailed explanation, such a procedure is possible, based on the few instances in which the distinction is made, and on other sources which help establish the approximate numerical ratio between masters and journeymen. Thus, through the introduction of an arbitrary but carefully determined cut-off point, it is possible to derive fairly accurate, average wealth figures for the various types of master craftsmen. The journeymen are probably badly distorted, but since they were wage-earners it is quite simple to locate them on the rank order, as a single category, using other means.

Thus, a fairly dependable ranking of more than fifty occupations can be derived from the schedules of the Eighth Census, based on the mean or median wealth of the sampled members of each occupation.[15] Interestingly, the rank order that I derived from the Philadelphia schedules contains no major surprises. Merchants, professionals and manufacturers in industries requiring heavy capital investment head the list, followed by agents, retail druggists and certain speciality craftsmen such as watchmakers, saddlers and cabinet makers. In the middle of the list are most of the craftsmen, along with grocers, tavernkeepers and other small shopkeepers. Lower, but not quite at the bottom, are carters and clerks. The rank order is completed with day laborers, servants, seamen and all types of unskilled workers.

Establishing the vertical dimension of occupations is a major step, but the step is not fully taken until it is established that this dimension remained fairly stable throughout the period under study. If we observe that at the beginning of the period laborers ranked significantly below shoemakers, we would naturally tend to regard a transition from laborer to shoemaker as indicative of upward mobility. But what would happen to this interpretation if we then discovered that in the interim certain

---

[15] The method of identifying masters suggests that the median would be the best average. But since the mean is less sensitive to variation caused by sampling error, and since many occupations contain but a few cases, it permits the ranking of many more occupations and is, therefore, probably the most useful average.

technological changes had reduced the shoemaker to the level of the laborer? Clearly, we would no longer wish to regard the transition as a sign of upward mobility. We might even go one step further and recognize all those who had been shoemakers at both periods of time to have been downwardly mobile. Actually, if we did discover significant changes in the occupational rank order, a better course would be to avoid using occupation as an indicator of economic or social mobility, and to search for a more stable variable.

Accordingly a second necessary procedure is the creation of several occupational rankings, sufficiently separated in time, and the computation of coefficients of correlation between these rankings. For the period 1820–1860, such a procedure involves the use of different data, as the census schedules are useless before 1860. Here is one instance where local tax records may be of vital importance, and in Philadelphia they allowed the creation of a comparable rank order for the very beginning of the period, 1820. Spearman's r (·759) and Kendall's tau (·625) both seemed to indicate that the occupational structure was sufficiently stable during the period to permit a study of occupational mobility.

It should probably be mentioned at this point that local tax records may be well stocked with pitfalls, and should not be used until they are studied thoroughly. The entries may mean something entirely different from what the investigator thinks they mean. They are probably not complete, and certain groups are probably systematically understated or excluded. They may even contain a good deal of dishonesty. As an example of the first point, the Philadelphia property tax was, since the tenant, not the landlord, was responsible for the real property tax, more of an occupancy tax than a property tax. This made the accumulation of a property inventory for any one individual quite impossible. What it did allow was the collection of a list of persons, along with the assessed value of their residences, and information as to whether they owned or rented the residences. The occupational rank order that ensued was based on something entirely different from total property, which is what property taxes are usually taken to reveal. An examination (using probate records) of the relationship between wealth and the value of an individual's residence produced the expected strong relationship, but the point remains that local tax records, like any document, must be thoroughly understood before they are used in historical research.

Having established the shape and stability of the occupational structure, we may return to the critical question of how closely this picture is related to economic stratification. Without a strong relationship between occupation and wealth, the inference of economic mobility from occupational mobility, while not invalid by definition, is highly questionable. The relationship is best explored through the analysis of variance, which answers the basic question, 'what is the significance of the variation in wealth *between* the ranked occupations as compared to the variation *within* each occupation?' Obviously, the relationship between the two variables, expressed as Eta^2, is stronger as the amount of 'between variation' increases relative to the amount of 'within variation'.

When the sample derived from the 1860 census schedules from Philadelphia County is subjected to the analysis of variance, the results are very interesting. When occupation is defined in terms of the rank order, that is, when each occupation is maintained as an entity, Eta^2 equals approximately ·17. When the rank order is collapsed into five 'classes', Eta^2 remains substantially the same, ·18. Four categories of occupations reduce Eta^2 slightly to ·157. Indeed, however we manipulate the data, even by omitting several occupations, Eta^2 remains at about the same level. Apparently, occupation, in *ante bellum* Philadelphia, accounts for about one-sixth of the variation in individual levels of wealth.[16]

How useful, then, is occupational mobility as a device for estimating economic mobility, when occupation explains only one-sixth of the variation of wealth? The relationship does not appear to be very strong. Of course, it is entirely possible that there is no other single variable that explains as much variation as occupation, but if that is true it merely argues against *any* uni-dimensional approach to mobility. Occupation may be the best available indicator of wealth, but it is apparently only a partially useful one.

When a little thought is given to some of the other variables that may be related to wealth, any surprise over the weakness of the relationship between wealth and occupation is dispelled. Within any occupation, there are men of different ages, nationalities and religions, men who practise their trades in more or less prosperous neighborhoods, men who come from poorer or wealthier families (and men who may or may not have received their due inheritances), and even men whose wives contributed smaller or larger dowries. Each occupation includes men with great and small ambitions and men with good and bad luck. Even when age is controlled, each occupation includes men who have been working at their trades and reaping their rewards for different lengths of

---

[16] The square root of Eta^2 is a coefficient of correlation, which is, therefore, about ·4 for occupation and wealth.

time. All of these different variables, plus many more, help explain the large amount of 'within' or unexplained variation in our 'uni-dimensional model'. Of course, even if we had access to data that could fit every variable that we could think of into a multi-dimensional analysis of variance, there undoubtedly would still be some amount of variation that would remain unexplained. The lesson to be learned is not that the world is perverse, but that it is complex, and that simplistic models of analysis should not be applied to complex problems.

Perhaps a better means of understanding just how strong a relationship we are dealing with would be to create a series of wealth intervals, and to visually assess the concentration of the members of each occupation within a particular interval. Or, the rank order of occupations can be collapsed in various ways to locate the categorization scheme that best concentrates the members of each occupational category in a distinct interval of wealth. With the Philadelphia data this best possible 'fit' is achieved only when the rank order is distilled down to three categories, and when the wealth intervals are kept fairly simple. Because of previously discussed shortcomings in the data, only the upper two classes can be compared:

Occupational Categories	Wealth Intervals		
	$6,000+	$500–5,999	Total
'Upper'	63%	37%	100%
'Middle'	18%	82%	100%

It should be readily apparent that these categories are not sufficiently distinct to support the inference of change in wealth from change in occupation. The overlap between each category is large enough to contain any occupational mobility that we are likely to observe. For example, assume that 10% of those who were in the Middle category in 1820 had moved into Upper category occupations by 1830. If we also assume, on the basis of the above table, that some 15% or 20% of the members of the Middle category were really wealthy enough in 1820 to be included in the Upper category, then we would assume that at least a portion of the 10% who improved their occupations did not increase their wealth. If these 10% were representatives of the entire Middle category in 1820, then we may speculate that 15% or 20% of them did not become wealthier as part of the process of changing occupations.[17]

[17] We cannot expect that occupational mobility and economic mobility were simultaneous events. If occupational mobility is a good indicator of either

But it is at least as likely that the mobile 10% represented the wealthiest members of the Middle category in 1820, that they were part of the group that should have been placed in the Upper category. If this were true, then the eventual movement of these men into the Upper category need not imply a single dollar of upward economic mobility!

Although we have no data with which to examine the relationship, we may assume that occupation was somewhat more powerful in accounting for variation in income than it was in accounting for variation in wealth. This would be especially true for salaried and wage-earning occupations. Of course, the majority of individuals listed in the city directories were proprietors, and the same factors, (age, ethnic group, and so on) that produced excessive variation in wealth undoubtedly produced variation in income. The variation could not have been as great, but the foregoing discussion is undoubtedly applicable here as well. In any case, we cannot simply assume that income levels can be predicted from occupation.

Thus far we have been judging occupation as an indicator of specific levels of wealth or income. As we have seen that occupation cannot be used to predict economic status within certain critical limits, we have implied that it cannot be relied upon to predict economic mobility. It is at least theoretically possible, however, that the correlation between occupational mobility and economic mobility may be greater than the correlation between occupation and wealth. Assuming that other variables, such as age, nationality, religion and residence would account for most of the variation in wealth left unexplained by occupation, it is entirely possible that the correlation between occupation and wealth would be very strong within each of the large number of 'homogeneous' sub-groups that could be created by breaking the sample down by these other variables. If this were the case, then we would assume that the correlation between occupational mobility and economic mobility would be correspondingly strong. Thus, for each individual in our sample, we could accurately predict changes in wealth by changes in occupation.

To illustrate this point, let us assume that ethnicity is the only other variable that explains variation in wealth, and that it explains most of the variation within each occupation. Let us further assume that the least wealthy members of each occupation were Irish immigrants, the average members were British immigrants and natives of non-Anglo-Saxon

previous or eventual change in wealth, then we should consider it a good indicator of economic mobility.

stock, and the wealthiest members were Anglo-Saxon, native Americans. We have observed that a tailor in one of our samples has become a druggist, and that there is a degree of overlap between the wealth of the members of the two occupations. Was the tailor upwardly mobile? He probably was, unless he discovered a means of 'changing' his ethnicity. If he were an Irish immigrant, we would predict that he rose from a poorer than average tailor to a poorer than average druggist. If he were a native of solid British stock we would predict that he rose from a wealthier than average tailor to a wealthier than average druggist. In other words, none of the three ethnic groups are to be found within the overlap between tailor and druggist, so that a change from one occupation to the other would necessarily involve economic mobility. We cannot tell how wealthy the tailor was, or how wealthy he became as a druggist, because we do not know to which ethnic group he belonged. Yet we can predict that at some time he improved his economic status.

The foregoing is based on two rather artificial assumptions – that the variation within each occupation can be sufficiently reduced by introducing new variables, and that these additional variables are permanent attributes of each individual. Neither assumption is entirely realistic. Not only is it unlikely that a multi-dimensional model could be constructed that would reduce the variation in wealth within each occupation to a point where the overlap between occupations would be eliminated, but it is also unlikely that the variables in this model would be permanent attributes of each individual. Ethnicity cannot be changed, but other variables can be. Thus, if we found that residence accounted for a large amount of additional variation, we could not assume that it remained constant while occupation changed. Perhaps a clerk could become a dry goods merchant only by moving to a neighborhood where the rents were cheaper and the incomes lower.

Nevertheless, it is possible that some of the overlap between occupations can be eliminated in this manner. If so, the likelihood increases that the correlation between economic mobility and occupational mobility is strong enough to support the inference of one from the other. It is unfortunate that we cannot measure the relationship directly, for it is the only way that we may truly understand the implications of occupational mobility. Data from other localities, of course, may well shed new light on this relationship. But until such data are located and analyzed, historians should remain alert for other variables that may be used, perhaps in conjunction with occupation, as a basis for inferring economic mobility.

If city directories are used in the study of mobility, one other interesting variable is available, namely, the residential addresses of the inhabitants of the locality. Directories may vary somewhat as to their presentation of addresses, but when the directory listings are used in conjunction with the excellent street guides that invariably accompany them, and with a good map of the locality, it is possible to locate practically any enumerated individual with a great deal of precision. If, furthermore, it can be demonstrated that residence in a particular neighborhood is indicative of a particular economic status, then a second variable emerges for the study of economic mobility.

Cataloguing the structure of an entire city is, of course, an extremely ambitious project. Local property tax records are of vital importance here, and can be used with great profit to define the character and boundaries of the city's neighborhoods, providing that the records allow the researcher to pinpoint the location of each property. But for almost any locality there are numerous other types of documents that can, and should be consulted in conjunction with the tax data. Local histories, memoirs, 'views', letters, newspapers and a host of other non-quantitative sources can probably be uncovered to describe the locality almost as completely as the tax records. These data provide a means for testing quantitative procedures, and help avoid the embarrassment of having a 'wealthy neighborhood' turn out to be a warehouse district.

The strength of the relationship between residence and wealth may be examined, of course, using Eta^2. But since the Philadelphia tax records are based on residential assessments rather than on wealth, and since these assessments vary considerably less than does wealth, Eta^2 for residence and assessments is a strong ·4. This is about the same amount of variation that is explained by occupation, when the latter is applied to the same data. In other words, it is likely that we may infer economic mobility from residential change or from occupational change with about the same level of confidence.

But how much is our accuracy improved when we infer economic or social mobility from changes within both of these dimensions simultaneously? When all of our variables are examined in a two-way analysis of variance,[18] the following is the result:

[18] The method utilized here was developed by C. Horace Hamilton in an unpublished paper, 'The addition theorem and analysis of variance in the case of correlated nominal variates,' as a far more manageable alternative to the method of fitting constants. Mr Hamilton's permission to use this method is gratefully acknowledged.

Total Sum of Squares (SSy)	1·000
Subclass Sum of Squares (SSy.ab)	·609
Variable A, Occupation (SSya.b)	·140
Variable B, Residence (SSyb.a)	·203
Interaction (SSy.axb)	·062
Correlation (SSRy.axb)	·204
Error (SSye)	·391

In this table the sum of all squares (SSy) is divided first into two categories: the 'subclass sum of squares' (SSy.ab) and the error, or 'residual sum of squares' (SSye). The first, SSy.ab, is in turn divided into four sub-categories: the amount of variation attributed to variable A (SSya.b), the amount of variation attributed to variable B (SSyb.a), the amount of variation attributed to 'interaction' between A and B (SSy.axb) and the amount of variation attributed to the correlation between A and B (SSRy.axb).[19] 'Interaction' refers to variation accounted for simultaneously by variables A and B, in other words, variation that is not additive when variables A and B are combined. In our data the interaction term is small, and need not concern us. Correlation, on the other hand, is of the utmost importance. It refers, in our case, to the distribution of occupations throughout the city. Different average ward assessments may be created in two ways: people with similar occupations may be clustered into distinct neighborhoods, or those of similar wealth *regardless* of *occupation* may be clustered into neighborhoods. The latter phenomenon (the tendency of wealthy people of all occupations to gather into the same neighborhood) is variation attributable to variable B, residence. The former (the tendency of merchants to cluster in one neighborhood, laborers in another) is the correlation between occupation and residence, and does not add to the amount of explained variation.

Owing to the strength of this correlation, occupation and residence acting together do not seem to account for any more variation in assessments than does either one of these variables acting alone.[20] Obviously, if knowledge of occupational category allows us to predict residential neighborhood, and if knowledge of neighbourhood allows us to predict the occupational category, knowledge of both of these variables is

---

[19] Correlation is equivalent to 'correction' in the method of fitting constants.
[20] The fact that the sum of squares attributable to both A and B is a bit lower than Eta² is, I trust, an artifact of the difference between the measures. The fact that SSyb.a is higher than SSya.b probably reflects the sampling procedure – all occupations recorded within a few distinct wards.

no improvement over knowledge of either one of them. It is quite important, however, that we distinguish between accounting for the total variation within a sample or population, and predicting an individual's wealth or assessment. The above table does not tell us that knowing where a shoemaker resides is irrelevant for estimating his wealth. It tells us, rather, that there will not be very many *cases* in which the second variable does not 'conform' to the first. Thus, if we can demonstrate that those shoemakers who live in residential zone 1[21] are wealthier than those shoemakers who live in zones 2 and 3, we are certainly entitled to distinguish between the residences of shoemakers in our city directory samples. Our table warns us, however, that we will probably find very few shoemakers in zone 1, and that our two-variable method, while perhaps perfectly valid, may not be particularly useful. The mean assessment for shoemakers of zone 1 in the 1820 Philadelphia tax sample is more than twice as high as the mean for shoemakers of zone 2. But out of 49 shoemakers in the sample, only five lived in zone 1.

Judging from these interrelationships between the static variables of occupation, residence and wealth, the addition of a second variable improves but little on the method of occupational mobility. On the other hand, a more direct analysis is that which relates the dynamic variables of occupational, residential and economic mobility. We have already seen that economic mobility cannot be directly measured with the available data. But nothing prevents us from assessing the relationship between occupational mobility and residential mobility. This relationship can tell us a great deal. For example, a strong positive correlation would seem to strengthen the idea that occupation is related to economic mobility. A strong negative correlation would suggest the opposite, that upward occupational mobility was typically achieved in Philadelphia only by moving to areas where rents and incomes were lower. But in fact, neither of these correlations appeared. Four correlation coefficients were calculated,[22] each pertaining to the occupational and residential mobility matrices of a specific decade. None of these coefficients ($G = -{\cdot}041$; ${\cdot}042$; ${\cdot}194$ and ${\cdot}157$) reveal a significant correlation in either direction.

It may seem at first that this rather surprising fact should place at least one and perhaps both of our variables in a very doubtful position as indices of economic mobility. Obviously, both cannot be strongly cor-

[21] A three-zone system of categorizing neighborhoods was utilized in Philadelphia.

[22] G is an estimate of Gamma. See Leo A. Goodman and William H. Kruskal, 'Measures of association for cross classifications III: Approximate sampling theory,' *Journal of the American Statistical Association*, 58 (1963), p. 323.

related to economic mobility if the correlation between them is so weak. But if occupational and residential mobility each bears a small but discernible relationship to economic mobility, it is quite possible that they represent different and *additive* aspects of economic mobility, providing between them a very good estimate of its magnitude and trend. The Philadelphia data remain inscrutable to the last. But the results of our two-way analysis of variance, and of our analysis of the relationship between occupational and residential mobility, do seem to argue for a reliable, two-dimensional inference of economic mobility.

In dwelling so long on the validity of studying vertical mobility through inferential procedures, we have slighted the rather critical question of whether or not such procedures are in fact feasible. Actually, prospects for the calculation of rates of occupational and residential mobility are not unlimited. For example, in Philadelphia, numerous attempts to calculate inter-generational mobility proved futile, and analysis was necessarily restricted to intra-generational, or career mobility. Perhaps more important is the limitation imposed by the necessity of focusing on a particular locality. Since we are tracing the individual careers of the inhabitants of the city, it is obvious that we are systematically eliminating those who migrated beyond the limits of our data. To the extent that the vertical mobility of migrants varied from the vertical mobility of those who remained in the city (whether these were natives or in-migrants), our mobility rates cannot be generalized. We can speak of the 'openness' of the city, but we cannot simply accumulate the findings of local studies until more is known about the relationship between vertical mobility and migration.

Within these limits, however, occupational and residential mobility can be studied. If city directories exist for a sufficient number of years, and if they are sufficiently inclusive, samples of names may be drawn from them and traced through subsequent directories. The samples must be large enough to provide for a considerable amount of attrition caused by death and out-migration of sample members, and by clerical error and an occasional confusion of identities. This latter problem may be minimized by establishing systematic guidelines for the exclusion of very common names. All surnames should be given their appropriate weighting, of course, but they should not be combined with very common given names. Thus, when random sampling places a John Smith in the sample, he should be replaced with an Ezekial Smith. The sample randomness is compromised but little, and a very serious difficulty is avoided.

Although the basic unit of analysis is the individual career, it may be wiser to trace careers over a shorter, specified time period. In Philadelphia, names were traced for ten years, and mobility rates were then calculated for a specific decade. A new sample was drawn for the next decade, without eliminating names that appeared in the earlier sample, a provision that tended to preserve a comparable age 'mix' in all samples. This procedure was repeated through all four decades, and rates of mobility were derived which allowed a comparison of trends for the forty-year period. It should be noticed that these do not describe the mobility of specific men over their entire careers, but rather describe the magnitude of mobility within specific decades. It is the decades that are being described.

The rates themselves are best described as a series of matrices, with the occupations or neighborhoods of the sample members at the beginning of the decade indicated in the columns, and those of the end of the decades indicated in the rows. This creates a diagonal of immobile cases, with all instances of upward mobility appearing above the diagonal, and all instances of downward mobility appearing below.

By utilizing proper coding procedures, the mobility rates may be calculated according to a number of different categorizations. The occupational rank order may be collapsed in a number of different ways, or even left intact to record each specific change. Occupational mobility can be broken down by neighborhoods, and residential mobility may be broken down by occupations and occupational categories. Finally, mobility matrices may be calculated to reflect movement along both variables simultaneously, which, as we have seen, may be the most valuable measure of all.

With each of these matrices, a great deal of information can be obtained about the nature of mobility in the American past. The difficulties involved in arriving at them are, of course, plentiful. Many of them, especially those involving the validity of the basic inference, are not yet overcome. But as long as historians retain their interest in the 'openness' of American society, the resolution of these difficulties should be moved to a place of prominence in contemporary historical research.

8 Voting behaviour 1832–1872

T. J. NOSSITER

Broadly speaking, there have been three major approaches to the study
of modern British elections from 1832 onwards: firstly, what might
loosely be called the Nuffield College campaign studies; secondly, the
social geography or ecological approach; and finally, the detailed sociological analysis of individual voting behaviour.[1] The choice of method for
a particular study has largely been conditioned by the kind of material
available to the researcher and this has inhibited the development of the
sociological investigation of individual behaviour. For elections since the
secret ballot was introduced in 1872, this has been dependent on the
expensive and time-consuming technique of the survey. Previously,
however, voting had taken place openly and was individually recorded
by law. Since in many places this information was often published in the
form of a booklet or as a supplement to a newspaper, it is surprising that
historians have paid so little attention to the study of individual voting
behaviour from 1832 to 1871. So far the only significant published book
on the subject is the somewhat limited coverage by Professor Vincent in
his *Poll Books*.[2] It seems therefore worthwhile giving an account of some
research in progress in this field.

    The writer has been working for some years on the social background
to voting behaviour in the period, using as data poll books, directories,
rate books and the original schedules of the census of 1851 in addition to

T. J. Nossiter (1970) *Political Studies*, XVIII, pp. 380–9.
[1] Recent books of interest in this field are: T. O. Lloyd, *The General Election
1880* (Oxford, 1968); H. Pelling, *Social Geography of British Elections, 1885–
1910* (London, Macmillan, 1967); M. Kinnear, *The British Voter* (London,
Batsford, 1968); J. Vincent, *Poll Books* (Cambridge, 1967).
[2] Vincent is mainly concerned with polls from smaller market towns rather than
the bigger industrial towns and cities.

the usual historical sources of private papers, parliamentary returns and newspapers.[3] The main aim has been to evaluate the extent to which social factors interacted with opinion, influence and corrupt practices in determining the outcome of mid-nineteenth-century elections and so to supplement such standard accounts of the political process as Professor Gash's *Politics in the Age of Peel*. At the very least this research enables us to provide a definitive answer to the vexed question of who is my ten-pound neighbour and at best yields fascinating insights into the relationship between voting behaviour and occupation, status, income, religion and political generation. This individual investigation has been complemented by the aggregate analysis of voting statistics in English urban constituencies to ascertain how far there was in any sense a nation-wide movement of opinion between elections and to what extent region-alism is discernible as an independent variable before the 1885–1910 period discussed by Dr. Pelling in his *Social Geography of British Elections*. An outline of the results of both these investigations is presented below.

Perhaps the striking thing about the electorate from the occupational analysis of thirty-three representative towns[4] was its pre-industrial character. Few of the new urban proletariat of the midlands and north were entitled to vote and insofar as the working class still voted after 1832 it was as old-style craftsmen. This assessment is confirmed by a precise estimate of how contemporaries saw the class composition of the electorate after a quarter of a century of Reform in an interesting par-liamentary return of 1866.[5] This shows the percentage of the electorate in each English and Welsh borough constituency deemed 'working class': infuriatingly, there is no indication of how the term was defined but it is, nevertheless, highly instructive. Overall one quarter of the electorate was classified as working class: in a number of big industrial centres, enfranchised in 1832, the proportion was very low indeed – in

[3] See 'Elections and political behaviour in County Durham and Newcastle 1832–74', (D. Phil. thesis, Oxford, 1968); 'Aspects of electoral behaviour in English constituencies, 1832–68', in E. Allardt and S. Rokkan (eds.), *Mass Politics* (New York, Free Press, 1970).

[4] Ashton (1841), Bath, Brighton, Cambridge (1866), Carlisle, Colchester, Durham, Exeter, Gateshead, Halifax, Hereford, Huddersfield (1837), Hull, Ipswich (1839), Leeds, Leicester, Lincoln, Liverpool (1832), Maidstone (1865), Manchester, Newcastle-upon-Tyne, Northampton, Norwich, Oldham, Preston, Reading, Rochdale (1857), Southampton, South Shields, Sunderland, Tynemouth, Yarmouth, York. Except where otherwise stated the calculations relate to 1852. Full details are available on request.

[5] Boroughs, Electors (Working Classes) Return, Parl. Papers 1866, LVII, 47, 243.

Leeds, as low as 7 per cent. The industrial working class of the north and midlands were denied a voice while the politically less conscious artisans of the south and the home counties voted in reasonable numbers.

The poll books and directories show that this middle-class constituency was numerically dominated by the retail shopkeeper (rarely less than 30 per cent and often as much as 40 per cent). The upper and professional classes formed anything between 10 and 20 per cent of the

TABLE 8·1 *Extent of Liberal support among occupation groups in designated constituencies, 1832–66.* Percentage of Liberal vote*

	No. of M.P.s	Enfranchised pre-reform or 1832	Date of election	Upper and profess. %	Manuf. and merchants inc. textiles† %	Retail %	Craft %	Drink %	Textiles where separated‡ %	Farm %	Shipping %	All %
Ashton	1	1832	1841	40	—	61	61	36	54	—	—	54
Cambridge	2	P.R.	1866	38	60	60	56	44	—	—	—	49
Gateshead	1	1832	1852	41	37	72	23	20	—	—	—	64
Huddersfield	1	1832	1837	61	70	55	57	41	50	12	—	54
Ipswich	2	P.R.	1839	36	60	60	46	54	—	21	58	50
Leeds	2	P.R.	1834	38	50	53	62	37	61	—	—	51
Liverpool§	2	P.R.	1832	50	64	48	—	—	—	—	—	45
Maidstone	2	P.R.	1865	44	50	55	56	40	—	—	—	52
Newcastle	2	P.R.	1832	61	—	75	63	68	—	—	—	65
Newcastle	2	P.R.	1835¶	38	—	86	70	—	—	—	—	?
Oldham	2	1832	1852	44	74	58	—	28	—	29	—	53
Rochdale	1	1832	1841	33	—	67	64	44	61	—	—	54
Rochdale	1	1832	1857	47	—	65	58	19	39	—	—	48
South Shields	1	1832	1852	44	—	83	89	61	—	—	17	63
Sunderland	2	1832	1845	38	—	60	50	48	—	—	24	44
Sunderland	2	1832	1852	66	—	84	84	83	—	—	50	63
Tynemouth	1	1832	1852	61	—	74	28	32	—	—	27	49

* Gateshead, Ipswich, Liverpool, Newcastle, South Shields, Sunderland, and Tynemouth, are drawn from my own research; the rest are calculated from information in Dr Vincent's *Poll Books*. The two sources are not necessarily comparable.
† Where inseparable.
‡ Textiles includes operatives.
§ These figures are based on a small sample.
¶ These figures are for the 60% of voters doubling or splitting.

electorate, although clearly much more in terms of social power, while
the drink interest was generally 10 per cent. The manufacturers varied
greatly in numbers, as one would expect, from as little as 5 per cent to as
much as 30 per cent. Thus between them, the shopkeepers and craftsmen might well make up half the average constituency: they were
obviously a significant force in local politics. It can also be argued there
cannot have been quite as many in this kind of electorate who were as
seriously exposed to external pressures against their real inclinations as
sometimes supposed, whatever was the case in the rural areas and some
of the smaller market towns. This was also an educated electorate in
which the vast majority were in a position to have political views of their
own. They were in fact, on both counts, rather different from many of
the county electors.

When the electorate is analysed in terms of party support by occupation, there are distinct signs that the major parties of Radical-Liberal,
Whig and Tory attracted disproportionate support from different occupational groups. Whatever may have been the case in factional Westminster, the accompanying table reveals that in the constituencies, there
was a remarkably consistent social basis to voting. The core of the
Radical-Liberal Party was the shopkeeping class and the artisans.
Marginally the former may have had the edge in radicalism but the
artisans outside the more venal market towns were also substantially
Radical. Lancashire is, of course, a partial exception to this general rule.
The Whigs were predominantly the party of the upper and professional
classes, the party of 1832 who had never advanced beyond it; and, it was
the Conservative Party which was the most nearly representative of the
social composition of the electorate as a whole, despite a tendency to
draw somewhat more support from the upper classes, the older free
trades, the shipping interest and the church. In any one election the
lines of demarcation might be blurred in a particular constituency by the
pull of influence, purse weight and the movement of public opinion but
this could not disguise the existence of long-term lines of social cleavage
in the electorate.

A number of constituencies have been examined in more detail from
the originals of the census enumerators schedules of 1851, Gateshead,
Bradford, Hull, Leeds and York, and their social characteristics compared with voting behaviour in 1852.[6] Since the time taken by such

---

[6] The census original schedules are available in the Public Records Office and
also usually on microfilm in the local reference library. I am indebted to Mr
Gordon Matthews for much of this work.

detailed research is considerable, the size of the sample had to be kept small, but even so as the table below shows, party support was significantly correlated with occupation in 1852 at the level of 5 per cent or better in three out of the five constituencies.

TABLE 8·2 *Voting, age and social composition from the 1851 census for the 1852 election. Significance levels (H_0 is rejected if p is equal to or less than 0·05 for chi-squared test)*

	Age cohort	Social composition	$N=$
Bradford	0·8	0·3	131
Gateshead	0·001	0·001	141
Hull	0·7	0·3	140
Leeds	0·05	0·02	142
York	0·3	0·001	156 and 308

This table also shows that in two of the five cases – despite the small numbers involved – the age of the voter was a significant variable in voting behaviour, not, however, in the sense of older voters having more to lose and inclining to conservation rather than change, but as a measure of political generations. The average age of the elector in these five constituencies was in fact, around forty-four years but there was only the slightest tendency for Conservative voters to be older than Liberal ones in two of four cases investigated; and this could be explained in terms of the structure of political generations.

TABLE 8·3 *Age of electorate by party from 1851 census and poll books*

	Age			
	Bradford	Hull	Leeds	Gateshead
Liberals	43	46	44	44
Conservatives	46	46	44	46
Splits	40	53	—	—
All voters	44	46	44	44

In fact the existence in some constituencies at least of generational dispositions to vote a particular way is one of the most interesting results of this investigation. Even in constituencies where the figures are not statistically significant there are still marked differences in the voting of five-year age groups in the following table.

TABLE 8·4 *Percentage Liberal vote by age cohorts in designated constituencies 1852*

Age	Bradford	Hull	Leeds	York	Gateshead
26–30	42 (25)*	46	59	64	70
31–35	50 (22)	50	45	71	86
36–40	46 (4)	59	83	79	42
41–45	42 (0)	72	36	61	84
46–50	40 (15)	65	50	74	56
51–55	38 (8)	65	60	71	67
56–60	44 (12) ⎫		75	⎫	⎫
61–65	50 (8) ⎬51		50	⎬71	⎬61
66+	29 (0) ⎭		57	⎭	⎭
Significance level	—	—	0·05	—	0·001

* Split votes.

Butler and Stokes have recently made much of the notion of the political generation in their *Political Change in Britain,* and it would be very important if we could show that a similar, if less developed, electoral geology existed in early Victorian England. Furthermore this is a clear case where sociological research far from denying the political content of electoral decision-making does much to confirm it.

The analysis of census originals and ratebooks also gives some indication that income and social standing, indirectly measured in the number of servants per voter and the rateable value of his housing, were also correlated with voting behaviour. In Gateshead, for example, in 1852 the mean rateable value – ignoring big industrial cases – of Whig voters' property was £50, Tory voters' £45 and Radical voters' only £22; while the average number of servants per voter was 0·95 for Whigs, 0·88 for Tories and 0·63 for Radicals. It could, of course, be objected that these differences might simply have reflected their occupational background. But the differences, though reduced still remain if we control voting by occupation: the mean rateable value of Whig shopkeeper property was £25, Tory £22 and Radical £18, and of Whig, Tory and Radical Licensees £50, £40 and £28. From this it is tempting to suppose that there was some justice in the common belief that the successful voted Whig or Tory and the less so Radical; but a more detailed investigation of this proposition for Bradford and Hull in the same election suggests the pattern was not so simple. The following table illustrates this by giving the average number of servants per voter in each major occupational group.

The numbers involved are too small in most cases for the results to be more than suggestive guide lines for further research but it is interesting to note that the differences (better-off professionals, and shopkeepers tend to vote Tory and better off manufacturers and craftsmen to vote Liberal) are in the same directions in both cases. It is certainly difficult to believe that all the differences in mean servants per voter are the product of chance alone; and in the long run it should be possible to

TABLE 8·5 *Servants per voter by occupational groups in Bradford and Hull, 1852*

	Bradford				Hull			
	Lib.	Cons.	Total	Voters N =	Lib.	Cons.	Total	Voters N =
Profess./Upper	0·27	1·25	0·82	23	1·0	2·5	1·56	24
Manufacturers	0·86	0·5	0·71	20	(1·8	0·83	1·38	13)
Retail	(0·44	0·86	0·75	15)	0·35	0·5	0·40	25
Craft	0·68	0·5	0·61	35	0·17	0·14	0·16	38
Drink Trade	1·25	1·33	1·31	21	(1·0	1·0	1·0	9)

establish voting patterns in terms of income and social standing. But it is hard to be as sanguine about the prospects of demonstrating the importance of religion in voting behaviour.

Few historians would doubt that religious affiliation was one of the determinants of voting behaviour after 1832 although they might disagree over the details, but proving it is quite another matter. In principle it would be possible to go through church and chapel records and relate individuals to details of polling but there are many objections both practical and theoretical to this approach. At the practical level there are few central repositories of such records and even where the local archivist has collected marriage registers and the like, there are substantial gaps. It would be not only a Herculean task to gather the data but also ultimately Sisyphean in view of its erratic survival. Even if it was available in some cases, it is doubtful how meaningful it would be because many married in church but attended other denominations, some men must have obliged the bride's family by going through ceremonies in her place of worship when it was not of his denomination, and finally because of the fluidity in religious attachments during the century as a whole.

The alternative is aggregate statistical analysis but here as well the problem is bedevilled by unknowns. First the membership of a religious

organization does not necessarily imply particular attitudes or conse-
quential actions in the nineteenth century any more than it does now:
secondly, we do not as yet know how far the members of a particular
denomination had the right to vote, even in the most prominent dissenting centres: thirdly, there is no means of discovering how a man evaluated
his religious allegiance compared with other social reference points for
voting; and finally, there is no way in which we can decide whether
where nonconformists occupied secular positions of authority the
ordinary elector voted with them because they were accustomed to vote
the same way as, say, their employers or out of religious conviction. The
former is at least as probable as the latter. Any adequate estimate of the
electoral influence of the religious factor is further complicated by the
difficulty of finding a satisfactory measure of the relative strength of
church and dissent at the time. The most obvious candidate is the 1851
religious census but its value is much reduced by the fact that it related
to the whole population – men, women and children – not the much
smaller and socially-biased adult and all-male electorate. In any case its
units were those of the registration districts not the parliamentary constituencies which often did not tally with each other at all closely. No
doubt these two problems help to account for the fact that two different
types of statistical test on this data showed no significant relationship
between 1851 religious returns and 1852 voting. The first test was by
means of a rank order correlation of the Conservative vote in forty-seven
constituencies in 1852 with the anglican attendance in 1851, which
produced the trivial correlation of only 0·236. A more sophisticated
investigation by means of regression analysis on a number of social and
economic variables in twenty-three constituencies showed no better
results. There was little sign of any statistically significant relationship
between any of the religious indices drawn from 1851 and mean
Conservative vote, 1832–80.[7]

Part of the problem with the 1851 census for our purposes is the large
size of the geographical units with which we are dealing. But shortly
before the secret ballot was introduced in 1872 a religious-based election
was held for the first school boards in 1871 with smaller and statistically
more helpful units of declaration. In a handful of cases similar wards
were used to declare polling in the 1868 general election and the 1871
school board election and we can compare these results by a rank order
correlation. In view of the fact that the initial board elections were
severely contested along religious lines and there was a high turnout, the

[7] See Table 8·6.

result of this test can be considered extremely important. The most striking case is undoubtedly that of Leeds where despite the 1867 Reform Bill which added many of the working class to the more religious existing middle-class constituency, the relationship over twenty districts was easily significant on a rank order test. The five most anglican districts in 1871 were also the top five Conservative polling stations in 1868 although in slightly different order. At the bottom of the rank order three of the five least anglican districts were among the five most hostile to the Tories in 1868. However, evidence from other boroughs is less clear-cut and it would appear that religion over-rode other factors only where dissent or anglicanism was particularly strong and when religious issues were especially salient as in the early 1870s.[8] Religion interacted with other social determinants in a complex way to produce the final electoral outcome.

Indeed if the sociological approach to nineteenth-century voting study is to be more than precise estimates of individual factors in isolation it has to go on to concern itself with this interaction. How can this be done? One approach might be to attempt a regression analysis of relevant social and economic data. This is still in an exploratory stage and must be treated with caution: the quality of the data going into the equation about any one constituency is not as good as one could wish; and the number of cases are not yet enough for real confidence. Nevertheless, so far details of religion, class, income, housing, press readership, the occupational composition of the electorate and other items have been gathered for twenty-three 'large towns'.[9] A preliminary computation suggests that the most significant predictor of mean Conservative vote between 1832 and 1880 was the occupational composition of the electorate. The percentages of the electorate engaged in the craft trades and in the licensed trade were significant at the 5 per cent level and the proportion in retail trade was not far behind. On the other hand a Pelling-type index of servants per hundred of the population had no predictive power at all and figures for religious attendance were also poor performers. Further investigation by the expansion of the analysis to

[8] The extent of religious division during the previous decades would clearly be a factor influencing these results.
[9] The following is the list of towns for which data has so far been collected together with their registered electorate in 1851: Bath 3,278; Brighton 3,675; Carlisle 1,134; Colchester 1,258; Durham, 1,157; Halifax 1,200; Hereford 1,013; Hull 5,221; Leeds 6,406; Leicester 3,853; Lincoln, 1,363; Manchester 3,921; Newcastle-upon-Tyne 5,269; Northampton 2,263; Norwich 5,390; Oldham 1,890; Preston 2,854; Reading 1,399; Southampton 2,419; Sunderland 1,973; Yarmouth 1,249; York 4,133; Exeter 2,501.

thirty-three other 'large towns' will clarify the relationships though statistically it should not alter the basic pattern. The table below summarizes the results of the preliminary investigation of the first twenty-three 'large town' over sixteen variables.[10]

The preliminary findings which have been summarized above of research on poll books, directories, census schedules and similar sources suggest the value of the individual investigation of early and mid-nineteenth century voting behaviour, indicating that occupation, income, status, religious affiliation and age cohort were factors which interacted with the more familiar ones of influence, corrupt practices and public opinion in determining the outcome of elections between 1832 and 1871.

TABLE 8·6 *Results of multiple regression analysis of social and economic data for twenty-three 'large towns' against mean Conservative vote, 1832–1880*

1. Working class in Electorate 1865	1·123
2. Servants/100 population 1851	0·188
3. Taxpayers as % of 1861 population	0·208
4. £20 + householders % 1861 population	−0·289
5. £20 + householders % taxpayers	1·311
6. £10–20 householders % of all householders	1·984*
7. Non-occupiers rated to poor rate	1·351
8. Methodism (attendance % pop. 1851)	−0·445
9. All old dissenters (same)	1·161
10. Press (ratio Tory to Liberal) 1852	0·905
11. Social composition of electors (craft %)	−2·351*
12. Same (retail %)	−1·519
13. Same (professional %)	0·531
14. Same (manufacturers and merchants %)	−1·237
15. Same (drink trade %)	−2·241*
16. Turnout	−0·208

Number of observations = 23
Independent variables = 16
Dependent variable = Mean Conservative % 1832–80
* —Significant at 5% level (= 1·895)

The aggregate analysis of voting statistics also yields valuable findings relevant in particular to the allied problems of when and at what pace the process of 'nationalization' of political life took place in England and

[10] I am indebted to Mrs Chew, Mrs Millington and Mr Thomas, research officers in the Social Studies department, University of Leeds, for their work on these computations.

whether the regional factor which Dr Pelling demonstrates in the nine-teenth century operated before 1885. Kinnear, Lloyd and Pelling are all concerned with this key question of the relationship between local, regional and national in English politics.

One of the most marked features of post-war British elections has been the uniform nationwide swing of opinion with little local or regional variation. In 1966, for example, half the constituencies had swings, within 1 per cent of the national average. Political life in Britain – with the exception of Ulster and arguably the Celtic Fringe – is effec-tively nationalized. How long has this been the case? Pelling would have us believe this has been so only since some time after 1910 as he makes use of the regional factor in his *Social Geography*. The differences be-tween the six-election averages for the Conservative and Unionist poll in the English provinces from 1885 to 1910 are almost as big as those between England, Scotland and Wales at the same time. In England the range is from 56·2 per cent in the South-East to 45·2 per cent in both Yorkshire and the North. This compares with 50·8 per cent for England, 43·0 per cent for Scotland and 38·6 per cent for Wales. Pelling admits that part of the regional variation in England can be explained in terms of difference in social class – something which he might perhaps have tested – but rightly argues that this is not the whole story. Regionalism does appear to be an independent variable at least by 1885. Nobody, however, has systematically pursued the question beyond that point.

Prima facie it hardly seems worth investigation. During much of the period from 1832 to at least 1865, politics was still highly local in character. The constituencies generally sought local representation of local interests in preference to tried party men who might be pre-occupied with national affairs; the imperial legislation occupied far less of parliamentary time than countless local and private acts. Elections were not single national affairs but a variety of elections in which local interests, local feeling and local candidates were weighed as much as the national issues involved in the dissolution. But what at first seemed obvious turns out to be surprisingly lacking in foundation. From as early as 1841 there were clear indications of regionalism in voting behaviour, though not yet of a definite 'nationalization' of electoral behaviour.

The standard deviations give us some measure of the extent to which the regional figures varied from the mean and so indirectly of the 'nationalization' of English politics in the nineteenth century. The 3·83 deviation for 1885 contrasts vividly with the 8·13 of 1880. There does

TABLE 8·7 *Rank order correlation (Kendall) of Conservative vote by region in English boroughs from 1832 to 1886 significance levels better than 0·05*

	1832	1835	1837	1841	1847	1852	1857	1859	1865	1868	1874	1880	1885	1886
1832	×													
1835		×												
1837			×											
1841				×										
1847	0·002		0·01		×									
1852	0·01	0·02			0·008	×								
1857		0·03				0·004	×							
1859				0·01				×						
1865			0·01						×					
1868						0·03	0·03	0·03		×				
1874				0·05	0·02					0·006	×			
1880				0·01		0·01	0·05	0·01		0·0007	0·001	×		
1885										0·01	0·001	0·005	×	
1886						0·03				0·008	0·02	0·005	0·02	×

TABLE 8·8 *Mean regional Conservative vote for English borough constituencies, 1832–85*

The calculations presented below are not strictly comparable with Dr Pelling's since I have had to distinguish between borough and county seats and ignore the latter in the regional averages. They are, however, based on the same regions and Conservative support.*

	1832	1835	1837	1841	1847	1852	1857	1859	1865	1868	1874	1880	1885†
North	25·79	36·17	47·34	39·75	37·17	33·09	30·28	35·95	35·59	30·61	35·16	28·5c	41·7
Yorkshire*	27·78	45·01	45·33	51·70	36·88	37·46	40·89	52·24	43·94	33·36	45·69	33·43	45·8
Lancashire	32·91	40·27	41·47	50·28	40·65	39·92	46·71	39·46	42·98	45·86	51·19	45·46	51·4
East Midlands	42·86	48·97	48·28	49·23	41·35	44·82	41·38	26·89	42·60	34·45	35·92	35·25	43·7
West Midlands	35·48	47·65	46·24	47·80	45·85	45·65	45·68	34·30	54·05	40·32	48·07	45·48	45·5
Central	44·76	42·64	54·65	49·66	57·09	43·68	43·45	48·93	53·33	33·83	37·83	31·22	44·7
East Anglia	35·14	56·04	55·39	51·33	51·63	53·51	47·63	56·65	53·86	42·75	53·50	49·89	49·2
Bristol	25·42	41·68	45·50	43·69	32·19	30·40	33·57	38·26	44·77	34·66	48·75	45·41	48·7
Devon and Cornwall	38·19	46·87	39·72	44·79	45·72	54·92	54·42	35·24	34·37	41·87	49·22	47·21	44·3
Wessex	38·45	36·96	52·29	50·43	48·44	43·48	37·91	50·36	45·20	40·62	55·55	48·14	51·5
South East‡	43·09	44·64	50·09	56·15	53·94	53·62	43·45	50·40	48·79	44·20	52·22	54·27	54·5
Mean	35·44	44·26	47·85	48·62	44·63	43·69	42·31	42·61	45·41	38·41	46·65	42·21	47·36
Standard deviation	6·59	5·46	4·72	4·25	7·41	7·77	6·38	9·00	6·41	4·93	6·82	8·13	3·83

* With the exception that I have assimilated the Peak-Don district into Yorkshire on the grounds that before 1885 there were too few constituencies to make a meaningful calculation.
† Pelling (adapted).
‡ Excluding London.

not seem to be much justification in a Whig interpretation of progressive nationalization over the years: the two least national in character were 1859 and 1880 while the three most so were 1837, 1841 and 1868. But it can be shown statistically that the detailed regional differences are most unlikely to have arisen purely by chance. The data from 1841 to 1886 is significant on Kendall's Rank Order Concordance (W) at a confidence level better than 0·001.

The regional figures can also be tested for rank order relationships between any pair of individual elections. The significance levels better than 0·05 are given in Table 8·7.

As can be seen from this there were three fairly distinct periods between 1832 and 1886. During the confused alignments of the 1830s there was no significant pattern of regional voting; but from 1841 for the rest of the life of the First Reform Act some patterning began to emerge even though it was not yet completely established. Finally from 1868 onwards the regional pattern becomes quite decisive and there are significant relationships not only between adjacent pairs of elections but also between all possible pairings. Until 1851 the outcome of elections appears to have been largely dependent on all manner of local factors but from then onwards political cleavages emerged along geographical lines. These regional differences appear to have been greatest between 1868 and 1885 becoming less marked thereafter and giving way after the First World War to an increasingly national pattern, disturbed only by such exceptional realignments as occurred in the 1920s.

This article has tried to demonstrate the value of two neglected ways of approaching the study of electoral politics in the early and mid-nineteenth century, individual investigation of voting behaviour and aggregate statistical analysis. The former helps to confirm the view that there was a distinct social basis to voting behaviour in Victorian England. It does not, of course, in itself provide an explanation but rather helps the historian and political scientist to know precisely what it is which has to be explained. The latter indicates that the local basis of politics was already breaking down from 1841 onwards and that although not fully established until 1868 the regional factor was important long before 1885. It can be argued that regionalism was an intermediate stage between an essentially localised political system and a nationwide one. In England the region serves as a link between the periphery and the centre in the second half of the nineteenth century.

Annotated bibliography

This short bibliography is for readers whose appetite has been whetted by what has appeared in this book. It is by no means a comprehensive review of the literature, more a series of pointers to recent works, which in their turn, of course, offer further leads.

INTRODUCTION

A common characteristic of all the articles in the book is their reliance on quantitative techniques. Until recently textbooks in statistics have not been geared to the particular needs and problems of scholars working with historical data. Happily the situation is now changing. For anyone working on English material R. Floud, *An Introduction to Quantitative Methods for Historians* (London, Methuen, 1973), offers a gentle introduction, which should quieten the fears of all but the incurably innumerate. It is particularly good on time series. Another short book offering a less comprehensive treatment, but one which gets one over the all important first hurdle is E. Shorter, *The Historian and the Computer* (Englewood Cliffs, N.J., Prentice-Hall, 1971). Most of this work is concerned with the use of the computer by historians. It deals with this, for many, equally frightening topic, in a very soothing fashion. A more daunting, but by way of compensation, more comprehensive treatment than either Floud or Shorter is C. M. Dollar and R. J. Jensen, *Historian's Guide to Statistics: Quantitative Analysis and Historical Research* (New York, Holt, Rinehart and Winston, 1971). This also contains a sixty-page bibliography which takes the form of a 'Guide to Resources of Value in Quantitative Historical Research'. Two recently published volumes, whose titles are self-explanatory, are V. R.

Lorwin and J. M. Price (eds.), *The Dimensions of the Past: Materials, Problems and Opportunities for Quantitative Work in History* (New Haven, Yale University Press, 1972) and E. A. Wrigley (ed.), *Nineteenth Century Society: Essays in the Use of Quantitative Methods for the Study of Social Data* (Cambridge, Cambridge University Press, 1972). The essays in both vary in degree of difficulty, but even the novice will find something of value. A particular mention, in this regard, needs to be made of the article in the Wrigley volume on 'Sampling in Historical Research' by R. S. Schofield. Not for the uninitiated, on the other hand, is another work edited by Wrigley, *Identifying People in the Past* (London, Edward Arnold, 1973). The essays in this volume are all concerned with 'nominal record linkage'; the bringing together of information about an individual from a variety of sources, using the individual's name as the linking device. The technique is widely used for the so-called 'reconstitution of families' by historical demographers. For an example of the latter see Küchemann *et al* above pp. 195–219. For a more elementary treatment of the 'reconstitution of families' method see E. A. Wrigley (ed.), *An Introduction to English Historical Demography* (London, Weidenfeld and Nicolson, 1968).

CHAPTER I

Erikson's essay should be seen in the context of a lively discussion. Works preceding his include Asa Briggs, 'Sociology and history' in A. T. Welford *et al.*, *Society: Problems and Methods of Study* (London, Routledge and Kegan Paul, 1962), pp. 91–8; W. J. Cahnman and A. Boskoff (eds.) *Sociology and History: Theory and Research* (New York, Free Press, 1964); T. C. Cochran, *The Inner Revolution: Essays on the Social Sciences in History* (New York, Harper and Row, 1964); B. Halpern, 'History, sociology and contemporary area studies', *American Journal of Sociology*, **63** (1957), pp. 1–10; H. S. Hughes, 'The historian and the social scientist', *American Historical Review*, **66** (1960), pp. 20–46; H. S. Hughes, 'History, the humanities and anthropological change', *Current Anthropology*, **4** (1963), pp. 140–5; M. Krug, *History and the Social Sciences* (Waltham, Mass., Blaisdell, 1967); P. Laslett, 'History and the social sciences', *International Encyclopaedia of the Social Sciences*, VI, pp. 434–40 (New York, Macmillan and the Free Press, 1968); I. Schapera, 'Should anthropologists be historians?', *Journal of the Royal Anthropological Institute*, **92** (1962), pp. 143–56; and S. Thrupp, 'History and sociology: new opportunities for co-opera-

tion', *American Journal of Sociology*, **63** (1957), pp. 11–16. The appendix
to S. Thernstrom, *Poverty and Progress: Social Mobility in a Nineteenth
Century City* (Cambridge, Mass., Harvard University Press, 1964)
entitled 'Further reflections on the Yankee City series: the pitfalls of
ahistorical social science' is a vigorous statement of the case. The same
theme is also admirably discussed in Barrington Moore Jr., *Political Power
and Social Theory: Seven Studies* (Cambridge, Mass., Harvard University
Press, 1966), Chapter 4. For the relevance of history to sociology see
C. Wright Mills, *The Sociological Imagination* (New York, Oxford
University Press, 1959), Chapter 8. A brief note on the relationship
between history, sociology and social anthropology is to be found in the
report of a conference held by the Past and Present Society in 1963 (*Past
and Present* No. 27, April 1964, pp. 102–8). For a study which pours
scorn on the claims of social scientists and 'new' historians alike see G. R.
Elton, *The Practice of History* (London, Methuen, 1967). This highly
readable account of his craft by a leading historian includes two gems,
that cry out to be cited. 'One would be more impressed' writes Elton,
p. 33, 'by the claims made for the "new methods" if the results proved
more striking and less predictable. Too often vast energies are assembled
and blows of enormous weight are struck, only to produce an answer
which is either obvious, well known or manifestly unhelpful.' And
again, on p. 39, he notes: 'saving the social scientist from himself (and
society from the social scientist) may be a worthy reason for studying
history . . .'

Works appearing since Erikson's lecture in 1968 include Phillip
Abrams 'The sense of the past and the origins of sociology', *Past and
Present*, No. 55 (May 1972), pp. 18–32; S. H. Aronson, 'Obstacles to a
rapprochement between history and sociology: a sociologist's view', in
M. Sherif and C. W. Sherif (eds.), *Interdisciplinary Relationships
in the Social Sciences* (London, Aldine, 1969), pp. 292–304; N. B. Harte
(ed.), *The Study of Economic History* (London, Cass, 1970), (a collection
of inaugural lectures delivered by economic historians over the last half
century); G. Leff, *History and Social Theory* (London, Merlin Press,
1969); D. C. Pitt, *Using Historical Sources in Anthropology and Sociology*
(New York, Holt, Rinehart and Winston, 1972); W. Todd, *History as
Applied Science: A Philosophical Study* (Detroit, Wayne State University
Press, 1972); H. Trevor-Roper, 'The past and the present: history and
sociology', *Past and Present*, No. 42 (1969), pp. 3–17; E. H. Tuma,
Economic History and the Social Sciences: Problems of Methodology
(Berkeley, University of California Press, 1971); B. R. Wilson, 'Socio-

logical methods in the study of history', *Transactions of the Royal Historical Society*, 5th ser., No. 21 (1971), pp. 101–18.

CHAPTER 2

The Achieving Society followed on McClelland's earlier work, reported in D. C. McClelland, J. W. Atkinson, R. A. Clarke, E. L. Lavell, *The Achievement Motive* (New York, Appleton-Century-Crofts, 1953). Two subsequent works are D. C. McClelland, 'Does education accelerate economic growth?', *Economic Development and Cultural Change*, **14**, No. 3 (1966), pp. 257–78 and D. C. McClelland and D. G. Winter, *Motivating Economic Achievement* (New York, Free Press, 1969). The latter begins with a summary of the work done on the *n* Achievement. The book as a whole is an account of some experiments conducted in southern India, designed to see whether, with appropriate training, the achievement motive could be increased among a group of businessmen, and consequentially their business performance enhanced. The book is noteworthy for the ingenuity of the experimental design and for the way in which the rather simplistic model, presented in the passage from McClelland cited in this Reader, has been elaborated to include a wider range of variables. For two articles bearing directly on the passage in this Reader see J. B. Cortes, S. J., 'The achievement motive in the Spanish economy between the 13th and 18th centuries', *Economic Development and Cultural Change*, **9**, No. 2 (1961), pp. 144–63 and N. Morgan, 'The achievement motive and economic behaviour', *Economic Development and Cultural Change*, **12**, No. 3 (1964), pp. 243–67. And for a couple of perceptive reviews of *The Achieving Society* see G. Katona, Review of David McClelland, *The Achieving Society*, *American Economic Review*, LII, No. 3 (1962), pp. 580–3 and D. Potter, Review of David McClelland, *The Achieving Society*, *Business History Review*, XXXVI (1962), pp. 470–3.

CHAPTER 3

The appearance of Professor West's book *Education and the State: a Study in Political Economy* (London, Institute of Economic Affairs, 1965), created a storm: a storm of abuse from the radical left matched in intensity by the ecstatic approval of the radical right. Most attention was focused on Professor West's proposals to abolish the state education system, as we know it, but his views on the condition of British education before 1870 did not go unnoticed. For something of this controversy one should read the four essays. *Education: A Framework for Choice* by A. C. F. Beales, Mark Blaug, E. G. West and Sir Douglas Veale, published in London by the Institute of Economic Affairs, 1967. For another essay by West which uses the same technique as the ones in this Reader, but takes the data from the nineteenth-century United States (in particular the New York state school system) see E. G. West, 'The political economy of American public school legislation', *Journal of Law and Economics*, X (1967), pp. 101–28. For some Canadian data see G. Loken, 'Perspective on change in educational structures in Alberta', *Alberta Journal of Educational Research*, XV, No. 4 (1969), pp. 207–23. For other recent works on English education before 1870 which have a direct bearing on points raised in the West-Hurt debate see B. I. Coleman, 'The incidence of education in mid-century', in E. A. Wrigley (ed.) (1972), op. cit.; N. Ball, 'Elementary school attendance and voluntary effort before 1870', *History of Education*, **2**, No. 1 (1973), pp. 19–34; R. Johnson, 'Education policy and social control in early Victorian England', *Past and Present*, **49** (1970), pp. 96–119 and M. Sanderson, 'Literacy and social mobility in the Industrial Revolution in England', *Past and Present*, **56** (1972), pp. 75–103. For a recent general survey of the history of education see A. Briggs, 'The study of the history of education', *History of Education*, **1**, No. 1 (1972), pp. 5–22.

CHAPTER 4

Of all the 'new' histories developed in recent years the 'new' economic history (or cliometrics as it is sometimes called) has been both the most vigorous and the most hotly debated. Fogel is the doyen of this new school, its most ardent advocate and most readable exponent. He has put forward his views in a particularly succinct and easily digested form in 'A provisional view of the "new economic" history', *The American Economic Review*, LIV, No. 3 (1964), pp. 377–89 and in 'The reunification of economic history with economic theory', *The American Economic Review*, LV, No. 2 (1965), pp. 92–8. A later, longer and more difficult article is his 'The specification problem in economic history', *The Journal of Economic History*, XXVII, No. 3 (1967), pp. 283–308. This last named journal has become increasingly dominated by practitioners of the 'new economic' history. For an article in it critical of Fogel see P. D. McClelland, 'Railroads, American growth and the new economic history: a critique', *Journal of Economic History*, XXVIII, No. 1 (1968), pp. 102–23, and for a whole issue devoted to the theme 'Economic history: retrospect and prospect', which sets the 'new' economic history in the context of the 'old' see Vol. XXXI, No. 1 (1971).

Much has been made of the unreality of the 'new' economic history; its apparent concern with 'what might have beens'. In beginning his review of the responses to the new developments ('As if or not as if: the economic historian as Hamlet', *Australian Economic History Review*, VII No. 1 (1967), pp. 69–85) J. A. Dowie brings this out clearly by citing the following extracts from three reviewers:

. . . Fogel is opening up a new branch of literature, quite unlike what has hitherto passed as historical knowledge and somewhat more analagous to science fiction. It consists of mathematical predictions about what the past could have been.   CHARLOTTE ERICKSON

. . . the applause comes from economists rather than historians, from men never exposed to methodology and often not even to history.
FRITZ REDLICH

. . . if Fogel had not written his book perhaps someone else would have written a similar one almost as valuable; should I therefore conclude that what Fogel has done is of little value?
MARVIN E. GOODSTEIN

CHAPTER 5

In his article Krause raised a number of issues which have remained at the centre of the debate in historical demography. One of these, the suggestion that fertility rates *might* rise in the currently under-developed countries was taken up immediately by Easterlin, as the extract in this Reader makes plain. On that particular issue time seems to have favoured Krause rather than Easterlin; see T. W. Fletcher and R. P. Sinha, 'Population growth in a developing economy', *Journal of Development Studies*, 2 (1965), pp. 2–18 and R. B. Tabbarah, 'Toward a theory of demographic development', *Economic Development and Cultural Change*, 19 (1970–1), pp. 257–76. For a review of the general questions raised by Krause, conducted at a fairly general level see H. J. Habakkuk, *Population Growth and Economic Development since 1750* (Leicester, Leicester University Press, 1971). For another overview, but one which keeps its nose more firmly in the local records, which are the life blood of this field of enquiry, see J. D. Chambers, *Population, Economy and Society in Pre-Industrial England* (Oxford, Oxford University Press, 1972). Both the Chambers and the Habakkuk volumes are eminently readable. For collections of key articles in the field, most of which have appeared since Krause's article see D. V. Glass and D. E. C. Eversley, *Population In History* (London, Edward Arnold, 1965); D. V. Glass and R. Revelle (eds.), *Population and Social Change* (London, Edward Arnold, 1972) and the Reader I edited entitled *Population in Industrialization* (London, Methuen, 1969). For a broad and stimulating coverage of the wide variety of sources available to the historical demographer (both China and Peru are covered, the former at length!) see T. H. Hollingsworth, *Historical Demography* (London, Hodder and Stoughton, 1969).

CHAPTER 6

'Space and distance can clearly be seen to be prime determinants of genetic structure . . .' (G. A. Harrison and A. J. Boyce, *The Structure of Human Populations*, Oxford, Clarendon Press, 1972, p. 129). Historical data can be tapped in order to show the nature of population movement as Küchemann *et al* above have demonstrated. They relied mainly upon parish registers for their material. Other authors have used listings (quasi-censuses) of various kinds e.g. E. J. Buckatzsch, 'The constancy of local populations and migration in England and Wales before 1800', *Population Studies*, 5 (1951), pp. 62–9; P. Laslett and J. Harrison, 'Clayworth and Cogenhoe, turnover of population, household and family structure in two English villages in the seventeenth century', in H. E. Bell and R. L. Ollard (eds.), *Historical Essays Presented to David Ogg* (London, A. & C. Black, 1963), pp. 157–84 and R. S. Schofield, 'Age-specific mobility in an eighteenth century rural English parish', *Annales de demographie historique 1970*, pp. 261–74. For this last mentioned article Schofield used a quite remarkable document, a listing giving not only the names, ages, occupations, religious affiliations and place of birth of the household heads and their wives, but also the names, ages, occupational and marital status of all their surviving children whether they were living with them or not. If they were not, then the list states where the children were living. The year is 1782, the place is Cardington in Bedfordshire. Such a document is, of course, extremely rare and falls more into the category of material used by the traditional historian than into that category the exploration of which this present volume seeks to foster. Two recent articles which are more directly related to the genetic side of the Küchemann *et al.* article are R. A. Cartwright, 'The structure of populations living on Holy Island

Northumberland' in D. F. Roberts and E. Sunderland (eds.) *Genetic Variation in Britain* (Vol. 12 of Symposia of the Society for the Study of Human Biology, London, Taylor and Francis, 1973) and G. A. Harrison and A. J. Boyce, 'Migration, exchange and the genetic structure of populations', in G. A. Harrison and A. J. Boyce (eds.) *The Structure of Human Populations* (Oxford, Clarendon Press, 1972), pp. 128–45.

CHAPTER 7

The publication in 1969 of S. Thernstrom and R. Sennett (eds.), *Nineteenth Century Cities: Essays in the New Urban History* (New Haven, Yale University Press) brought with it some of the detailed findings discussed generally in the Reader articles by Blumin and Thernstrom. The articles in question were S. Blumin, 'Mobility and change in antebellum Philadelphia' and S. Thernstrom, 'Immigrants and Wasps: ethnic differences in occupational mobility in Boston, 1890–1940'. In the same genre were H. G. Gutman, 'The reality of the rags-to-riches "myth"': the case of the Paterson, New Jersey, Iron and Machinery Manufacturers, 1830–1880' and P. R. Knights, 'Population turnover, persistence and residential mobility in Boston, 1830–60'. A more recent review, S. Thernstrom and P. R. Knights, 'Men in motion', *Journal of Interdisciplinary History*, I, No. 1 (1970), pp. 7–35 indicates that 'urban frontier' mobility was very high (thus confounding earlier findings) and suggests a need to re-examine the concept of closed ethnic or class ghettoes. For the use of nineteenth century English census material see the essays in E. A. Wrigley (ed.), *Nineteenth Century Society: Essays in the Use of Quantitative Methods for the Study of Social Data* (Cambridge University Press, 1972), especially W. A. Armstrong, 'The use of information about occupation. Part 1. A basis for social stratification', pp. 198–225.

CHAPTER 8

Although political historians have produced a large number of studies of political contests in particular constituencies, (for an excellent and seemingly comprehensive bibliography see H. J. Hanham (ed.), *Dod's Electoral Facts*, Brighton, Harvester Press, 1972) there is little that can be described as psephological in character. Nossiter reviews some of the latest studies in his 'Recent work on English elections', *Political Studies*,

XVIII, No. 4 (1970), pp. 525–8. His original works in this area are
'Aspects of electoral behaviour in English constituencies, 1832–1868'
in Erik Allardt and Stein Rokkan (ed.), *Mass Politics: Studies in
Political Sociology* (London/New York, Free Press, 1970), pp. 169–
99; 'Shopkeeper radicalism in the nineteenth century' in T. J. Nossiter
et al., *Imagination and Precision in the Social Sciences* (London, Faber
and Faber, 1972), pp. 407–38; and *Influence, Opinion and Political
Idioms in Reformed England* (London, Faber and Faber, in press).
What has become known as the Nuffield approach to the study of
elections, (the name comes from the work done on recent British
elections mostly by Fellows of Nuffield College, Oxford) has been used
by Trevor Lloyd in his *The General Election of 1880* (London, Oxford
University Press, 1968). A study which makes extensive use of poll book
material is R. W. Davis, *Political Change and Continuity 1760–1885:
A Buckinghamshire Study* (Newton Abbot, David and Charles, 1972.)
For a minuscule study (with a grandiose title!), involving the use of
record-linkage techniques in the analysis of electoral contests, as recorded in poll books, see my 'The Mid-Victorian Voter', *Journal of
Interdisciplinary History*, I, No. III (1971), pp. 473–90.

Index

rank order correlation, 258
rates of growth, 35–6
regression analysis, 36, 206
Spearman's r, 240
standard deviation, 261, 263
statistical significance, 40, 49–50
statistical sources, attitudes towards, 107–8
statistics, interpretation of, 114–
15, 135, 158 *ff*
T tests, 44
time series, 230
variance, analysis of, 241, 245–6

railroads, U.S.A.:
and availability of farmland,
122–7
charges of, 144, 152
economic growth, influence on,
121
and internal combustion engine, 152–3
manufacturing, effect on, 130–9
'social savings' of, 143–50
space programme and, 150–3
steel industry and, 135–42
technology, effect on, 139–43
telegraph industry and, 142–3
Reading, 252, 259
religion:
entrepreneurship and, 48
in British 19th-century education, 84–5
rent, theory of, 124
research needs:
early factory labour, source of,
225
historical demography, 182–3,
193
n achievement in literature and
sermons, 41, 46
private and parochial schools,
influence of, 65
voting behaviour, 257
Rochdale, 87, 103, 252–3
Ross, 62
Russia, 188
Rutland, 73–4, 96, 100, 112–13

Salford, 73, 75, 84, 88, 100, 108,
112
Sampling:
of city directories, 229, 248
of entrepreneurs in Industrial
Revolution, 48
and the historian, 15
from poll books, 11
random, 144
by sociologists, 15
unbiased, 48
from U.S. federal census, 239
Scandinavia, 156, 166–7, 180
school:
attendance at, 101–3, 114, 116
definition of, 94–5, 108–9
turnover of, 69, 97–8, 116
Scotland:
education in Highlands and
industrial areas, 61–2
parochial schools in, 60–5
private schools in, 60–5
production of entrepreneurs in,
48–9
quality of education in, 63–5
social mobility:
causes of changes in, 224
and economic mobility, 237
historical study of, 230–1, 236
and occupational mobility, 234
problems of analysing, 229–30,
237–49
of skilled workmen, 225–6
in U.S.A., 4, 222
in western world, 221
sociologist:
attitude towards history of, 16,
221–2
concepts of, 21
data of, 14–16, 22–3, 25
explanatory system of, 22
field of, 19
and historical data, 25, 232
language of, 17–18, 21
as participant historian, 27
relationship with his data, 22–3,
223–4
time sense of, 20–22, 26